心理门

Psychological Gate

伶点金 著
S Jing Goldtouch

Billson International Ltd.

Published by
Billson International Ltd
27 Old Gloucester Street
London
WC1N 3AX
Tel:(852)95619525

Website:www.billson.cn
E-mail address:cs@billson.cn

First published 2025

Produced by Billson International Ltd
CDPF/01

ISBN 978-1-80377-127-4

©Hebei Zhongban Culture Development Co.,Ltd All rights reserved.

The original content within this product remains the property of Hebei Zhongban Culture Development Co.,Ltd, and cannot be reproduced without prior permission. Updates and derivative works of the original content remain the property of Hebei Zhongban. and are provided by Hebei Zhongban Culture Development Co.,Ltd.

The authors and publisher have made every attempt to ensure that the information contained in this book is complete, accurate and true at the time of printing. You are invited to provide feedback of any errors, omissions and suggestions for improvement.

Every attempt has been made to acknowledge copyright. However, should any infringement have occurred, the publisher invites copyright owners to contact the address below.

Hebei Zhongban Culture Development Co.,Ltd
Wanda Office Building B, 215 Jianhua South Street, Yuhua District, Shijiazhuang City, Hebei province, 2207

心理门·守护幸福

1 在爱里消失的人 1

2 爱之晕轮 4

3 我是爱之"寄生者"吗? 6

4 爱之"暴躁狂" 10

5 我不做"暴躁狂" 12

6 异地恋,你安全吗? 16

7 做个安全依恋者 19

8 爱情里的选择权 22

9 慈爱诚实、公义平安、相遇相亲 26

10 我们在同一个世界淡伤包容珍爱 30

心理门·心理影视密码

1 "卑鄙的我":如何重生(一) 37

2 "卑鄙的我":如何重生(二) 40

3 "卑鄙的我":如何重生(三) 42

4 小黄人:在亲密关系里如何快乐依恋?(一) 44

5 小黄人:在亲密关系里如何快乐依恋?(二) 48

6 《港囧》:你心里还有哪些囧让你坐立难安? 52

7 从《寻龙诀》中认识正念疗法DBT之超然力量 58

8《芈月传》•女人篇：浅析人格特质对社会关系的影响 64

9《美人鱼》心声：我是自恋但不狂妄 72

10《西游记》白骨夫人：善力的自由 77

11 从《盗梦空间》与伯特·海灵格谈梦境系统 83

12 从《魔法老师》识别善良的智慧 88

心理门·倾听儿童

1 因材施教才是最合理的教育理念 94

2 尝试采用区别增加来管住你的小嘴巴 96

3 如何做一个情商高的父母 99

4 如何让你的孩子拥有强大的内心？ 101

5 走出逝去的阴霾，从抽动中解脱 104

心理门·我们的情绪

1 为自己做一个"转移计划随身带" 108

2 您是否能全盘接受这样的自己？ 112

3 释梦——一个心理师的梦境分析 116

4 重识自我的价值 121

5 致心灵书 125

6 优质标签的背后——还原别人眼里"万能"的我 129

7 由重庆两幼童坠亡案引发的思考 137

8 有时候我们要学会哀悼哀伤 141

9 为什么有的人难以与人建立亲密关系？ 145

10 绘画疗法真的能治愈受伤的心灵吗？ 148

11 怎样的亲密关系才叫高质量的关系呢？ 151

12 愿我拥有蒲公英一般的人生 154

13 咨询笔记之咨询师如何在咨询中克服选择冲突 158

14 如何走出焦虑的心境？ 161

Psychological Door · Guarding Happiness

1 The Ones Who Disappear in Love..166

2 Love Halo 169

3 Am I a parasite of love?..173

4 Love's' Fury Madness' 177

5 I won't be a "hot tempered maniac" 180

6 Are you safe in a long-distance relationship?..184

7 Be a Secure Attachment Holder 188

8 Choice in Love..192

9 Loving kindness and honesty, righteousness and peace, meeting and matchmaking 197

10 We are in the same world, indifferent, tolerant, and cherished.................202

Psychological Gate · Psychological Film and Television Password

1 'Despicable Me': How to Rebirth (Part 1)...211

2 "Despicable Me": How to Rebirth (Part 2) 215

3 "Despicable Me": How to Rebirth (3)...218

4 Minions: How to enjoy attachment in intimate relationships? (1)...........221

5 Minions: How to enjoy attachment in intimate relationships? (II)..........225

6 "Lost in Hong Kong": What other troubles do you have in your heart that make you feel uneasy?..231

7 Understanding the Transcendent Power of Mindfulness Therapy DBT from "The Dragon Quest Technique"..239

8 "Mi Yue Zhuan" • Women's Chapter: An Analysis of the Influence of Personality Traits on Social Relationships..247

9 Heart of the Mermaid: I am narcissistic but not arrogant 258

10 Journey to the West: White Bone Lady: The Freedom of Good Power 265

11 Discussing Dream Systems with Bert Hellinger from Inception 274

12 Identifying Kind Wisdom from 'Magic Teacher' 280

Psychological Gate · Listening to Children

1 Teaching students according to their aptitude is the most reasonable educational philosophy 287
2 Try using differential addition to control your small mouth 291
3 How to be a parent with high emotional intelligence 294
4 How to give your child a strong inner self? 297
5 Step out of the haze of the past and free yourself from the twitching 300

Psychological Gate · Our Emotions

1 Create a "transfer plan" for yourself to carry with you 305
2 Can you fully accept yourself like this? 309
3 Interpretation of Dreams - A Psychologist's Dream Analysis 315
4 ways to recognize one's own value 321
5 books for the soul 326
6 Behind High Quality Labels - Restoring the 'omnipotent' Me in Others' Eyes 332
7 Reflection on the Death Case of Two Young Children in Chongqing 342
8 Sometimes we need to learn to mourn and mourn 347
9 Why do some people find it difficult to establish intimate relationships with others? 352
10 Can painting the rapies really heal wounded souls? 356
11 What kind of intimate relationship is considered a high-quality relationship? ... 360
12 May I have a life like a dandelion 362
13 Consultation Notes: How Counselors Overcome Choice Conflicts in Consultation .. 367
14 How to get out of an anxious state of mind? 371

心理门·守护幸福

1 在爱里消失的人

A good feeling of song…

It can prove that truth. We live so truely. Correcting the mistake again and again.Because our knowledge is existent in our brain ,our blood and our soul forever.

一首美妙的歌的感觉……

它能够证明真理。我们活得如此真实。一次又一次地纠正错误。因为我们的知识永远存在于我们的大脑、我们的血液和我们的灵魂之中。

Love your neighbor as yourself.

要爱人如己。——《旧·利》19：18

"不会吃饭，不会睡觉，什么都要人陪着，你刚刚离开一会儿，她就哼哼唧唧，但只是用目光四处找人。"

"她这是怎么了？"

妮妮刚来访的时候，是被两个闺蜜带着来的，神情麻木，对外界刺激几乎没有任何反应。因为失恋的缘故，她不能正常地工作、生活，甚至连行走、吃饭、睡觉都退行到一个婴儿的状态，累坏了闺蜜们。

有一种人，在亲密关系中，叫"寄生者"。

过度依赖，担心被遗弃、厌弃、离弃；于是紧紧地依附，以满足对方的一切作为全部或大半精神支柱，为了对方放弃社交生活、独处的时间、灵性思考与修行，甚至是原本正向积极的喜好、价值观。这一类人，在婚恋情感或其他亲密关系中，称之为"消失的人"或"寄生者"。

而这一类人，虽然其中也不乏男性，但因为男女思维方式大多迥异的缘故，所以，这里谈及的"消失的人"多以女性为主。

美国心理学专家贝芙丽·英格尔在她的《爱他也要爱自己》一书中也谈到"消失的女人"，为何会牺牲自己的主体性与自尊，错失追求个人成长的机会呢？

一旦亲密依赖关系出现问题，这样的被迫抽离，几乎让这一类"寄生者"无法接受。有的无法回到以前的生活，甚至衣食住行都退行为婴儿状态，苦闷、憔悴，食不知味、夜不能寐，感官失调，自卑自罪，失眠焦虑，甚至是抑郁，导致部分社会功能明显受损。

妮妮在稍微清醒一点之后，开始疯狂地宣泄情绪，连自己已经不知不觉做了一个怨妇都不知道。

"他让我不去参加闺蜜的生日聚会，我就不去；他让我不穿短裙子，我就把家里的短裙全丢掉；他让我不准和陌生人说话，我就不说话；他让我卸载掉微信和QQ聊天工具，我就卸载；他让我多看书，我就多看书，而且还必须看他给我选的书籍，尽管我从不喜欢看书和学习；他甚至都不准我看《煎饼侠》《屌丝男士》这类喜剧片，说我够白痴了，再看可能更智商为零了……我都做到这份上了，他还想怎样？"

等情绪宣泄完毕之后，她的能量耗尽了，陷入了抑郁，并伴有躯体疼痛、无力感的症状。

妮妮认识这段感情的男主人公是通过微信摇一摇的功能。一见面，妮妮就为男主角风流倜傥的外表、揶揄风趣的幽默感、小细节的体贴入微、不菲的工作收入等特质深深吸引。

她几乎在心里感叹："哦，我的上帝呀，除了他，我再也遇不到这么好的男人了！"

或许是这样的思维一开始就给了她"抱紧了别撒手"的暗示，两人迅速进入热恋，从相聊甚欢到发展成亲密关系，不过短短一个月的时间。

可自此之后，妮妮就从一开始的被迫接受被男主人公改造，到主动地配合被改造，乃至到最后的"强迫症依恋"。

现在，这段关系里的"男主人公"突然消失了，连句"道别"的话都没有。他倒是抽刀断水，绝情绝义，而妮妮一个人心里忽然空出了好大一个空洞，平时习惯依赖的肩膀突然消失了，她的魂灵无处相依，整个人轰然倒地，行为退行是再正常不过了。

"你当时为什么从来不拒绝他的强迫改变呢？"我问她。

她眨巴眨巴泪眼，问了一个看上去很让人啼笑皆非的问题："我……我可以吗？"

这——有点像一个5岁的孩子在家里拉着妈妈的衣角问，自己是否可以上厕所一样那么令人哭笑不得。

"你知道通常心理学层面上，寄生者分为三种类型。"我看着妮妮的眼睛说。

"那——您说说看，我是哪种类型？"

妮妮到底属于哪种寄生者呢？

《心理门 · 守护幸福》1—在爱里消失的人

本期【心理门】解语：当我们只关注现实的残酷、生活的困境，我们就不会更多关注如何积极去面对这些，是等待别人施舍，还是思考如何去创造美好、守护幸福？毕竟每一种创伤，都是一种成熟。

2 爱之晕轮

To shun evil is understanding.
远离恶便是聪明。——《旧·伯》28：28

上一期节目我们提到，在恋爱关系中，妮妮因为失恋，而退行成一个"巨型婴儿"。我告诉她，这是一种"寄生者"，那么，她到底属于哪一种"寄生者"类型呢？

我们这里从心理、社会关系、生物学角度分析成因：

第一，依赖性人格障碍型"寄生者"，几乎没有个人主体的存在感和价值感，只能通过依附外界客体来获得存在感，**依赖性很强，而且对抽离与遗弃相当恐惧**。这样的人格障碍，需要建立长期的咨询关系，耗费心理师极大的心力，才能有所改善。但总体而言，这样的人格障碍如果和先天遗传有关，被彻底治愈的几率相当低。但也有资深心理师通过沙盘游戏或催眠治疗，成功治愈过此类人格障碍的案例。

"你属于这一种吗？"我问妮妮。

妮妮想了一会儿，摇了摇头，"我没遇见他之前独立性不算特别强，但也不算上面说的那种。"

"那你很幸运，并不属于先天遗传的人格障碍。"我说，"因为那样的话，想要改善，会有点难度。"

"啊，还有后天的吗？"妮妮问。

"这就是我们接下来要着重谈到的社会关系环境和心理层面的分析。"我点点头。

鉴于妮妮说的"再也找不到这么好的人"，在心理学上，是一种"晕轮效应"的误导。正是这种晕轮效应，导致两个人在还未真正完全了解就走进了亲密关系，发展成高开低走的"速食爱情"。

那么什么叫"晕轮效应"？

晕轮效应又称"光环效应"，是指当认知者对一个人的某种特征形成好或坏的印象后，他还倾向于据此推论该人其他方面的特征。本质上是一种

以偏概全的认知偏差。就好比我们常常容易得出"一个外表光鲜亮丽的人一定是一个心灵美好的人",可实际上呢?

这样的效应会影响我们在认知层面上的组织、决策和判断,无论是在朋友关系上还是在恋人关系上,都会产生"择友不善"的后果。即被外在的元素迷惑住了心眼,譬如外貌、对方的身份、地位、优越的物质条件等等,却忽略了仔细审视彼此的内心世界、精神层面是否合适,三观是否合得来,这样精神层面的两个人彼此是否能够接受?

而不是等到两个人很快陷入爱情之后,才发现彼此不合适,那就势必出现一方拼命想控制,产生分离焦虑,那样的关系里没有幸福,只会让人窒息。

"你是受了这样的影响吗?"我淡然地看着她。

"哦,这个该死的晕轮效应,我好像……是有一点迷恋那样的人。"妮妮对着手指头,低下头去,"不过,我想,我还有点悲伤。"

"你是指悲观情绪化,对吗?"我更正她提出的概念。

易悲观情绪化。像妮妮这类女人,太在意别人对自己的看法,害怕因为拒绝改变而不被人接受或讨厌。诚如妮妮所言,"我担心我不改变,会给他一种一意孤行的形象。"可实际上,反映的是我们自己内心对自己的拒绝和不肯定,内在的自我没有足够的信心支撑,怎么可能从外在评价上得到恒定固守的自我价值观肯定呢?

"我还有点不太明白。"妮妮问我。

"不懂啊,这样,我举个例子,比如,如果一个人说你是胖子,你会介意吗?"

在我淡淡的声音后,就是妮妮的笑声。

因为她很苗条,她自己也知道。

"没办法,这是我的前男友要求的,他说过,如果我成了胖子,他就不要我。可我现在依旧苗条,他还是不要我了。"

同时,自卑、敏感多想,也是造成"寄生者"人格的成因之一。这里不再赘述。

我察觉到她的沮丧,就跟她开玩笑,"看,这也是上一段恋情当中一个明显的好处。当然，现在还有很多的好处，都是有关成长的。我们有时候要经历疼痛，才能真的引发思考和逐步成熟。"

然而类似妮妮的情况，要如何杜绝"寄生者"现象出现呢？

《心理门 · 守护幸福》2 爱之晕轮

本期【心理门】解语：很多时候，我们相信的，其实仅仅是我们愿意相信的，那么表象与本质同时显现，什么才是真实的呢？

3我是爱之"寄生者"吗？

Man does not comprehend its worth.
智慧的价值无人能知。——《旧·伯》28：13

上篇文章中，妮妮因为失恋成了爱之寄生者，而依赖性人格障碍、晕轮效应、悲观情绪化、自卑敏感多想等都是后天导致这种现象发生的成因。我们每个人都想获得完美的爱情，从亲密关系中获得温暖与可靠恒定的安全感，没有人愿意做爱之寄生者，那么要如何才能杜绝自己成为亲密关系里的寄生者呢？

1. 让情到浓时的时间拉长一点。

在当今这个活色生香的花花世界，认真客观地做好一个观察者，抛开恋人光鲜亮丽的外在条件，包括身份、地位、财富、幽默感、蜜语甜言，甚至是一些体贴的小细节；从思想精神层面去了解这样的人，他到底是一个怎样的人？只有这样，才可以认识到真实的对方，而这样的他，是不是那一个适合我们来谈一场不那么荡气回肠却又值得你花费一点小心力去细水长流的那一个人。这个办法，相信也是克服恋人关系里"晕轮效应"的杀手锏吧。

2. 做真实的自己，诚实的表达真实的思想。

不要因为你的他不喜欢，你就隐藏起这样的自己，长此以往，就算他和你在一起了，也不是爱真实的你呀，而是爱你假装出来的那一个人；始终不是你，那么这场爱情，除了各取所需，还有什么值得珍贵的意义呢？所以，如果两个人是真实的相爱，那么，我可以照顾你的感受，但不能因为爱你，而失去原本的自己。彼此接受真实的对方，坦诚以待，才是一段开启在平等真实当中的亲密关系的好方法，而不是彼此隐藏。我记得刘若英说过一句话，当你找到一个不用担心在他面前需要收腹的伴侣时，那证明你的"真命天子"或"天女"出现了。真正的命中人，有一个共同的特质，就是可以自在相处的人。

3. 拥有自己独立的生活、工作、爱好、专业，那些……除了优雅的意中人，还能值得你欣喜的，或值得骄傲的地方。

有些女士，擅长烹饪、插花、品咖啡、绘画、雕刻、写作、音乐等等……这些可以算作是一种爱好，如果稍加培养和用心，还能把这些爱好变成骨灰级的专业，做到业内最好的那一个层次，把它变成钱。然后再用钱来进阶更高阶的梦想，不断完善自我，这样，就算是哪一天，你的心上人跟别的妹子跑掉了，那你也不至于像案例中的妮妮那么凄惨，搞得自己跟个怨妇或"巨型婴儿"似的。这里谈及的专业，和梦想有关系，这会在以后的婚恋情感节目中专门来谈，如何为我们选择的梦想负责。但这要放在古代应该算得上是一门技艺吧。只是这个时代，早已不推崇"女子无才便是德"那一套了。

4.珍惜你的"影子人格"者。什么叫影子人格呢？

心理学上，每个人都有一个阴影面的人格特征，就如一个内向的人，其实内心深处也是喜欢外向活泼的色彩；而一个不善言辞的人，内心是对巧舌如簧、运筹帷幄的社交达人充满向往的。

而具有"影子人格"的人，正好能弥补我们阴影性格面的另一面，而社会关系心理专家认为，如果找到这样的阴影人格，自己的人格通过相似互补的原则，在与之交往中不断地习得，就能成功弥补心灵上的缺失和不足，从而成长为完善人格。

人最难改变的是先天继承的性格特征，但可能更难改变的，是面对欲望时我们脆弱的人性，而"影子人格"者恰好在一定程度上可以使我们这部分得以完善，逐步完美。

只是很多人在遇到适合自己的"影子人格者"之后，在熟识的基础上，总是开始不知不觉尝试改变对方，把他改变成自己想要的那个样子。如果对方总是强迫你改变，那说明，他或许并不是真爱你，他爱的，不过是他心里深藏着的那一个人，所以才会在现实生活中，强迫眼前人不断改变成那个人的样子，而不是爱着真实的你。

就像妮妮在遇到好好之前，其他的人都是过客，都是来给她上课的"老师"，或需要授课的"学生"，在遇到自己的"Mr.Right"之前，就努力成为一个独立的主体，即便是一个人，也可以很自由自在很快乐地安排好自己的一切生活，一直到，遇见那个和你一样独立快乐的人，完善人格的人为止。

这样，"妮妮"和"好好"相遇，才可以变成一句简单平和却真正契合的一句——"你好"。

最后，请抱着平和的态度去恋爱吧，同时关注内在修行美好，秉持一颗内外兼修的心灵，坚持美好，在这个世界是一种特立独行。

诺贝尔文学奖得主萧伯纳说："此时此刻在地球上，约有两万个人适合当你的人生伴侣，就看你先遇到哪一个。如果在第二个理想伴侣出现之前，你已经跟前一个人发展出相知相惜、互相信赖的深层关系，那后者就会变成你的好朋友。但是若你跟前一个人没有培养出深层关系，感情就容易动摇、变心，直到你与这些理想伴侣候选人的其中一位拥有稳固的深情，才是幸福的开始，漂泊的结束。"

高层次的爱，是可以跨越于欲望和心瘾之上的大爱，是真实的付出，心灵的交流和爱的情感流动中的修行。

无论是哪一种，如果是真的——请珍惜已经拥有的，为了未来那个更好的自己努力做好现在吧。

《心理门·守护幸福》3——我是爱之"寄生者"吗？

本期【心理门】解语：佛经有云，人之所以痛苦，是因为正追求着或许是不适合自己的梦想，心灵被蒙蔽着，但总有一天，会找到答案，因为有快乐因子在指引。

4 爱之"暴躁狂"

Resentment kills a fool, and envy slays the simple.
忿怒害死愚妄人，嫉妒杀死痴迷人。——《旧·伯》5：2

英国生物学家达尔文说过："人要发脾气就等于在人类进步的阶梯上倒退了一步。"暴躁是一种不良的个性品质，遇事不顺发急，到底是你不会安抚内在的自己，还是允许它轻易地驾驭你呢？

第一次见到妮妮的时候，她穿着洁白碎花长裙，长发飘逸，皮肤白皙，精致的五官透出一种伶俐的气息。

她来找我，只有一个问题关键词："暴躁"。

她和好好很相爱，两个人在一起六年多了，三观正常，个性相似又互补，唯一的矛盾就是，她常常会因为一点芝麻大小的事就口出恶言，甚至是失控地摔东西。

一开始她以为这只是女人使的小性子，吵闹之后，好好一贯宠着她，可最近，她渐渐发现自己的小性子在不知不觉间升级。前不久，一次争吵，依旧是因为油盐酱醋茶的小事，她狠狠地摔门，却不小心压伤了好好的手指，造成指骨碎裂的后果。

妮妮对这件事愧疚非常，深深明白自己的过分，而好好的包容，让她更加希望能得到改善。其实妮妮在办公环境并不会这样，在平时的人际交往里也不会如此，最多是有点小野蛮，但不影响她的正常人际关系。

"我只想偶尔做他的野蛮女友，不是想做人见人憎的暴躁狂。"

上述案例的来访者妮妮，是一个暴躁症心理问题患者，但她有强烈想要改善的欲望。

暴躁有相当的情境性，并不是在任何场合都会出现的心理问题。而可笑的是，暴躁往往是出现在当我们面对很熟的朋友或亲人之中才会暴露无遗，而在面对陌生环境中反而可以得到控制。

为什么会这样呢？

这里我们暂时抛开先天性格基因遗传的元素，仅从后天心理成长来分析原因：

其一，从心理潜意识层面上，我们知道，我们的亲人朋友可以容忍我们，甚至是无比宽容，就像是被妮妮伤害了很多次的好好，一如既往地宠溺着她。继而她的潜意识会知道，就算她再如何暴躁，好好都会原谅她。

而相反面对较陌生的环境，比如办公室，为了保持自己的气质和自尊，即使受到不利于自己的刺激，妮妮也会尽量忍耐。

而这类患有暴躁症的人，无论男女，其实对自己身边最亲近的人给予的无意识伤害是最深的，而亲人朋友的真爱与宽容也是造就"暴躁症"的"温床"。

其二，是在我们成长的历程中，接纳的认知理念的非一致性。比如，在妮妮的身边，如果她因为暴躁症伤害了好好，而导致有内疚心理从而想要改善，但她同时又接受着身边另外一些人的"建议"：

"哪个人能一点儿没脾气呢？兔子逼急了还咬人呢？更何况，这件事上，一开始就是好好不对，惹了你生气，不是吗？"

"老虎不发威，他当你是病猫啊？可不能由着他，改天就蹬鼻子上脸了！"

这些反复的声音频繁出现，而与妮妮的愧疚感交织在一起，无助于她的意识清晰，反而会增加更强烈的受挫感。尤其是有些人的个性特征上，对周围的环境具有很强的被暗示性的时候，就更容易导致烦躁和暴躁。

其三，这种有暴躁症的人，通常她的原生家庭里一定有一个十分严厉的"教导者"形象。在我们还未成年的时候，稍有过错，或没有按要求去做，或又做不好的时候，就会遭遇"教导者"的严加训斥，甚至是体罚。

这种做法会造成两种不良的后果：第一，使童年期的我们感到不满和压抑，这种不满和压抑会在以后相应唤起这种情绪的场合中被爆发出来；第二，教导者的举动，在无意识间，为童年期的我们提供了一个效仿的暗示。这就是为什么一旦有这样的环境出现的时候，暴躁症和攻击性行为就会爆发出来。

导致暴躁症最后一个原因是，某些疾病或生理调节的因素（常常熬夜晚睡）引发心理的烦躁不安、易发怒的行为。

《心理门·守护幸福》4——爱之"暴躁狂"

　　本期【心理门】解语：这个世上没有不生病的人，只要对症下药就一定会有改善。就如同我们遇到种种挫折和痛苦，皆是难免，但只要抱着幸福的愿望，抱持苦乐成长，就能驱散迷雾见阳光。找到每个人心底的那朵纯白色莲花吧。

————The End————

5我不做"暴躁狂"

　　I will speak out in the anguish of my spirit,I will complain in the bitterness of my soul.

　　我灵愁苦，要发出言语。我心苦恼，要吐露哀情。——《圣经·诗篇》42:4

那么要如何纠正暴躁症呢？

首先，和妮妮同样有心理问题的人，需要了解暴躁症的以上成因，并且明白这种不良个性品质是可以通过长期的自我觉察与心理治疗或亲友间的不断提醒，逐渐形成正向的行为模式，从而达到得以纠正的目标。

第二，在心理治疗上有一种"内观疗法"，即引导来访者学会凝视内心的那个小孩，看着他在沟通不利时在一旁大吵大闹的样子，然后看着那样的哭闹的孩子，你会有什么想法？

这是一种积极的自我觉察方式。

不管是处于哪个年龄阶段，出现这样的状况我们不难发现，那个暴躁的坏脾气小孩子，还很稚嫩，他多么需要你的呵护和提醒。你要尝试做他的理想父母或理想伴侣，一直陪着这样的自己，不断地提醒。

当然人都有脾气，但有时候发脾气的确可以起到很好的让事情进展的效果，而且我们发脾气的对象有区别。

有的人，你发发脾气可以起到很好的作用，但有的人，你发脾气不会起任何好作用。他除了能在那一刻轻松占领你的理智和处理问题的头脑以外，还会伤害对方好重，而这些愿意忍受你发脾气的人，通常都是你身边最亲近的人。试问如果不爱又何来包容呢？还由着你内心的顽皮小孩子任性胡闹？

他们是愿意用默默的爱包容你的人。如果你觉察不到这一点，就势必在每一次发脾气的时候，把他们当作是惯性的垃圾桶，还认为可以毫不顾忌地发泄坏情绪？说尽世间你能找到的、搜罗来的一切恶毒的话，来释放你的坏情绪。

可后果呢？

事后，你看着他们因为你释放发泄的负能量与不良情绪无比苦痛，你又会伤心、难过、自责，觉得如此不应该……有这样的自我觉察很好，那么就要学会控制脾气与情绪，学会安抚那样的内在自我，那个小孩子，尽我们所能让他平静下来，而不是让他驾驭你，对吗？

元朝张光祖在《言行龟鉴》中也提到："君子所养，要令暴躁邪僻之气不设于身体。"由此可见，除了要学会包容、宽容之外，就算是为了我们拥有一个健康的体魄，也是需要合理科学地调节我们的情绪的。

(It is a flower like a dragon but like a dragon turtle.)

自我觉察之后，就要悉心关注你内心的那个顽皮小孩子，他是如此需要被爱，需要被关注，他的伤心、难过、痛苦，还有他的不舒服……做他的好父母，耐心地陪伴他，在他又要发脾气顽皮的时候，提醒他一下。

比如：**用逻辑的思维及时紧急干预感性的情绪，可以快速数数，但要有点难度的**，比如："1+3=4""3+5=8""5+7=12"……如此类推，奇数类或偶数类相加，紧急调用逻辑思考能力来控制或选择性遗忘不良的情绪瞬间。等完全冷静下来，再思考，下一步理性的我，应该怎么做？

这和有些人在心绪不宁时念"清心咒"是一个道理，第一是思考，第二，是为自己能安抚好坏情绪增加坚定的信心。

第二，深呼吸，感觉清净的气息从外部自鼻腔进来，顺着呼吸道，一直到肺部，再往下感知，一直到肚脐眼的位置，在禅修上，这个位置叫"脐轮"，然后再经过一个呼吸，把体内的浊气排出来。这种深呼吸的自我正向暗示法，一般性的怒火，在5-8次这样的呼吸后可以平息下来。

第三，阅读。"俗话说，书中自有颜如玉，书中自有黄金屋"，多阅读带正能量的书籍，让自己纷乱的心绪，在正向的书籍中得到安宁。

第四，**让自己浸泡在户外大自然风景优美的环境当中**，大自然对一切的负能量都有一种神奇的净化作用，就如同，一条被污染的河流，在保持不再继续接触和产生污浊之后，经年累月，可以慢慢重新变得清净。**这就**

如同我们的心灵，不管之前有多么阴暗，只要从此往后，和那些容易产生负能量或负面情绪影响的环境保持安全距离，再加上自身的强烈想要得到改善的心愿，那么持之以恒，就能重新获得心灵的温暖，完成自我疗愈和心灵成长。

第五，早睡早起，养成合理科学健康的生活作息习惯。

只有我们内心真的拥有了强大的温暖和真正成熟完善的人格，才能拥有感受快乐、获取幸福的能力，内心有了阳光，才能把这样的光与温暖传递给身边的朋友们，让身边的朋友也因为你而温暖快乐。

最后，当我们与亲密关系的人发生了矛盾的时候，如果自身不具备合理沟通、理性解决问题的沟通能力，什么都要等着对方来解决，那么自己在问题解决上，始终都是被动的。如何让自己从被动的接受，变成具备主动解决问题的修心达人，也是一门心理学社会关系中的必修课。

《心理门·守护幸福》5——我不做"暴躁狂"

本期【心理门】解语：每一个改善都会那么的不容易，甚至是痛苦的，可为了心爱之人重展的欢颜，或身边的朋友释怀的笑脸，也为了未来那个更好的自己，我们都需要努力，慢慢地……你会发现，你所做的努力，一切都是如此的有意义。

6 异地恋，你安全吗？

For the ear tests words as the tongue tastes food.
耳朵试验话语，好像上膛尝食物。——《旧·伯》34：3

导语：

"你爱我吗？"

"爱。"

"真的？"

"真的。"

"真的真的是真的？"

"真的真的是真的。"

"嗯……可以再说一遍吗？"

"你——怎么总是不信？"

我们每个人在婴儿期的心理发展，是需要建立信任感，克服怀疑感，从而才能拥有希望的良好人格品质。

在这一时期，我们是否获得了良好的母婴依恋关系，直接影响着我们内心的安全感。而安全感，也是你是否能够在经历一场荡气回肠的异地恋时，顺利走向终点，收获幸福的重要心理密码。

美国著名心理学家斯滕伯格的爱情三角理论中，指出爱情包括三要素：激情、亲密、承诺。

要想收获完美的爱情，这三者缺一不可。

亲密是指恋人之间相互关心、呵护、照顾、终日厮守的愿望。

但当遭遇异地恋的恋人们，亲密的元素就不得不大打折扣，于是安全感就成了解读异地恋完美爱情的重要密码之一了。

"你今天怎么没说晚安？"在妮妮的责问声中，好好的睡梦完全被惊醒了。

"唔，我忘了。"

"那你现在在干嘛?"

"睡觉啊……"好好明早还有一个会,一天的工作让他异常疲惫。

"和谁?"

"你到底在说什么呀?"好好有些生气。

哪知电话那头的妮妮"哇——"一声哭出来。

"你是不是不爱我了?"

"你怎么了?"好好被妮妮的哭声彻底惊醒了,开始有点慌乱,也自责刚才自己的语气是不是重了。他花了好长时间才哄得妮妮不再哭了,细细一问原因,妮妮的反常居然是因为:

"你……你都没有道晚安。"

妮妮与好好在一年前相爱了,但美中不足的是异地恋。妮妮要求好好每天下班必须一个电话,晚上临睡前,要一声晚安。有时候,妮妮会打电话过去,可每天同样的话题,同样的时间,同样的问候,两个人都有些乏了。

对于妮妮的怀疑,好好一开始还会尝试解释,可随着时间的流逝,他现在居然感觉到心累了。

可他的回避,却让妮妮的安全感迅速下降,继而猜疑、追问也越来越多了。反反复复好多次,起初好好都会在妮妮哭泣之后第一时间出现在她的身边,但好好一旦离开,妮妮又开始了上述类似情况的分离"反抗",或哭泣,或焦虑,或食欲下降,甚至是失眠。而好好被妮妮折腾得越来越累心。

他明确地希望妮妮能够更加独立一些。可这样的冷漠表示,换来的是妮妮变本加厉的猜疑。到最后,两个人对这段关系都不想忍受了,只想赶紧逃离。这场异地恋以失败告终。

虽然是好好最终的冷漠与倦怠为这段感情画上了句号,但不可不说,其实是妮妮在这段亲密关系中严重缺乏安全感,不断地猜疑,才导致了后来的事。

缺乏安全感的人,永远会做一些事,来毁灭内心对一段亲密关系的真实信任感。

通常会出现两种情况:要么是拼命监控对方,查岗,查聊天记录,甚

至是跑去打印对方手机的通讯记录单，不难发现这是由缺乏安全感而衍生出现的控制欲。

而上述案例中的妮妮，只是因为好好没有说晚安，她内心的安全感一旦下降，就开始猜疑不断，以致于自己都厌恶这样的自己。

尽管从某种程度上来说，妮妮缺乏安全感，是因为和好好异地恋的缘故，但究其根源还是因为妮妮缺乏的安全感，导致的一定程度上的分离焦虑。

如果说我们的伴侣亲密关系就是在寻找"理想父母"的复刻模板，再通过"现实父母"的方式来呈现童年依恋方式的话，在心理学上，有一种依恋称为"反抗型依恋"。

这类依恋关系的人，会因为缺乏安全感，时刻警惕母亲的离开，对母亲离开极度反抗，非常苦恼。母亲回来时，既寻求与母亲的接触，可又随时警惕着下一次的分离，于是会在亲密关系相处中，表现出既想拥有亲密关系，又时常反抗，就跟上述案例中的妮妮是一个模板。

这是缺乏安全感导致的一种反抗型依恋关系形式。

本期【心理门】解语：我们常常会因为内心的需求想要控制对方，但其实控制是双向的。当你控制一个人的时候，你或许感到一切处在掌控之中，你安全了，但实际上，你也是在被这份注视而受掌控。掌控你的不是别人,而是你自己的选择方式。在婚恋关系中尤甚如此,没有纯粹安全的依恋关系,这份安全感,需要内在给予,而非外在。倘若内在增加了一份定力,自然就减去一份猜疑与痛苦。若是让人感觉心安的幸福依恋关系,是不需要控制的,就让我们来思考,是不是这样?

7做个安全依恋者

He is like a tree planted by streams of water,which yields its fruit in season and whose leaf does not wither

要像一棵树栽在溪水旁,按时候结果子,叶子也不枯干。——《旧·诗》1:3

缺乏安全感导致的第二种形式是无爱感。

下面我们就来看看第二种情况:

妮妮和好好在一次相亲会上一见钟情,可惜是异地恋。妮妮总是让好好觉得他在与不在都无所谓,妮妮依旧自己玩自己的。这让好好很有挫败感。

"我周五会过来,我们一起吃顿饭吧。"好好在电话里积极地建议着。他以为妮妮会表现出很开心的模样。

可妮妮这头只换来了一个轻描淡写、不冷不淡的"嗯"。

他以为是自己安排的节目让妮妮不感兴趣,于是又建议一起去看电影。"听说白百合主演的《捉妖记》上映了,我记得你说过你喜欢看这类影片,吃过饭,我们就去看吧。"

还是一个"嗯"。

好好百思不得其解,难道是自己的魅力不够吗?为什么明明妮妮已经是自己的女朋友,却还是一副不咸不淡的样子呢?小别胜新婚啊。

到了周五,公司临时通知开会,好好带着歉意,打过去电话说不能来了,妮妮也一副无所谓的样子,没有想象中的失落感。

两个人不得已分手的那一天，好好问妮妮，"你爱过我吗？"妮妮并不否认对好好的爱，可是，究其原因，是什么导致妮妮这样的态度和方式去爱呢？

与其恐惧分离，还不如不爱。这便是妮妮的无爱感，她已经没有爱人的能力了。

在亲密依恋关系中，有一个心理学名词叫"回避型依恋"。这种情况相当少数，在婴幼儿期，被称为是无依恋婴儿，亲密的抚养人在与不在都无所谓，但从根本上而言，还是缺乏安全感导致的，和第一种案例一样，都属于消极依恋。

还是妮妮和好好的异地恋故事，第三个案例。

与前面两个案例截然不同的是，妮妮和好好是一对已经5年异地恋的恋人了，可感情却若"人生初见般美好"。

"今晚你吃得什么呀？"好好在微信上问。妮妮拍下一碗白粥，附上一张小脸儿惨白的自拍照。

"怎么了？你生病了？"好好急忙打来电话焦急地问候。

"嗯。有一点小感冒。昨晚踢被子着凉了。"

"都怪我没有在你身边照顾，我马上请假回来看你。"好好立即向人事部请假。

"诶，不用请假，干嘛耽误工作呀？我又不是小孩子了。"

可好好还是赶了回来，他的关怀和细心呵护，并非停留在蜜语甜言上，让妮妮明白并肯定，自己在好好心里是唯一的。

妮妮本身就不缺乏安全感，而好好的真实呵护，也更加深了她内心深处的安全感。

有时候，妮妮会把去看的电影片段发给好好，然后好好会在另一个城市也看一遍，到周末相聚的时候，两个人再把有趣的话题聊一聊。

已经五年了，可两个人，还是如初恋一般，总有说不完的话题，制造不完的新鲜感与浪漫。

五年，是妮妮和好好规定的异地恋期限，两人也最终修成正果。在这五年里，两个充满安全感的恋人，都一直在为真正的相聚努力着，奋斗着。五年也足够实现各自的一段梦想，等聚到一起的时候，再携手，向下一个梦想进阶。

第三个案例里的两个人，都是**安全型依恋**，他们互相视彼此为安全基地，当恋人在场时会感到足够安全，能够在陌生的情境里积极地探索和操作，譬如更加积极的实现梦想。对恋人的离开或在陌生城市里面对陌生的人事物，也不会有强烈的不安全感反应。

而说到安全感，到底从何而来呢？

准确地来说，安全感的建立，是在三岁以前。如果在婴儿期得到的关注不够多，安全依恋没有能够良好地建立，那么在后期成长过程中，如果能在无条件的被给予爱的环境下，重新完成亲密关系的复刻，在心灵成长上有一定的自我觉察，并拥有强烈想要修复的欲望，那么心灵上或许可以在积极的引导下，获得新的成长。

这样"自我疗愈"的安全感，等同于"安全型依恋"。需要一个亲密关系的人一直给予无条件的积极关注来完成，也可以是在这方面有经验的心理师，正向地运用咨询技巧导引改善。此时，来访者如果将过去重要人物的情感投射太多到分析者身上，那么"移情"便产生了。

一个真正有安全感的人，安全感是来自于内心深处，而不是来自于别人的心灵寄托。唯有自身建立了牢固的安全感，心灵才能获得更大的成长。而拥有强大安全感的人，是更能够完成自我实现的，在人生规划中，也更容易获得极大的成功，也容易拥有幸福。

身处异地恋的恋人们，可以通过发达的通讯媒体方式来传情达意，休息日小聚，让恋人爱上你的思想灵魂多过于你的身体，这或许是异地恋最大的一个优点了。但最好在这段恋情上，制定出一个合理的规划：包括如何努力地真正在一起以及一个异地状态的时间。

如果没有这个期限，那么异地恋就如同看不见出头之日的万丈深渊，让"在一起"三个字变得如此遥遥无期，不切实际如夜空里的烟花，虽然璀璨，但也不过是你人生爱情路上的昙花一现，又有什么意义呢？

就好比我们实现目标一样，如果超出了期限，却丝毫不见起色，那就真的不得不考虑一下未来的路要怎样调整前行了。

祝愿天底下所有的妮妮和好好，有情人终成眷属，相信应该相信的，坚守应该坚守的，收获属于自己的那一份真爱。

本期【心理门】解语：若是因为恐惧而希望永远蜷缩在"壳"里的人，那是否等同于选择永远让自己处于"孵化期"，拒绝长大。要知道，虽然走出来注视这个世界的多姿，会有可能受伤，但若是把每一道岁月给予我们的伤疤变成某种经历过的"勋章"，那我们或许可以从中获得将来行走的更加安稳顺利的力量。

8 爱情里的选择权

like silver refined in a furnace of clay, purified seven times.
纯净的言语，如同银子在泥炉中炼过七次。——《旧·诗》12：6

导语：你不懂为什么你没有喊停，就有人擅自决定停止？你不明白，明明你心向明月，却偏偏襄王有意，神女无情？

英国现代杰出的现实主义戏剧作家，诺贝尔文学奖的获得者萧伯纳说过："人生有两出悲剧。一是万念俱灰；另一是踌躇满志。"

在爱情与婚姻里，无论是悲剧还是喜剧，也无论是谁，每个人都拥有选择的权利。当爱情褪掉魔力的华丽外衣，就只剩下现实的残酷需要面对，理智地抉择，或许也是一种真正的成熟吧。

一位朋友，前不久发私信询问我：很久以前，他就想和女友分手，很清楚知道他们没有结果，可不知为何，每次做选择时，他都异常艰难，似乎自己无法做出正常的满意选择，而且严重的时候，还会很恐慌，惊慌失措，甚至是汗流浃背，导致最后无法选择。而这样的情况，也仅仅出现在感情抉择上。说到这一点，连他自己也觉得啼笑皆非。

英国现代杰出的现实主义戏剧作家，诺贝尔文学奖的获得者萧伯纳说过："人生有两出悲剧。一是万念俱灰；另一是踌躇满志。"

在心理学上，有一个名词"选择恐惧症"，也称作选择困难症。选择恐惧，显而易见是不自信和逃避责任的心理，缺乏自立意识，害怕失败。患上这种病的人面对选择时会异常艰难，她甚至会陷入究竟是选择吃了晚饭沐浴好，还是沐浴后再吃晚饭好，这样的日常生活纠结中。好在以上的个案只发生在情感的选择上。

出现难以抉择的情况，排除开情感本身具有错综复杂性的特点，就个体而言，造成这样的原因，主要是：一，**不能确定自己内心最重要的需求，无法获得心理平衡**；二，**害怕承担抉择的后果**；三，**对自我不满，将对不满"投射"出来变相反应，逃避自己**。

我们姑且称这样的现象为爱情选择困难症吧。与这类现象的反面：有一种人，或有过很多经历，或在这方面虽然经历不多，但悟性很高。在选定自己婚恋的对象的时候，一旦选定，常常是比较忠贞的。也就是说在他的内心世界里，男女到底要发展成怎样的关系，他应该在这段亲密关系里得到什么，他能给对方怎样的承诺与责任的担当，已经是十分清楚了。这样的人，对婚姻的追求比较得当，在选择上更为理性。比如，不仅要合得来，而且都要能够很好地彼此生存，促进进步，或互利成长。结婚要让双方都得到更大的空间和更大的成功机会，或更能够满足我们对事业、对社会关系、对自我发展的心理需求。也就是在较为成熟的婚恋关系里，这样的选择配对，是一加一大于二的。比起仅仅依赖感性为生的亲密关系，更为稳妥牢固。

也就是说，选择一个既有情感又在多方面适合自己的人，更能够给一段亲密关系带来牢固的安全感。

另外，我发现，但凡有选择恐惧症的朋友，都或多或少有追求所谓完美的强迫症倾向。

如何来克服呢？

这里，我们只就此个案来浅析：

首先不妨问问自己，我有多么了解这样的自己，在这段亲密关系里，我到底想要什么样的生活，得到什么样的成长，然后，我能付出的是什么。我们可以暂时不看回报，但一定得清楚我们付出的底线在哪里。

如果对方想要得到的，远远超出了你能给予的底线，那就仅仅能依靠委曲求全的扭曲自我意识，才能换取短暂的聚合，而这样的关系，是不堪一击的。

在一段成熟的婚恋关系里，如果已经清楚了以上这一点，那么想要管理自己，坚定地接受一种选择，也并非是难事。当面临选择困难时，我们可以尝试只选择其中一项，不去考虑更多，只专注于"适合"二字，坚定地完成这一选择。当选择完成时，也不用后悔，不做对比，只要相信自己的选择实际上已经是最适合自己的正面心理暗示。

通过这样的正面积极心理暗示，从而彻底摆脱情感选择障碍的阴影。

如果实在太纠结想弄清楚脚下的路应该如何走，那也可以采取"对比优劣"的方式，来帮助自己进行更加明晰的选择。例如，在上述个案里，当这位朋友感到比较困难而不知如何抉择的时候，可以在身边拿出纸笔，一边列出做这个选择的十项优点，在另一边列出不做这个选择的十项缺点，两相对照，就一定能够帮助自己，更清晰地看到自己选择的结果，从而帮助下决定。

同时，我们都应该在亲密关系相处当中，学会自我欣赏。

只有发自内心的自我欣赏，才能在这样的基础上，真正懂得欣赏别人。让亲密的彼此，多一些鼓励和欣赏中获得的成长，由此加强和促进亲密关系的良性发展。

这一点同样适用于亲密的朋友关系、父母关系，以及身边和谐人文环境的打造。

只要做到了以上几点,内心的安全感得到了由内而外的夯实,就更能懂得自己该何去何从了。

在爱情与婚姻里,无论是悲剧还是喜剧,也无论是谁,每个人都拥有选择的权利。当爱情褪掉魔力的华丽外衣,就只剩下现实的残酷需要面对,理智地抉择,或许也是一种真正的成熟吧。

真正成熟的人,生活的方式是平稳的,很多选择也是趋于这个方向,也从而拥有了获得从内心微笑出来的幸福的能力。在与周围平稳祥和的关系里,平和淡然到一个眼神就已读懂一切,了然于胸。所以……感恩我们所拥有的,让心灵充满满满当当正能量的爱,妥帖安稳,灵魂便富有而满足。有了这样的幸福的能力,这世上还有什么想要的美好是我们不能创造与拥有的呢?

《心理门·守护幸福》8——爱情里的选择权

本期【心理门】解语:在爱情里,我们每个人都拥有选择的权利,少一点痛多许多快乐与幸福,感恩。愿所有的阴暗里都能盛放一朵纯白色的莲花,似水年华,懂得珍惜与真爱,静默闭眼,心下了空,惟愿安好。

————The End————

9 慈爱诚实、公义平安、相遇相亲

Love and faithfulness meet together;righteousness and peace kiss each other.

慈爱和诚实，彼此相遇。公义和平安，彼此相亲。——《旧·诗》85：10

近期"出轨男是否值得被原谅"这个话题，似乎又被炒热了。就像是蛋炒饭这类家常菜谱，反复炒，也不觉得腻味。

昨夜那个找我咨询、在视频里哭诉到无比哀痛的女人，一直在为上述问题苦恼、焦虑，还失眠。

"那你打算怎么办？"我听了近50分钟，在咨询快结束时才问她。

"我不打算怎样，我打算和那男人鱼死网破，他要和我离婚，和外面的小妖精在一起，那我一定要他脱层皮，让他以后都害怕女人！"那女人咬牙切齿，恨得牙痒痒。

我没有说话，只是把扑在桌面上的小镜子照给她看。

她忽然愕然，顿住，"老师，你怎么……"那是一张狰狞扭曲的面孔，她自己猛然间也意识到了。

"其实你不发脾气的样子，五官很精致，近乎完美。"我淡淡道，"只可惜，再美的女人，也有被人审美疲劳的一天，如果你们的情意只是建立在外表之上，同时缺乏心灵深度的灵魂相依相伴，所以，不会长久。你这样做，他是有可能会害怕，因为害怕而回到你身边，但是，他不是怕所有女人，而是怕把你自己变成这样面孔的女人。"

"那我不管，总之我不好过，他也别想好过。"女人陷入歇斯底里中，全然忘记了他们初遇时的美好，而这美好，即便已是过眼烟云，难道就一定要全盘否定？

"如果他选择回来，你还要他吗？"

这一问，却把女人问住，"不要……要吧，不过还是要他脱一层皮才可能……。"

女人已经想好了怎样的复仇计划，不管那男人怎么选，她都一定是要把他对她的伤害十倍奉还的。

她这么做，无非是要让他知道，他曾经插在她心口上的匕首，让她有多痛！

"一定要如此吗？"

她陷入了矛盾中。

关于婚姻爱情以及两性关系中的"出轨"问题，很多女人都在精神上有类似"性洁癖"的情结。女人在心灵深处在意性关系，就如同男人在脑子里在意金钱一样，不过也有特例的情况，这里只是谈普遍的情况。

或许两个曾经深爱的人，被深深地彼此伤害过、背叛过，再勉强合在一起，挤在一个屋檐下，于双方而言，或许早已爱意不在了。那么现在女人的纠结是因为什么呢？

第一，性关系的独占性。这就是为什么那个女人既想那个男人回来，可其实在心灵上，也是不能再接受男人的了。这样的情绪反应，通常也与人格特征有关，偏执的人容易有，依赖型人格也容易有，即"你属于我，你曾经属于我，所以即便我不再需要你了，你也不能有选择新欢的权利。"

第二，尚未形成独立完满的人格，对自我独立生活、独自面对未来的恐慌。这类现象的发生，通常和自身的经济能力、独立能力以及自信心有极大的关系。很多人喜欢把两个人在一起描述成习惯，其实就是这个隐因在其中。当两个半圆的人遇到一起，合成一个圆，那么即便不爱了，或背叛了，但其实谁也离不开谁，除非再找到合适照顾自己的人。这一点，于男人，于女人都是如此。除非自我人格已经成长为一个圆满的圆，那么，此时可言"来去自留，悉听尊便。"

第三，心灵深处的创伤并未愈合。不仅需要修复，也尚处在你来我往的彼此还击式的伤害阶段，执着于继续彼此伤害纠缠。你不会快乐，他也不会幸福，但两个人宝贵的下半生就耗在这样的事情上了，毫无意义，亦无未来。

这样的情况，一直到什么时候呢？到彼此的能量都耗尽，都疲惫不堪了，就会有想停下来的欲望，然后才可以在独处中，想到要疗伤的那回事。然后才有更多的求助于亲朋好友，但最好是心理咨询师。

第四，当下的婚恋社会价值观。出轨的一方是否值得原谅？此文姑且定义为男性出轨的角度，因为社会价值的既定认可度，很多时候，同类问题并不具备同等对待的能力。譬如女方出轨，通常都会只有"离婚"一条路，没有之一。而男方出轨，譬如前半年的"文章"，网络上那段期间"渣男"骂语铺天盖地，可半年后，马伊琍太太的大度原谅，夫妻俩又一同出现在同一部影片里，拍片复出，又是一条"好汉"，还不用等十八年。从整体现有社会观而言，关于出轨，对于男人仍旧是宽容的居多。

我的这位来访者纠结的原因，还有一个，就是综上第四点，因为社会价值的倾向，似乎这年头，你不认可，你就是"怪人"。

可，是不是这样呢？每个人都生而独特，不要因为从众效应而忘记了自我。

现实是，你被人伤害了，严重背叛了情感，因为一部分大众认可和接受，你就没有选择的权利了吗？

男男女女都有选择新欢的权利，那么，你也一样有选择未来新生活的权利呀。关键是，你想要什么样的生活？你希不希望有一个新的未来？或者，你自己给不给你自己这样选择的权利？

对于每个人来说，个体感受才是最重要的关键。男人可以选自己所爱，远离原本的家庭，女人也一样可以选让自己愉悦的方式生活。"一别两宽，各生欢喜"，这句分手金句里诠释着一个深沉的含义：你最需要关注并且尊重的首先是你自我内心的需求和感受，而不是管谁怎么看，谁怎么说，大众评审又怎么言论。每个人都有各自的生活，无论如何，除了茶余饭后的谈资，也决定不了各自真实的人生。

你或许可以选择一个劈腿的伴侣继续去适应生活，当然也可以收拾好一切旧行囊，迈开大步往前走。有时候，我们之所以犹豫不决，是因为习惯，也因为害怕改变旧有的框架模式，去迎接新的创新与新的认知结构体系的重建。但往更深层面自我探索，还有一个小小的自卑受虐的小人儿在心灵那里，或许他藏在你的潜意识层面，需要你去认真仔细地倾听着——你心灵深处的声音：我，想要的到底是什么？

王尔德说"自恋是一个人浪漫的开端"，那些犹豫不决，不知道该不该原谅出轨伴侣的亲密爱人们，你们所犯的最大错误是不够自恋。你不相信自己值得被专一对待,不相信自己将来会遇到更好的伴侣,不相信离开一个劈腿伴侣,生活终将五色斑斓、多姿多彩。

这个世界上只要还有一个不出轨的伴侣,他就会撞到你的怀里,或许还是个帅哥或美女……至少得是一个彼此合适的人。如果你有这样的自信,只要你有这样的自信,那么,是否原谅出轨伴侣就根本不是一道难题。

当然,这里所言的自信,并非盲目的自我催眠与正向强化法的随便滥用。诚如有人常道:王婆卖瓜自卖自夸,那你也还得先有可以值得人一买的瓜,而且最好还是香甜可口。

所以,发挥自己已有的优势在此基础上建立起来的自信,才可在彼此的和谐关系里,保持你的品质,可拥有慈爱与诚实、相遇与相亲,乃至在懂得不失去自己优品的自我懂得与自我珍惜里,拥有富足的内心安宁。

那么我们应该如何重建自我的价值,抑或是重新认识自我的价值呢?

《心理门·守护幸福》9——慈爱诚实、公义平安、相遇相亲

本期【心理门】解语:倘若我们一辈子都在做着自欺、欺人、被人欺的重复,那么"真心相待"便已是最基本的人生修行课业。首先我们能做到的,至少是对自我的那个小人儿真诚,苦乐幸福都是自己的改变与抉择。就如同改变与否,全在于你心灵的声音,相信美好,相信自己,终会安然。

10 我们在同一个世界淡伤包容珍爱

Love can use wisdom, kindness, courage to forgive love of self deception, finally embrace each other.

爱能用智善勇敢包容爱的自欺欺人，最后拥抱彼此。——《旧·箴》10：12

心理学知识与哀伤处理：或许有个人在物理空间上与你相距遥远，有些人可能会把这样的体验理解为彻底或永远失去了这个人，那么，很可能就会陷入哀伤。如果不能体验到彼此之间曾经享受过的美好情感，也可能导致丧失感或空虚感。分离焦虑，与"现实"不对等的想象，或者有关愿望或梦想与现实严重不对等时，都有可能导致丧失感或空虚感。这就是哀伤体验。

在此，我们就《从你的全世界路过》介绍两种哀伤体验及处理方式。《从你的全世界路过》（英文名：I Belonged to You）改编自张嘉佳同名小说，由张一白执导，邓超、白百何、杨洋等人主演的爱情、文艺、微喜剧电影，于2016年9月29日在中国上映。

"滚什么？"

"滚床单。"

"陈末老师，你好，我是幺鸡。"

"幺鸡你好，我是白板。"哈，嘿呼～

这就是陈末。

一个看上去对什么都无所谓的男人，一个好似口无遮拦连新来台里的小姑娘实习生都要不正经一番的男人，心底却一直藏着一句话，一段似是而非的曾经，一个空缺需要补位的温暖。

"如果没有住进你的心里，都是客死他乡。"

每天和王牌DJ小容（杜鹃饰）针锋相对，只因陈末从大学时代开始就已经与清高的杜鹃势均力敌，从年少轻狂到死鸭子嘴硬的那一句"谁娶你是倒了八百辈子血霉了，这样吧，我吃亏点，我娶你。"

片中展示了三段爱情，如果以现实结合心理学观点，准确地说，应该是两段似是而非的朦胧，一段真实的情投意合，以及三段错过。

虽然影片有不少的戏份是在讲述陈末以外的两个兄弟，以及他们演绎的爱情模式，或者说不同角度的人看待爱情的方式。

这部影片里，因为幺鸡的善意撮合，杜鹃饰演的小容曾对陈末说过这句话：对你来说，相爱就可以。对我来说，适合才重要。

在此，请原谅我，只想就心理学的哀伤处理方法来分析陈末的情感模式。

最初陈末以为自己爱慕着杜鹃，却在杜鹃一句"不适合"后，变得颓废不堪，宛如一个"废材"。

以前，他随便脱口一句，就可以通过电台的电波，温暖很多人的心灵。"我希望有个如你一般的人，如山间清爽的风……只要最后是你就好。"

或许很多人都不明白，遇到幺鸡之后，却被幺鸡一句话戳中要害，"你曾经温暖过那么多人的心，怎么到你这儿就不行了呢？"

You know you can

那是因为给予温暖者，自己也正处于缺乏温暖期或自我调适期，所以，会出现影片中陈末出现的对自我价值感的自我贬低，吊儿郎当，口无遮拦等……

"为了什么男人的冰箱总放着甜点……"

《不说》是由黄伟文作词、李荣浩作曲并演唱的歌曲，是电影《从你的全世界路过》的"路过版"主题曲，整首歌，我只截取了这一句，是因为陈末就是一个需要"冰箱里常存甜点"的大男孩。

对待情感体验，如果不懂得适度，恰如这冰镇，就会弄丢自己的前进方向。唯一能唤起温暖的，唯有温暖。所以陈末在失去了内心爱情体验的温暖之后，只会在其他温暖自然生发时，比如兄弟情义，才会表现得像个还有温暖的人。

在我们人生历程中，每个人都可能会经历重要的失去。所以，需要以一种迅速处理哀伤的方法来灵活应对处理不同的心灵哀伤。

若从最粗浅的层面看，似乎大部分人都更多关注到了陈末的情感失去，所以他获得了幺鸡这样一个纯净水一般的女孩子的形象来拯救，这样的陪伴与宽慰也是一种对陈末的情感失去的紧急哀伤处理。

并在影片的最后，他获得了一个启示，那就是他保留着幺鸡这个纯净的女孩子的纪念品，一个毛猴子的面具，选择了放下那段不适当的似是而非的情感，选择了继续向前走。

虽然，他似乎错过了幺鸡，还在节目里请求整个重庆的收听他的节目的听众都为他闪灯寻找拯救了他的那个曾同在一片星空下的幺鸡。

当整个重庆为他的美好愿望祈福的时候，陈末在不知不觉中，已经又获得了他事业的回暖及全新的高峰，那些听众的闪灯就是最好的证明，也正是他对幺鸡这样的纯净水好姑娘美好印记的特别思念。

而且，即便没有了幺鸡，他也已经可以选择继续向前。

有些人，把爱情的温暖体验与事业的自我价值感联系在了一起，这样的人，通常不会把失去爱情体验的温暖感受表现出来，只会在某种体验失去的时候，抓紧另外一种体验来暂时替代，这样或许也可以修复部分哀伤，却不能完全修复。

这属于哀伤处理方式中的自我疗愈的方式，也是一种沉默以对的淡然哀伤自我疗愈方式。

淡淡的，就好

影片中人物角色的设置，颇为错位的是，陈末并不沉默，以吊儿郎当的方式来隐藏哀伤，是一种另类的沉默，唯有幺鸡这样的纯净水作为"药引"，才能开启他的自我哀伤自我疗愈的方式，而小容却才是那个终极沉默的自我哀伤处理者，她需要的是被正确的人正确的理解。

"多希望有一个像你的人，但黄昏跟青春无法相认……你爱默默倾听全世界，请往前走，不必回头。"这首林宥嘉演唱的影片插曲，正是小容的自我哀伤处理的一种自我解毒与自我疗愈的历程，也正是小容的选择——请往前走，不必回头。

或许很多观众是处于更多的同情陈末的这一边，反而忽略了看上去坚韧不拔的小容。学习和工作上，她始终站在比陈末更高一筹的位置，从互相较劲的同学友谊到工作中的"最佳拍档"。

只是，她想要的爱情体验不仅仅是情感的愉悦体验，更有事业工作上高品质的齐头并进。所以，在通透地明白了自己真正想要的是什么样的未来时，她会对自己心理上的哀伤，情感缺失方面的哀伤隐藏得很好，而且自我疗愈以憧憬未来的高品质生活，以精专的工作来要求自己。

陈末曾经为了似是而非的爱情体验差点弄丢了自己的路，而小容，很清楚自己想要的未来恋人与家庭以及事业的蓝图的模样，所以，她在暂缺的情感体验中或许有空洞的哀伤体验，但她很巧妙地把这部分空洞与孤独感，用精专的工作体验来弥补，以这样的等待，来换取她想要的美满的完美的未来。

如果说，小容有哀伤需要处理的话，那就是，她原本以为的那个合作人突然携款潜逃，留下她一个人独自承受。

这样的哀伤里，就不仅仅有情感体验方面的空缺造成的孤独感，更有事业方面，与她所憧憬的未来方面暂时不对等的自我价值感的缺失。这样的双重心理哀伤是属于严重的哀伤。而这一点，或许更多关注情感体验其次才是自我价值感明确的陈末，到影片最后，也能随着时光获得了真正的理解。

也或许小容的这一面，或许绝大部分观众不能理解，但我想，陈末会给予她最沉默的特殊的理解与成全。

小容是一个贪慕虚荣的女子，或者是一个彻头彻尾不解风情的事业型女性吗？

可小容真的是一个这样的女人吗？

从你的全世界路过，如果只是路过，我就在终点等着你，只要最后是你就好！

阿白，绣球花的话语是什么？我忘了……但我还是想说：remember hope

她要的那个最后，只有真正理解她的人才能明白，才能无论是从情感体验方面还是事业精专的高度方面给予与被给予。她细腻的心灵深处，那里虽然有自我修复，但却有在她与现实全然不对等的"理想"的太长等待中，需要被全然治愈的哀伤，对于小容这样非同寻常的女子，除非，是现实与理想划上等号，她心理的哀伤才可以得到全面的处理和痊愈。

"到对方心底瞧一瞧，体会彼此什么才最需要，别再寂寞的拥抱……"

这首电台情歌（《从你的全世界路过》电影电台版推广曲，是由火星电台制作。）

所以，从最初的不理解，也注定了，陈末与小容最初那段时光的最熟悉最陌生最亲密以及最疏离，而陈末因为幺鸡这个"药引"出现，因为，幺鸡深切地理解他，让陈末在沉默中学会了理解与成长，以及那份特殊的对幺鸡这样曾为他撑伞的女子特殊的思念印记。

就恰如他或许会在影片最后片尾曲结束后，问，"幺鸡你想要什么?"

而幺鸡不会回答，就好比，一个消弭于风中的恬然微笑，也释怀了陈末那原本或许放不下的心结。

这首《你在终点等我》片尾曲是由姚若龙作的词，轻轻读来，感觉有些别致：

> 我一直追寻着你心情的足迹
> 被所有的人误解都要理解你
> 准备好当擦亮你天际的浮云
> 你却在终点等我笑里有雨滴
> 我甘愿成全了你珍藏的往昔
> 只想你找回让你像你的热情
> 然后就拖着自己到山城隐居
> 你却在终点等我住进你心里
> ……

小容、陈末都随着幺鸡那自然消弭于金色阳光中的笑意，了然释怀了一切，懂得了该放下的过去，以及该迎接与拿起的未来，不回头，向前走，就好。

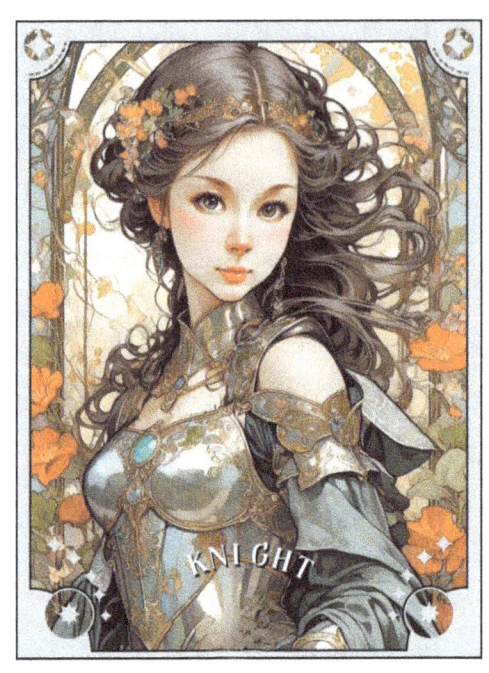

《心理门·守护幸福》10 我们在同一个世界淡伤包容珍爱

本期【心理门】解语：在心理哀伤得到妥善处理并治愈的那一刻，真正对的人，将拉进最美好的私人珍藏版记忆，恰如时光最美好的印记，挺起胸，抬起头，迎接美梦成真的、完美的、现在与未来。

心理门·心理影视密码

主要简介：从热门或经典影视剧中，除了看到乐趣、滑稽、搞笑、悬疑、紧张、奇幻的创意，我们还可以看到什么不一样？从心理师的视角，又有怎样奇特的见解？且看心理师是如何看待这些新奇、独特的影视剧奇观的呢？相信这部心理影视密码会给您不一样的感想。

1 "卑鄙的我"：如何重生（一）

Blessed is the man who does not walk in the counsel of the wicked or stand in the way of sinners or sit in the seat of mockers.

不从恶人的计谋，不站罪人的道路，不坐亵慢人的座位。——《旧·诗》1: 1

上映资料：《神偷奶爸》是 2010 年上映的喜剧 3D 动画片，由环球影业及 Illumination 娱乐公司制作，克里斯·雷诺德和皮埃尔·科芬担任导演。

我很偏爱这类成长主题的电影，而不在乎它是科幻、魔幻，悬疑推理或是动画电影，只要内容对味，充满令人珍惜的温暖。

《卑鄙的我》又名《神偷奶爸》，是由环球影业出品的 3D 动画。剧情大概是：一个把成为"世界第一大坏蛋"当作事业和梦想来实施的大坏蛋格鲁，不甘落后于一个嚣张的新人盗贼——矢量的不公平竞争行为。于是他决定比卑鄙、比无耻，决定领养曾经向他贩卖饼干而被他拒绝的三位孤儿——玛戈、伊迪丝和艾格尼丝。他利用她们进入矢量的城堡售饼干的机会实施偷盗，打算计划成功后再偷偷处理掉她们。然而在平凡的日常相处中，格鲁却对这三个小女孩产生了感情。为了不影响周密的盗月计划，格鲁不得不将三个孩子送回了孤儿院。而当他的计划成功后，矢量却绑架走孩子们。结局是格鲁营救了三个小鬼，月球回到了宇宙。

故事的最后，一个卑鄙无耻的大坏蛋成了名副其实的"神偷奶爸"，完成了成长，能够感受被爱，也能付出爱。

那么，一个内心冰冷的人是如何形成以及他是如何修复自我、获得重生的呢？

幼年共情失败会直接导致自恋型脆弱。在孩童时期，我们很需要父母给予被关注、被赞誉、被守护陪伴的感觉。如果在这一时期，孩子能获得成功的长期共情，那么，他内心的需求得以满足，内心那个孩子成长的能量没有固着，他也能顺利地身心成长。

共情是人本主义创始人罗杰斯提出的，是指体验别人内心世界的能力，即打开心眼看世界，类似用你的眼看世界。在共情状态下的关系中，沟通是无障碍的，无论是接纳者还是被接纳方，都会有感同身受的内心体验、情感以及思维。这一点，在我的一部都市小说《曼曼无双》里也提到过。

而影片中的格鲁，从小并没有受到这样的待遇。他的母亲似乎是他童年时期唯一的监护人，但她似乎一直在埋头做自己的事。对于孩子来说，即便是坐在一旁，但很可惜，她更多关注的是自己。童年期的格鲁无论怎样想吸引他母亲的注意，得到的都是漠视的回应。

可有一天，他发现还有一种方式可以引起母亲的注意，那就是当他使坏的时候，他能得到母亲的一两眼关注。虽然目光停留的时间仍旧短暂，但对一个内心极度渴望父母关注的孩子而言，这无疑是等同于发现了"阿里巴巴的宝藏"。

那样的短暂关注，对于一个孩子而言，是全然不够的，但这并不影响格鲁这样童年期共情不足的孩子饮鸩止渴。

于是，他学会藏起自己的失望、不被理解、不被关心，甚至感觉不到爱也没有关系。他的心逐渐变得冰冷，学会把自己的身体和心灵的痛楚隔绝开来，寄情于做一个大坏蛋。这样似乎感觉不到伤害，反而他成了四处伤害别人的人。他忽略掉对自我的了解，内心固着在那个感觉不到爱的恐惧点上。

于是在影片里，我们可以看到，他走在大街上，看见一个为冰淇淋掉在地上哭泣的孩子，他抿嘴一笑，从身后变戏法一般做了一个小狗形状的气球给那个孩子。可正当关注到那个孩子脸上破涕为笑的模样，他又用针把气球"噗"的扎破掉，一脸漠然地走开。

其实，他不是坏蛋，他只是在用这样的方式告诉每一个他遇到的孩子，这个世界是残酷的、冰冷的、漠视的，你唯有变成卑鄙无耻的坏蛋，才可以不被伤害，哪怕我们再也感觉不到爱。这也是格鲁的母亲在童年期传递给他的爱的"诠释"。

而遇到那三个孤儿院的孩子，她们天真烂漫的笑脸，是否就是他重获新生，拥有感受爱与被爱、完善自我成长的转机呢？

破除这条魔咒的咒语是：获得真爱与关怀，一直到他懂得真实付出的那一刻。

我不禁想起当下很多"陪伴"在自己孩子身边的父母，玩着手机，关注着股票、陌陌微信，做着各种自己的事，以为这样就是陪伴。可身体在，心灵却不能更好地收获彼此链接。至少，每一次身边的孩子要唤许多次我们那个特定的称呼——"父母"，方能回神关注孩子一两眼。

如果爱，就身心长久地护持与陪伴，方为真实。毕竟像"卑鄙的我"——格鲁那样长大以后能遇到帮助自己完成成长的人，如此幸运儿，这样的机会并不多，不是吗？

本期（心理门）解语：极善与极恶，往往就在一念之间，想要呆在哪里，就看你是否愿意让负性情绪驾驭你的行为。

2 "卑鄙的我"：如何重生（二）

The price of wisdom is beyond rubies.
智慧的价值胜过珍珠。——《旧·伯》28：18

《卑鄙的我》这部影片一共拍了两部。第一部中，让冷漠的格鲁遇到了三个甜心小可爱。或许这是命运的安排，好让他学会一些东西。

他是如此冷漠，如此不耐烦，把自己是个"大坏蛋"这句话挂在嘴边。为了利用三个萌娃进入竞争对手的城堡盗取缩小枪，他不得不暂时和她们在一起。他告诉自己，这仅仅只是一段时间。他不要依恋，只做大坏蛋。他或许意识到自己是"爱无能"者。

爱无能，又可称为情绪无能者（Emotional incompetence）。他们以冷漠示人，以各种逃避来避免自己进入深刻的依恋关系中。如果广义理解，这里的"爱无能"者，不仅仅指爱情，而是代表一切深刻依恋亲密关系的无能为力感。

究其原因，很可能是内心深处有一个被冰冻的地方，仍旧没有得到疗愈。所以，一旦遭遇深层的依恋情感，就本能地回避与蜷缩起来。

于是，他忽略三个萌娃对自己的明显依恋和友好。他不懂尊重，也无需尊重，他最初还不会这些。所以，当他拿狗食盒子当她们的饭盒，拿导弹残次品给她们做睡床。当最小的艾格尼丝可怜巴巴地真诚请求他讲一个故事时，他选择了惯性逃避，留给她冷漠的背影……

爱无能者只是在用如此方式不断地强迫性重复，告诉别人，"我曾经被这样冷漠狠心的对待过。"那是他心灵的声音，只是连他自己都未觉察到而已。

一切都是那样的情有可原。你无法强迫一个还没学会行走的人立刻跑起来。但关键是，如何让这样的人总有一天懂得与学会，完成这个初步的成长，这才是疗愈的关键。

其实，或许在影片中格鲁的心中有想要快乐依恋的需求。为什么这样认为呢？看看围在他身边那一群呆萌傻乐的小黄人就一目了然。

无论遇到多么糟糕的情况，都会呆萌傻乐，对 boss 无限崇拜，没有怀疑，绝对依恋与忠诚。这是小黄人最大的特质。不过，这样的要求，也只有机器人才能做到。格鲁根据自我的内心需求，把它们设置成了唯命是从的呆萌傻。在他的世界里，已经在童年期接受了足够多的冷漠相待，所以，他厌倦一切反对的声音，只要崇拜、快乐的欢呼声，还有绝对的忠诚。但如此设定，也限制了自我的成长。

一直到他遇到了三个孩子。

为什么发生他内心改变与自我疗愈功能启动的是这三个孩子呢？

第一，三个孩子都是孤儿，也非常渴望被爱、被关注，可以完成强烈依恋（让爱无能者可以感觉到），哪怕那是一个一开始对她们不太好的收养者。

第二，无论爱无能者如何抗拒，空间上的近距离都会在慢慢的朝夕相处中，拉近心理距离，从而完成每个人的心理回报。处于近距离已经是一种自然而生的心理回报了。这就是为什么很多异地恋会无疾而终的原因。

第三，当格鲁把三个孩子骗到游乐园想要抛弃她们的时候，因为无良奸商的攻击，他从三个幼童眼睛里、脸上、神情中，看见了失望、沮丧、难过、被忽视的无力感……

这种心理学上的感同身受现象，无意间开启了格鲁的自我疗愈功能。因为他从无处相依的孤儿身上仿若看到了童年期的自己，那个被母亲长期忽视冷漠对待的人。

影片在一片孩子与小黄人的欢乐声中结束，格鲁完成了自我疗愈，打开了心扉，和三个孩子建立了深刻的依恋关系，从而有史以来学会并懂得了尊重彼此的需求，还有——责任感。

因为，片尾，他用自制的毛线手指绘图册给孩子们讲三只小猫的故事，好有爱……

如果他不能完成第一部自我成长的这些要求，就不可能在第二部遇到露西后，拥有感受到爱的能力。当然，这是另一个话题了。

本期（心理门）解语：在心灵成长道路上，唯有不断向内探索，分析隐藏起来的潜意识，才能明白自己真正的需求，从而获得完善自身的内驱力。

3 "卑鄙的我"：如何重生（三）

For evil men will be cut off.
作恶的，必被剪除。——《旧·诗》37：9

恋爱中的 S.V.R 理论：相识、相似、互补

在一片激昂呼声之后，《卑鄙的我》第二部隆重上映。原本立志成为一个国际大坏蛋的格鲁，金盆洗手，开始担负起成为三个小可爱的好爸爸的责任，并放弃了原本与恶人联盟的联系，着手建立自己正经的商业王国。但随着一种名为 PX-41 的病毒被抢，特工露西出现在他的生活里。而同时，原来的恶人联盟的最强关联也不愿轻易遗忘格鲁，他以前的犯罪伙伴蒙迪亚哥出现，并想方设法逼迫格鲁答应再次犯罪合作。

面对这些，格鲁的最终抉择在影片最后那幅全家福照片里已经做了最好的诠释。

如果从心理学研究分析，当旧有的罪恶关联再次叩响心门，无穷诱惑蜂拥而至时，最好的自制力和心智是有效杜绝诱惑的武器。

可格鲁是如何做到的呢？

第一，在上一期文字里已经提到，他拥有了三个小可爱，并在心灵上和她们建立了深层的依恋关系，懂得了责任的意义。每个人都应该为自己的行为负责，为自己周围的人际关系负责，为自己的事业蓝图负责，为自我管理负责。

第二，他在懂得一个男人应尽的责任之后，还遭遇了爱情——露西。

如果说，三个孩子赋予他懂得的责任感，那么露西的出现，是教会了他学会自己变得强大，重塑完整的自我价值体系，从而增强了心智的力量，克制心瘾。

这里不得不谈到恋爱中的 S.V.R 理论，爱情从相识到结婚必然经历三个阶段：相识、相似、互补。

第一阶段：无论男女，不可否认都容易受到外表美丽的异性吸引。美丽的事物容易带给人感官的刺激体验，这是相识阶段。本片中的格鲁和露西并没有这个体验，因为露西并非属于那种特别漂亮至妖至冶的类型。所以，两人的相识，从"冷冻光线"到"电击口红"，仅仅只是特工与罪犯之间的较量。可抛开了外表的吸引度进入了解的感情，或许才是很多女性梦幻式的完美爱情追求。诚如我一部小说里女主角无双曾感叹："有没有这样一个人，在我又老又丑的时候依然爱我？"

对于如此梦幻理想式的完美爱情要求，我持保留意见，毕竟一家之言，并不能代表全部。但不可否认，这样的人，或许真的会有。

第二阶段：价值观相互认同。但这个阶段会逐渐让对方的思想、态度、价值观等慢慢呈现出来。这个阶段的真实融合性是决定二人相处是否愉快的重要因素。相似性在这一阶段会被得以重视，包括不知不觉的模仿。人都是互相学习的高等动物。在格鲁最后以露西惯常出招的模式击败了昔日的犯罪伙伴蒙迪亚哥时，被绑在导弹上的露西脸庞上露出一种被认可的窃喜道："吼……他偷学我。"

第三阶段：进入婚姻，更加注重互补性。成熟稳定的婚姻关系，应当是男耕女织，各施其职。两人身份角色不同，赋予的婚姻中扮演的角色的责任不同，但地位却是均等的。如此平衡的关系，才是一段可以相互成长的婚姻关系维系长久的"法典"。

就如影片中格鲁和露西，抛开二人险象环生的爱情经历不谈，但格鲁的最小的女儿艾格尼丝因为缺乏对"母亲"的概念，她无法朗诵出对母亲的赞美诗的感觉。而露西的出现，让这个大家庭得以完整，填补了三个孩子心灵上对母爱的空白，也无意间疗愈了格鲁自小对"爱"的错误认知。更重要的是，拥有独立智慧见解的露西还是格鲁事业成就的好伙伴。在以上几点上，露西的作用和功能都不是随机的。

其实，无论爱情，还是婚姻，从人际关系而言，就是我们的一场身与心互相疗愈成长。好的婚恋关系应当是相互滋养型，任何一方有失偏颇，都会造成能量的阻塞或单方耗尽，不能长久互持。

4小黄人:在亲密关系里如何快乐依恋？（一）

Turn from evil and do good;then you will dwell in the land forever.

离恶行善，就可永远安居。——《旧·诗》37：27

上映资料：《小黄人大眼萌》是一部 2015 年的美国喜剧动画电影，该影片由凯尔·巴尔达、皮艾尔·柯芬执导，桑德拉·布洛克、皮艾尔·柯芬、史蒂夫·卡瑞尔配音，由照明娱乐公司和环球影业联合出品。

该影片讲述了小黄人的历史以及他们要找到强大的新主人，并辅佐他完成作恶事业的故事，背景涉及伦敦、纽约等几个大城市，该片于 2015 年 9 月 13 日以 3D 及 IMAX 3D 格式在中国上映。

妮妮带着一脸倦容出现在我咨询室门口的时候，我正在看 2015 年 9 月 15 日刚刚上映不久的《小黄人大眼萌》。这是《卑鄙的我》这部成功电影的外传，作为拥有独立语言体系、每一个都个性鲜明的小黄人，称它们是"抢镜专业户"一点都不为过。

或许是妮妮累了，这一次她来访，一点都没有不耐烦，而是陪着我把最后一点结局看完，才说："要是我也有小黄人这样招人喜爱，该有多好？"

"难道现在的你还不招人喜爱？"我合上电脑笑着反问她。妮妮的问题，和大多数拥有亲密关系的人一样，在每一段恋情之初，她很能吸引异性的目光，可就是在恋情进展过程中，亲密的链接关系却越来越弱。

但凡亲密关系，都会从初始状态相互吸引，逐渐进入相互了解相知的阶段。而每一个人作为独立的个体，都不可能是完美重合的高度相似体，若要让一段亲密友好的关系良性推进，当然磨合是不可避免的。

可妮妮的问题就出在无法正确地面对双方的矛盾，并采用有效调和的方法上。她就和影片里的小黄人一样，一开始那么想要依恋亲密关系中的伴侣，可却缺乏像小黄人般的依恋优势特质。

一旦遭遇矛盾，哪怕只是一件小事，当伴侣告诉她，双方都需要一定的空间冷静的时候，妮妮就会采用一种极端的方式去紧追不放，常用的方式是"攻击获得关注"。即"我生气，我愤怒，我攻击，甚至我拔刀相向，其实不过是想让你关注我，爱护我，让我感觉到你爱我。"

这类"疯狂爱人"在遭遇矛盾的时候，不能成功将自己从负面情绪高峰值里抽离出来，而是不管不顾，近乎丧失理智地追逐"亲密链接体"的所有关注，甚至不惜除掉所有阻挠她获得亲密链接的"障碍物"。

最典型的范例是耳熟能详的金庸笔下《神雕侠侣》中的人物李莫愁。

"问世间情为何物，直教人生死相许"，赤练仙子李莫愁在与陆郎的情感关系中是一个失败角色，她不是输在没有美貌，没有足够异性吸引力，更不是输在没有良好的外在条件，包括如日中天的事业、家世、教育等环节，而是输在不会调节婚恋关系中产生的矛盾。

陆郎希望她脾气和谐温婉点，不要动不动发怒伤及无辜，随便乱杀人，她不管，她说，我爱你，然后杀一个人，或一掌就伤一片她认为或许会靠近她陆郎的人，因为她的认知里，已经把这些当作了对她的"攻击体"，而无需再将"道义"放在理智的层面。

这要放在妮妮这段关系里，就是她和好好在进入恋爱深层了解关系阶段中，她猜忌、怀疑，并通过不断地查好好的手机通讯记录、短信、QQ、陌陌等聊天交流工具来获得一种内在缺失的安全感。而这样无中生有的怀疑、猜忌，正是最伤害这段亲密关系最严重的心理元素之一。

这里我们需要谈及心理学上一个关于PU的概念，即亲子不确定性（Paternity uncertainty，简称PU），原本指男性对后代的不确定感。当然女人是永远可以确定肚子里的孩子他爹是哪位，可男性在这一点上，却始终都会无可避免地受这样的关系不确定性困扰。

有人说，不是可以做亲子鉴定吗？

可数据事实是一回事，可人的认知是根深蒂固在脑海里，通过特定的事件触及，导致的神经传递反映，跟着就是情绪高峰值下做出不当的处理关系的行为。

就如同，小A从小讨厌吃鸡蛋，可有一天有一个人或某个事实告诉她，吃鸡蛋可以帮助她变得更加聪明，试问一个从小到大都被自己厌恶的事物，能因为这个事实，就导致她彻底改变说，"哎呀，我好喜欢。"

于个体固有的认知而言，这就好比天方夜谭，不是吗？

除非认知改变，否则难以接受，也不可能改变惯常的处理行为模式。

这就是为什么妮妮不管遭遇何种亲密关系，都会猜忌怀疑一样，和事件本身无关，只和她的认知有关。当我们提到女人PU高，意思是她看起来让男性不怎么放心，当我们提到男人PU高，意思是他对所有的女人都不怎么放心。无论如何，这毕竟关系到亲密关系进展中，某一方对另一方的情感投资甚至涉及后代的投资此问题上。

这类"疯狂爱人"在婚恋关系中,她的情感矛盾处理和表达需求的方式,其实是起反效果的。

你无法让一个被你的"火药包"反复炸得断胳膊瘸腿的伤病员,回头再次迎向你的数度反复攻击。

就算是你养的宠物狗,在你狠狠抽打它,鞭笞它,甚至拿刀割伤它,当它选择逃离或躲到床底下、缝隙里,你这个时候依然孜孜不倦俯下身子趴在床边,对里面瑟瑟发抖的它呼唤,"乖,来,我爱你,我需要你,快出来。"

试问,那只满身是伤的小狗会出来吗?

连狗都如此,更何况是人?

所以在亲密关系里,要想关系获得良性推进,采用不断毫不顾忌对方感受的"攻击"来获得关注的方式,是不可取的。

就像被无数小三小四插足的婚姻家庭主妇,抓狂、愤怒、伤害、纠缠、攻击所有,包括你的爱人,和小三小四一起痛打,那样的方式,并非能让你的爱人明白,你其实是需要他的爱,而是赶走他,更快地使你们的婚姻城堡崩塌,灰飞烟灭。

如果需要关爱,需要爱人回头,首先学会爱自己,好好表达需求,良性沟通,才是上策。

不是有句话讲过百千遍:"爱我,就请好好说话。"而小黄人在表达亲密依恋关系上,始终都是一个成功的表达体。

5 小黄人:在亲密关系里如何快乐依恋？（二）

No king is saved by the size of his army;no warrior escapes by his great strength.

君王不能因兵多得胜。勇士不能因力大得救。——《旧·诗》33：16

无论是《卑鄙的我》第1、2部还是《小黄人大眼萌》中，我们不难发现，小黄人身上始终都有鲜活明亮的快乐元素在闪闪发光，深深地吸引着人们唇角上扬。

从一个人呱呱坠地起，不管他身份贵贱高低，人生都难以保证不遇到任何挫折，因为这个世界上根本没有"纯净的情绪真空地带"。

完全自我地活着，不顾周围人的感受，可称为自私；但过度在意周围人的言行举止，不断朝内进行自我暗示，接收所遇之事，由内我意识中固有的认知反应，导致一重重烦恼，这样的处理信息方式，会让人身心疲惫，比起前者也是不相上下，好不到哪里去。

我们痛苦烦恼的根源在哪里？

有些人以为是他们遇到的事，懊恼自己一生运气不好，总是不顺，可其实静心一想，烦恼痛苦的根源不在于我们遇到什么事，而在于我们脑海中固有的认知，这与我们从小所受的教育以及所遇得出的人生经验有关系，但正是这些认知的存在，导致我们在遇到某些特定的事件或符号时，脑海里固有的认知引导我们产生这样或那样的想法，从而烦恼便滋生了。

一言以蔽之，即认知导致了烦恼，快乐与烦恼的关键转换点，不是我们所遇之事，而是我们所想决定的。

诚如影片中的小黄人，不管是遭遇绑架到大恶人联盟，还是被注射了PX-41的病毒改变生物基因，它们都始终能从自嘲和伙伴间的互相嘲笑中找到发自内心的笑容。因为它们这种单细胞生物的脑子里并没有感觉到自己是在遭遇不幸的认知。没有此类认知，就自然没有烦恼。

所以，想要真正快乐，就需要改变固有的认知，即我们从前看待同类问题的看法。这项工作是一条漫漫长路，可以由专业的心理师来帮助有此困扰的人进行行为认知疗法，改善不合理认知，甚至重塑缺损人格。

认知是指一个人对一件事或某对象的认知和看法，对自己的看法，对人的想法，对环境的认识和对事物的见解等。

认知行为治疗认为：人的情绪来自人对所遭遇的事情的信念、评价、解释或哲学观点，而非来自事情本身。正如认知疗法的主要代表人物贝克（A·T·Beck）所说："适应不良的行为与情绪，都源于适应不良的认知。"

例如，一个人一直"认为"自己表现得不够好，连自己的父母也不喜欢他，因此，做什么事都没有信心，很自卑，心情也很不好。治疗的策略，便在于帮助他重新构建认知结构，重新评价自己，重建对自己的信心，更改认为自己"不好"的认知。

认知行为治疗认为治疗的目标不仅仅是针对行为、情绪这些外在表现，而且要分析病人的思维活动和应付现实的策略，找出错误的认知加以纠正。

这里不得不提到——认知"ABC"理论：A指与情感有关系的事件（activating events）；B指信念或想法（Beliefs），包括理性或非理性的信念；C指与事件有关的情感反应结果（Consequences）和行为反应。事件和反应的关系：通常认为，事件A直接引起反应C。事实上并非如此，在A与C之间有B的中介因素。A对于个体的意义或是否引起反应受B的影响，即受人们的认知态度、信念决定。

就像婚恋咨询案例中最普遍的例子，妮妮因为很长一段时间在家里得不到正常的沟通交流，开始怀疑长期出差外地的恋人存有背叛的行为，以致于恋人的父母也对她的态度有异，似乎对她不冷不热，在家里成了一个可有可无的人，她不仅沮丧、焦虑，更加感觉不到在家里的存在感。

她来访的时候，1个小时几乎都以泪洗面。而后，我问她，如果你的恋人长期出差外地，但其实是在为你今年的生日准备一份别致的礼物，包括恋人的父母也负责了隐瞒这个惊喜的工作，你还会哭泣吗？

她愣愣地看着我，眼睛忽地睁大："当然不会。"

我告诉她，你的不快乐情绪，都是因为你悲观的想法和理念导致的，而并非那些你所遭遇的行为，是不是这样？

这就是为什么古语有云："世上本无事，庸人自扰之。"

"您的意思是说，其实是我的想法，我那样的思考结论导致了所有的不快。"她似乎明白了什么。

她离开的时候，转头嫣然一笑看我，"我现在没那么难受了。谢谢您。"

看着她离去的背影，我掀开田园镂空白纱帘，一缕阳光透进屋里，俏皮地跳动到我刚为自己做的小黄人性格测试上。

我们的生命很短，既然快乐是一天，痛苦也是一天，那为什么我们不为自己选择快乐地活着？

人生当中，有的人执着于对错，有的人执着于得失，可世事本就无绝对，从某些角度看，或许某个人在某一个点上是赢了，他不过是执着于"一定要赢"这个有失偏颇的认知理念，可换个角度，他或许却失去了身边那些本应该珍惜的那份适度的谈笑风生自如的温暖。

这里不是说我们不可以为自己所求执着于觉受，而是若那份执着带着毁灭身心的力量，让你不快乐，感觉不到幸福的气息，越发像一丝在暗夜里哭泣的魂灵，那么，或许这个时候你就需要一个专业的心理咨询师。

他能帮你在认知层面区分出哪些是合理的理念，哪些是不合理的，需要我们改善和摒弃的。

如果是良善的认知或执念，又不会伤害你身边在意的人或无辜的人，那么就尽量善执吧，这时候，越是憧憬，越要风雨兼程。

但若这份执，导向的是恶的那个因果，我们是否还能坚持着自己的得而去伤害周围的人？

真的汉子（无论是男人还是女人），但凡属于高智商高情商的理性品质之人，都应该做得到拿得起也放得下。

心存善念，其心自清净。

因为从来，快乐与幸福都只能是你自己给自己，如果你的心灵还没有这样的功能，那就一定要想办法学会它。

从心理学层面，除了"分散注意力、放松训练以及全面坦然接受所遇之苦"，更有一系列让自己可以转向快乐的活动，不要等到情绪很压抑时才进行这些活动，学会定时安排这些可爱的活动，因为类似锻炼的活动，可以使体内分泌止痛的内啡肽，让你立即就感到愉悦（以下只列举"小黄人快乐依恋法"的一部分吧）：

——和朋友在电话里聊天；

——吃巧克力（它对你有用）或别的喜爱食品；

——外出拜访朋友；

——在家里招待友人；

——吃你最爱的冰淇淋；

——做做美容；

——锻炼是抑郁杀手；

——组织一个有意义的派对；

——去图书馆；

——去书店看书或新碟片；

——做做瑜伽，打太极或报名一个班学习新的生活技能，有益身心；

——去公园或安静地散散步；

——祈祷或沉思；

——骑自行车；

——旅游，攒够积蓄；

——游泳；

——学习一门平时不敢挑战的外语；

——做点刺激的事（冲浪、攀岩、滑雪、跳伞、骑摩托车、划独木舟、对着隆隆火车尽情尖叫）；

——球类运动（篮球、保龄球、手球、高尔夫、桌球、壁球）；

——回忆你最爱的电影、话剧的台词或歌词；

——加入一个公共讨论组织，写一篇演讲稿；

——充足睡眠，早睡早起，身体作息有规律才有利于内分泌稳定；

——做拼图游戏或实地 CS；

——参加一个烹饪班或学一道新菜；

——用毛笔或手指画画花、树、人、漂亮的房子；

——阅读各类正向书籍……

愿每个人都找到内心的那个可爱小黄人，找到属于自己的快乐，我是乐观智慧稳重的戴夫（Dave），你是谁？

6《港囧》：你心里还有哪些　让你坐立难安？

All is riddle,and the key to a riddle...is another riddle.
所有的事物都是谜团，而解开一个谜的钥匙……是另一个谜。
——Emerson爱默生（美国诗人、散文家、哲学家）

上映资料：《港囧》是由北京真乐道文化传播有限公司、北京光线影业有限公司等联合出品的爱情喜剧影片。影片于2015年9月25日在全国上映。

徐峥饰演的徐来，是一个内心充满无数闷骚的青年，或许青春最初他想要走的是文艺范儿的路线，可命运作弄，他却不得不被现实与岁月打磨成了一个设计女士内衣的小商人——中年谢顶男。

他的小舅子蔡拉拉，是个热爱电影的文艺2B青年。

"请问你的梦想是什么？你第一次给了谁？你是不是早泄？"

"我发现你内心有许多小秘密哦……"

"你居然背着我拿了一个套！"

"不是，那是人家发给我的。"

"我发现你内心有许多小秘密哦……"

影片基本从以上这些足以令一个成熟男人内心几近崩溃的对话开始，它为我们展开了一个怎样令人坐立难安的故事呢？

这是一个男人和两个女人的故事，只是被蔡拉拉这个二货给掀开了遮羞布——而已。

大学时代的徐来，怀揣着画家的梦想进行演讲，在充满自信的一片掌声中回到座位上，这时候，前排的油画艺术美女杨伊转过头，对他说："特文艺。"这无疑对于同样拥有油画艺术梦想的徐来而言，是一种恰如其分的褒奖和鼓励。

然而这时，后排的管理系富二代女孩子蔡波却提醒他说，裤子拉链没拉好。

呃……这样的提醒虽然是善意，但也是真实的事实，把内心正沉浸在无限遐想的徐来拉回了现实中，并暗示他，梦想和现实毕竟存在着太大的差距。

从心理层面来看，随着奖励减少而导致态度逐渐消极，随着奖励增加而导致态度逐渐积极的心理现象，在社会心理学中被称之为"阿伦森效应"。

阿伦森效应也指人们最喜欢那些对自己的喜欢、奖励、赞扬不断增加的人或物，最不喜欢那些显得不断减少的人或物。

在首次见面上，徐来的内心里，杨伊无疑是远胜过大大咧咧的蔡波的。当然，两个人走在一起，产生感情，经历初恋，还有两人拥有共同的艺术梦想这一共同的爱好，自然会有说不完的话题。

但抛开婚恋情感中的相似性和共同话题那些不谈，仅仅从阿伦森效应来看，我们详细分析徐来的内心，为什么影片最初他会选择杨伊，而不是蔡波呢？

其实主要的原因是内心的挫折感在作怪。

阿伦森效应的实验是将实验人分4组对某一人给予不同的评价，借以观察某人对哪一组最具好感。第一组始终对之褒扬有加，第二组始终对之贬损否定，第三组先褒后贬，第四组先贬后褒。

此实验对数十人进行过后，发现绝大部分人对第四组最具好感，而对第三组最为反感。

阿伦森效应的关键点在于奖励的递减。虽然影片中最明显的只有这一个场景展现了蔡波和徐来的相遇，但也暗示了他们以后的相处法则。

阿伦森效应提醒人们，在日常工作与生活中，应该尽力避免由于自己的表现不当所造成的他人对自己印象不良方向的逆转。同样，它也提醒我们在形成对别人的印象过程中，要避免受它的影响而形成错误的态度。

蔡波让徐来明白的是生活中现实的法则，与理想化的生活自然有天壤之别，比如一个油画系的才子毕业后却设计了内衣，而且还是"倒插门"去妻子的家族企业，不仅入赘，还要为了妻子的整个家族事业奉献而奋斗，而不是为了自己的梦想。

内心的不甘与挫败感，不断升级的挫折感，以及两个人一直没有后代，都在导致二人隐藏的情感危机，最后与初恋情人的旧情难了，自然也就在徐来躁动的内心里萌发了。

长期的压抑和不平衡感，才会导致角色去抗争现状。

于是，打着陪伴老婆及家人来香港旅游的幌子，徐来踏上私会大学初恋情人之路就是必然。

"我希望在意大利一个小地方开一个小画室，在那里实现我画家的梦想。"这是徐来年轻时理想化的梦想。

而初恋的恋人杨伊给予的回应却是，她选择放弃这段恋情，接受成为国外交换生的机会，远走他乡。

在前面文字中，曾提到了"阿伦森效应"，虽然在初见时，徐来见到蔡波和杨伊两位他未来生活中产生重要影响的女性时，蔡波一句"你裤子拉链没拉好"，让杨伊这位鲜活甜美的女子在徐来心目中认可度迅速飙升，但随着故事情节的发展，杨伊留给徐来的是一个未完成梦想的背影，刻有青春的痕迹。除了遗憾，还有"阿伦森效应"的递减。

而蔡波从认识徐来起，就默默守候他。在他和杨伊恋爱时，她偷偷待在一旁，不敢靠近。等杨伊离去了，在徐来失落孤独时，她给他捧上热气腾腾的盒饭；他大学毕业，投递自荐书遭遇挫败时，她带他去了他们的家族企业，让他成了一名内衣设计师，成就了他在一个家庭中养家糊口"顶梁柱"的角色；她带着他们唯一的遗憾——一直没有孩子，但还不忘徐来年轻时的意大利小画室的梦想，借着一家到港旅游的机会，偷偷约见老外卖家，神神秘秘，只为了给他一个惊喜，这是她来港的小秘密，尽管她并不知道徐来也藏着一个小秘密；而她在大学时代就已经为他做出了牺牲和选择，偷偷放弃了做交换生的机会，而不告诉他一丝一毫，徐来是从后来约见初恋杨伊后，听杨伊说出来才得知的……

不难看出，杨伊和蔡波代表的是两个鲜明的社会女性特征。前者注重梦想和自由，喜欢像自由小鸟一样自由自在地展翅飞翔，不断尝试生命的自我探索神奇的旋律；而后者蔡波，无疑是贤妻良母的家庭典范，就连提醒徐来吃药这种小事都要录好音妥帖周到地放在他的衣袋里，关怀步步随行。

这是两个截然不同的个体，影片中的二位女性在各自成长追求上没有交集，而当今社会上，也不乏这样的实例，真正能将两种人性角色完美重合的女性，微乎其微。

可不管如何，综上可见，蔡波作为妻子的角色，她对于徐来的"阿伦森效应"却是递增的。

她不仅是维系着徐来入赘尴尬身份的纽带，也是整个大家族和谐共处的"润滑剂"。

在家庭中，这样的女性是用爱与默默奉献来平衡关系的，她的作用如此重要，就如同盐，每天的饭菜里都得有，可又容易让人在日复一日、细水长流的日子里忽略掉她的重要性。

尤其是正在经历中年危机的徐来，当再次得知了初恋的消息之后，内心充斥着悸动、不甘，以及当年那一次次未完成的亲吻以及性幻想……这些信息的轰炸，都让徐来完全忘记了妻子——这个付出角色的存在，而且还是默默的付出。

所以他必须要去见初恋，这是他内心难耐的悸动和梦想。

《港囧》从某种意义而言，其实讲述的还是类似徐来这样的男人青春流逝的岁月中，对待中年危机的生活态度与个人从中获得的成长。这里我们不得不谈到另外一个心理学效应——契可尼效应。

契可尼效应指一般人对已完成了的、已有结果的事情极易忘怀，而对中断了的、未完成的、未达目标的事情却总是记忆犹新。

比如，写一段话，没有写完被中途打断了，在你做其他任何事的时候，心里会一直记挂着这件事；又或者，我们常常被某一本解谜的小说迷住了，是一口气读完还是放下它明天再读，或许多数人会选择不知不觉地阅读下去，哪怕会到凌晨3点；同类现象会出现在一部连续剧的碟片上，我们也会看完，津津有味。

之所以出现这种现象，是因为人们天生有一种办事有始有终的驱动力。

不信？请试着画一个圆圈，但你不要完成它，过一会儿你再看它一眼，你的思维里，是否很想把它画完整。

对，完整，完形，不想有缺憾，这是多数人对于契可尼效应的正向积极的运用，但是还是有些人会走向极端：

要么就是永远完不成一件事，要么就一定要完成，不完成就一定不舒服。

这两种人，都需要调整他们的完成驱动力，他们很可能都是心理仍旧滞留在婴儿水平或童年期的人（通常是因为婴幼儿期没有获得足够的安全依恋造成的），而且这类人群还拥有巨婴的可怕特质：偏执、非黑即白、完美主义，把想象等于现实即幻想，甚至是妄想症等等，而其中最可怕的特征还有全能自恋——即把自己幻想成一个无所不能的人，所言所做都只有正确，也只能正确，这样的人，是惧怕失败的。

半途而废的人，半途而废的原因是担心做完一件事会遭到旁人的挑剔或苛责，那么就索性不做完，那样就不会有人来苛责他做不完的作品了。而另一类必须要做完的人，也同样具有惧怕失败的心理特征，因为他的字典里，没有失败，他不能接受"全能的自己"有失败的事情发生，也自然屏蔽了从失败中总结思考获得经验的机会。

而我们目前的社会，"巨婴"心理的人还是有相当数量，在《港囧》这部影片里其实是有两个"巨婴"的。

第一个明显的巨婴当然是"蔡拉拉"（包贝尔饰演），他的契可尼效应体现在那部拍摄纪录片的VD上，就算是人家小夫妻kiss，姐夫徐来上洗手间，他也照拍不误，完全不顾旁人感受，而为了一部VD也会跳下天桥，不管不顾，根本连自身安危都可以不负责任，这就是典型的巨婴。

而另外一个不太明显的"巨婴"，便是徐来。

虽然表面上看他很成熟，人也步入中年，可当他遭遇日复一日毫无激情的细水人生，无微不至像盐巴一样存在的贤惠妻子，他在遭遇传宗接代这件事与蔡波整个家族"撕逼"的坎儿上，他终于爆发了，把所有的积怨和不甘都用愤怒爆发出来，发泄出来，包括放弃了梦想，又是入赘的身份，为一个家族事业当牛做马等等……

他或许可以也值得发泄的，但，他却用愤怒的方式把这些遭遇都无限放大了，反而忽略了一直陪伴在他身边，在整个家族中默默做着和谐努力的妻子蔡波。

而他心中那个未画完的圆，就是再次与初恋见面，再续前缘，这种行为，在某种层面上，只是他作为青春将逝，祭奠梦想的一种心理安慰罢了，缺乏理性的思考。

只是，遭遇中年危机的人，在这种情况下，或许都会忘记现实中自己的责任，包括在家庭里一个角色应该肩负的责任。蔡拉拉忘记了自己已经是一个可以对自己行为负责的成年人，而徐来忘了家里还有一个为他默默奉献像盐巴一样爱他的妻子。

那么要如何才能避免我们受到契可尼效应负面的影响呢？

首先，在执行一件事之前，先掂量它的价值，如果从长远规划来看，你的付出和得到会严重失衡，不符合正常态的价值观，那么就果敢放弃吧，那是你的理智要你放弃了它，而不是你失败，学会把有限的精力和时间投注到人生更有意义和更有价值的事情中。

再次，如果第一步不存在问题，那么就制定一个合理的近期、中期、长期规划，把如何实现的步骤写在纸上，结合实际来规划从 A 方法到 B 目标的过程，如果在规定的时间段内，你能明显感觉到有所进步或收获，那么目前的方法或目标才是适合你耗费宝贵的时间追求的，反之，就应该改变方法或更换目标。

最后，需要训练自我控制的能力，告诉自己即便是没有做完，那也可以停下来的，停下来思考一下，目前自己的状态，是否真的适合自己，如果不是，那么就勇敢纠正吧。

其实在影片的最后，徐来也真的明白了，真正适合自己的人，不是自由追寻梦想的初恋，而是无微不至默默为他做了很多牺牲的贤惠妻子。

这一点点明白，多么难得与不容易，因为，这意味着主角勇敢地完成了又一次自我深入探索与思考，从中年危机的巨婴状态获得了真正的成长，这一点，比什么都重要。

本期（心理门）解语：当你有能力面对生活和困难的环境，或者有能力以希望、内在力量及勇气去衡量自己的过去得与失的深入思考，最后做出改变时，你已经从一个巨婴，获得了勇敢跨出第一步行走的成长机会。

7从《寻龙诀》中认识正念疗法DBT之超然力量

上映资料：该片于2014年8月开机，2015年12月18日上映，以3D、IMAX 3D、ScreenX等多种版本同步上映。

When you have eliminated the impossible whatever remains, however improbable, must be the truth.

当你排除了所有的不可能，无论剩下的是什么，即使是不可能也一定是真相。

——Sherlock Holmes 夏洛克·福尔摩斯柯南道尔笔下的名侦探

寻龙分金看缠山，
关门如有八重险，
一重缠是一重关，
不出阴阳八卦形。

《寻龙诀》的这句口诀，出自精通《十六字阴阳风水秘术》风水八卦的果敢司令——胡八一，摸金校尉。

这部仅仅上映一周，票房便大破 9.5 亿元的奇幻惊悚悬疑大片，主要讲述的是：九死一生的摸金三人组胡八一、Shirley 杨以及好友王凯旋正打算金盆洗手之际，忽然无意中从一个重头买家的交易中获悉了"彼岸花"的信息，从而开启了胡八一和王凯旋二人关于二十年前初恋"丁思甜"的尘封记忆。

本文开篇的摸金口诀，在剧中，不只一次地出自胡八一之口，用于分金断穴。原著的这段话，其实是改编自唐代风水大师杨筠松的代表作《撼龙经》。但此处，作为一名原创心理咨询师，我并不是想和读者们讨论风水八卦、奇门遁甲之术，而是从心理学的角度，来看看这部影片中展现的某个心理科普知识点——正念疗法 DBT 之超然力量。

第一，找到并认识自我的超然力量，如此内心会更加有力。

或许我们每个人，都会在某些生命际遇的某段时刻，感到过绝望或无助。或遭遇巨大变故、不幸，亲密关系突然断裂或忽然失去健康，苦心经营多年的业务濒临破产，甚至是被侵害……彼时，当事者的内心易出现乏力、焦虑、孤独，甚至是睡眠失调、食欲减退、意识狭窄、躁狂、抑郁、创伤后应激障碍（PTSD）等症状。

倘若，在这些关键时刻，拥有对非凡力量的信仰，反而能帮你在困境重重中重新找到自我的力量之源，重拾人生的信念或目标。

我们所谈到的这种正念疗法中认识你的自我超然之力，并不是非要我们去信仰上帝或宗教，它可以是一件客体事物、可以是一句话，甚至可以是一段重要关系中的良善之力。找到这样的超然力量的前提是，我们得深信不疑。这样的正能量的信念，在心理学上的解释是，相信心存良善之力、美好的、神圣的、崇高的、非凡的事物，能帮助我们度过某些极其困难的时候，以内观疗法或森田疗法结合运用，以达到忍受痛苦和自我疗愈的抚慰功能。

而这样找到自我信仰信念的方法，即找到自我的超然力量，是帮助我们度过艰难困苦的心理密码。

第二，以内观疗法为例，找到自我的力量之源，充分感受它。

内观疗法（NaiKan Therapy）1953年由日本学者吉本伊信提出。吉本认为："要想知道自己是不是有信心，可以去查查过去一天天度过的日子。"

它的核心要义是以内观禅修为基础，关注、面对、觉察，主要围绕三个主题，针对与自我链接最深的某段重要关系内观不断思考反省：他为我做了什么？我为他报答过什么？我给他带来了什么困扰，有哪些？

关注呼吸，自我觉察，关注当下的感受，直至发现每个人心中（这里指自我）原有的智慧与爱，从而明心见性，达到心灵成长、稳定平和的目的。

具体的操作方法，可以找有此操作经验的心理咨询师来辅助练习。内观疗法不仅仅是来访者快速有效治疗类似夫妻关系不和、非社会行为、成瘾、强迫症、神经症等身心疾病的好方法，更是许多心理咨询师应该长期熟练掌握用于排解舒缓自身工作压力及负性情绪的良药。

这里，我们不得不回到开篇提到的《寻龙诀》摸金口诀，一一展示影片中每个人的信仰之力，认识《寻龙诀》中的超然力量。

胡八一由于经常接触古墓、古尸这类容易令人产生负性幻觉的元素，所以，他的信仰显然是倾向求助于道法玄宗奇门遁甲之术，这是他内心的超然力量，并总是能在他遇到危险时，临危不乱，打通机关，寻得生门。

由黄渤饰演的探路先锋王凯旋，是胡八一最铁的哥们儿，60年代内蒙古插队时，和老胡"竞争"追求丁思甜。后和胡八一重逢，开始摸金校尉生涯。生性粗放豪爽，看上去好似没有什么可以点燃他内心的小宇宙，但象征初恋对象丁思甜的"彼岸花"便是他超然力量的生死密码。

"就算是开在阴曹地府，也为你采回来。"这是二十年前他对丁思甜许下的承诺，而小丁的死，不仅成了胡八一心理的创伤，也更在王凯旋的心灵深处打了一个死结。

两人看上去都未曾放下心里搁了二十年的丁思甜，可其实是对当年她的死的内疚与无奈，从而都烙印下了心灵创伤。

舒淇扮演的Shirley杨，美籍华人，美国海军学院毕业，做过《国家地理》杂志摄影记者。爱好考古，回国遇到胡八一、王凯旋，形成稳定的组合展开探险之旅，过程中对胡八一产生感情。个性典型的"色厉内荏"，无论表面上表现得多么不在意，可其实，对胡八一生死相随的爱，便是她内我的超然力量。

这里还是需要提到杨颖主演的丁思甜，她和Shirley杨其实有许多共同点，都是美貌与智慧并重，而且能在关键时刻理性杀伐决断。丁思甜说："不砍断那木头，咱仨都走不了……"她的自我牺牲情节，正好展示了她识大局的理性从容。

那么，她当时的超然力量是什么呢？居然能让一个弱不禁风的小女子舍生取义，义无反顾护住两个大老爷们儿？

"她当初那么做，就是要你们好好活着。"Shirley杨在墓穴中一句话道破天机。

"生存"便是丁思甜的超然力量，但她活不活不要紧，关键是要他们二人好好地活下去。

这里让我想起了剧情中还有设置一个反面对比人物，她的超然力量也是关于"生存"的，只是，别人活不活不重要，关键是要她自己活下去。这个角色就是身患重病的喜马拉雅无上尊师应彩虹。

为了活下去，她不惜装神弄鬼，不惜拖众人身犯险地，她视他人性命犹如草芥，不值一提。

借用在墓穴刚启之时，她说过的一句话："人活着，总是需要一点精神。"

是的，当我们运用自我觉察，内观疗法，感知自我，找到了属于自己的超然力量之时，我们便会变得平静，从而感受到前所未有的稳定与强大。有的人，或许会去图书馆阅读一部大部头的正能量书籍；有的人，或许会徒步登山，观赏雪峰浩渺的冰雪世界；有的人，或许会诵念经文；也有的人选择去教堂，在天主神像前祷告忏悔；有的人，透过天文望远镜，仔细观察星空中的星辰，想想宇宙中微渺的自我；有的人，去宽广的草原安静地平躺，感受那样的无拘无束；或者是禅修打坐，运用内观疗法思考人生中那个可以给自我力量之源的重要关系的人事物，到底是个什么样子，他有什么特殊之处，可以给自我心灵带来安抚沉静的力量……

当再次遭遇变故和困境之时，想象内我深处就是那个力量之源，他可以是信仰，也可以是某个总会给你带来安宁的地方，或可以是某个人；这时候，再来看看，把自身想象置身于当中，那么此时他会如何处理当下的问题和困难呢？

第三，《寻龙诀》之主题——探索生命的奥义。

Shirley 杨和胡八一的一段讨论当中，曾提到，你看到的并不是由你的双眼决定的，而是由你的大脑决定的，即移情与反移情。

当众人在古墓中彼岸花开时，因为受到陨石的影响，众人产生了负性幻觉。

胡八一再次见到了死去的丁思甜，而仿若又回到了二十年前的那一天，只不过逃出洞穴的两个人，不再是胡、王二人，而是胡八一和丁思甜。

这段幻觉，从动力学角度分析，其实揭示的是胡八一潜意识的创伤，表达了真实的愿望。

我们有时候回忆过往的一些事件，挖掘难忘的记忆，这样的情况的确是有的，但并非常常。可并不排除有一部分人，会常常追溯过去的记忆，尤其是那些引发负性情绪的记忆，从而导致强迫症（OCD）——这种焦虑障碍，往往来源于自身，而自己越是极力反抗，却始终难以自控，如"强迫思维""强迫疑虑""反复检查"以及"怕脏、穷迫洗涤"等。

这一部分人，或许会花很长时间来思考过去已翻篇的事件，做错的事，或未完结的事件，从而产生内疚、后悔、焦虑、自我冲突等负性情绪。那么，就可能产生两种情况，要么沉溺于过去，要么幻想在未来，如此一来，注意当下的感受部分显而易见就少了。

但《寻龙诀》当中解开胡八一心结的这一段剧情，给了我们探索生命的奥义：

原本，这段幻觉中有美貌智慧的初恋爱人，有辽阔美丽的草原，有亲密无间的依偎，这是胡八一对过去这段创伤的自我抚慰潜意识，就好比梦一样，只是他潜意识的某种愿望，幻觉中什么都不缺少了，可当胡觉察到丁思甜胸前佩戴的像章是反向的，他的自我觉察力猛然醒觉，意识到，这仅仅是幻觉，而与当下的人际关系更好地活在当下才是生命的意义呀。

要想拥有摸金司令这般高度自我觉察能力并不难，从第一个深呼吸开始，感受我们的呼吸，那样的气息通过你的呼吸道进入你的身体的感觉，是怎样？是深还是浅？自我的心理感受，当下是焦虑还是平静？是兴奋还是淡然？是开心还是抑郁情绪？

再看看周围的环境，看看双眼能看到的事物，他们带给自我的感觉是什么？哪些是自我的感受，哪些是那些事物真实的属性，而并非自我的投射。

当你感受到这一切时，这便是当下，这便是现实。

倘若感受到当下的心理情绪，是在痛苦，或不舒服的负性情绪，那么用理性的科学的心理学处理方式，譬如用以上正念疗法痛苦承受的技巧来尽快消除当下的负性情绪吧。等负性情绪消失了，再去思考到底是什么导致的这样的感受。

本期（心理门）解语：生命的意义在于，活在当下，尽量活得更真实，当可以正确地认识自我之后，包括美好的，抑或是丑陋的，就能够学会慢慢地完全接纳那样的自我，经营好自己，自然能善待他人。

8 《芈月传》•女人篇：浅析人格特质对社会关系的影响

上映资料：该剧于 2015 年 11 月 30 日在东方卫视、北京卫视首播。

Faith is not just a mind dominated thought, it is a mind that can control the mind.

信仰不只是一种受头脑支配的思想，它也是一种可以支配头脑的思想。

——Robert Oxton Bolton

《芈月传》并不是寻常的宫斗小剧，所以与昔日《甄嬛传》相比更显磅礴大气，因为这部剧的落脚点并非在讲述数位女人为争皇宠相互倾轧、钩心斗角，而是，随着芈八子的权力之路扶摇直上，在权力与虐恋糅合之中，宫斗也不过是"小儿科"而已。

后宫、前朝、虐恋，芈八子的人生之所以精彩，和她的人格特征是密切相关的。在此，就从心理学的角度，分析《芈月传》中的典型女人，择其机要，浅谈《芈月传》中的两类典型人格特质。

人格，拉丁文"persona"，本意是指古罗马时期的演员表演戏剧时所戴的面具。一直到 19-20 世纪，它才由人的外貌类型，逐渐演变为自我主观的概念，逐步倾向于心理学，演变为当下"人格"的含义。

人格（personality）是指一个人的思维、情绪和行为的特征模式，及其背后隐藏或外显的心理机制。它反映了个体在社会与生活环境中一贯表现出的行为模式，即在一般情况下个体表现出来的稳定而可预测的心理特征。

说得浅显易懂一点，就是一个人的生存行为模式是具有稳定的表现方式的，而这些也决定了个体的行为导致的发展走向以及对个体社会关系的影响。

在这里，我们就先以芈月为例，分析那些漂亮女人们的内在人格是怎样的？

芈月：忠于自己，不屈不挠，不卑不亢。用心理学观点一言以蔽之，低神经质、高宜人性、高严谨性、高开放性（创造力）。

当年，因为芈茵的频频陷害与无中生有的污蔑，芈月被威后软禁下毒，小命危在旦夕。可即便挨了板子也要坚持说实话；后因秦惠文王去世，芈月与儿子嬴稷流落燕国为质，从昔日尊荣之地落入困顿苦厄之所，又因芈茵与官府勾结，陷害其偷盗，害死了芈月身边视为亲人朋友之人，更令她也身临险境。

虽然明白是"欲加之罪何患无辞"，但她仍然坚持表明自己：没有做过就是没做过！还华丽丽地抡了欺凌弱小的狗官一鞭子，在她的骨子里有不逊色于英雄男儿的铮铮铁骨。

在恋情上，芈月曾有过三段恋情。

虽然与青梅竹马的春申君黄歇、柔情沉稳相伴的秦王、霸气执着的义渠王结局尽皆不同，但每一段皆为至真的情意：

幼年时期，她从厨房偷馒头分了一个给那个一脸傻萌的小公子，到以师徒戏称教"小呆子"春申君抢鞭子，再到大殿上，那一曲身形婉约的少司命祭祀舞间的眉目传情，她与黄歇的情意纯美如斯，至真至纯，若花蕊初露，淡香扑鼻，温馨隽永。

其后，芈茵逼婚黄歇不成，转而利用威后迁怒于她，不得已，她作为媵侍，随芈姝公主陪嫁秦国，身份潦倒，十五岁的年纪与三十而立的秦王嬴驷相距甚远，只是，她的才智聪慧还是令秦王刮目相看，自然识得她不同于寻常女子，他给她呵护与陪伴，他虽贵为一国国君，却也是她的夫。在黄歇黄公子已经"过世"好几年之后，秦王的耐心倾听与呵护，此"老伯"竟如此暖心，才再次让芈八子打开心扉。

两段情感是无法比拟的，若非要拿黄歇和秦王的情意相比较，那在嬴驷即将去世的那一集，这个昔日倔强不轻易落泪的芈八子却哭成"泪人儿"，称道出那一句"老伯待我如父如兄"。

单从这一句，也可以看出芈月是一个坚持做真我的人，哪怕是嬴驷弥留之际，她也不想就夫妻情分上欺骗他分毫，他们始终是亲情大过于儿女情长，在这一点上，跟黄歇的两小无猜纯情不能相较，与后来义渠王之间的男欢女爱激情也不能相比。所以嬴驷才言，"最后还是如父如兄"，还流下了一滴帝王的泪水。

他最爱的是眼前这个小丫头真诚相待这一点，可这一点在与他的情缘结局的评价上也到底是有点伤怀遗憾的。

在秦惠文王过世之后，芈月的命运再度遭遇挫折与颠沛，再遇义渠君，与他结下情缘是在他一度命在旦夕之时，为了鼓励他生出活下去的勇气，她道："你不是要我做你的女人吗？那活下去，只要你熬过了这一关，我就答应你。"义渠君，他爱慕她近乎到了迷恋的地步，为她身犯险境，为她挡掉惠后的暗箭飞矢，只因她唤他一句"黑马驹子"，他便憨笑如孩儿。于他，她或许有感动，有激情，有同情，也有利益的迫不得已。

一直到三十岁上下，芈月在义渠王与弟弟们的帮助下，排除万难一步步登上至上的王权之位，成就了这个历史上的秦宣太后。

是命运的安排？抑或是"性格决定命运"？

答案是人格。

这正是心理学者们多年研究得出的结论：人格的特征影响着个体的社会关系，包括恋爱关系、职场关系的发展。

人格的特征与遗传、生理因素、环境因素皆有关系。本文暂时回避掉羟色胺、多巴胺、去甲肾上腺素等神经递质或先天遗传因素对人格的影响，仅就人格在朋友、家庭、恋爱、职业中的互相关系层面进行分析——

以芈月为例，低神经质、高宜人性、高严谨性与高开放性（创造力）对个体获得较为成功的社会关系与个体成就发展具有积极的作用。

其一，神经质的高低决定了个体面对挑战和挫折的态度和恢复能力。

1. 低神经质的个体在某种程度上抗打压能力较一般个体强，俗称"神经大条"或"小强家族"。曾有心理学家经过实验得出，同样的外在刺激对于高神经质人格特性的个体而言，其在内在发生的反应与影响要远远超过低神经质个体数倍层级，其倍率层级又因个体差异不同而不同。

首先，就芈月的经历和她的反应而言，她并非一个斤斤计较、小肚鸡肠之人，这一点是由她具备低神经质的人格特质决定的。

面对一次次遭遇磨难，却一次次如"小强"般活得欣欣向荣，并把每一次历劫，都看作为一次往更高处进阶的岁月淬炼。

当然，从认知层面分析，这与一个人的根源性思维方式也有显著的关系，而在每一次遭遇挫折时，脑部产生的思维是正性还是负性，直接决定了个体会有什么样的情绪反应。

譬如，芈月被威后软禁时，她苦中作乐，自忖道："好，我就在这儿住几天，看你们能拿我怎样。"若是换做红楼梦里的林妹妹，别人还未动手，她就先挖坑埋了自己，一边挖还一边唱一曲自怨自艾的《葬花吟》。

低神经质的反面是高神经质，那么高神经质具备什么样的特征呢？

2. 高神经质的人，对外界的刺激反应通常会更为敏感，甚至出现病理性的反应。当然也并不是完全认定这种人格特征不好，要相信任何一种特质都具有两面性，就看个体怎么善用这些"天赋"。

看看剧中的芈茵、芈姝两位公主，再看看红楼梦里的林妹妹，便一目了然，她们应当是属于一个"长耳朵兔子"系列的。

比如，在芈茵偷盗夜明珠这一节，她若非高神经质的人格特征，便不会事先发现威后会彻查此事，也不会立即就采取行动。只是自保没有错，可为了自保伤害别人的利益，便势必会为自己以后的前行道路埋下大坑，无论是社会关系、恋爱关系还是职场发展关系皆是弊大于利。

由于高神经质的人或许时常处于情绪波动或岌岌可危、或一惊一乍当中，对个体的身心健康发展而言，思维、情绪会较普通人复杂纷乱，也容易产生过重的精神压力，不利于身心。

人作为一个精气神的主体，其精力是有限的，倘若把身心灵的精力过多耗费在过于复杂的思维、烦乱的情绪当中，那么能用在个体正向发展上的精力自然就少了许多。

这一点，对于个体的长远发展是不利的。

其二，个体的社会关系和谐度，在一定程度上取决于宜人性的高低。

平衡的宜人性，考察的是个体对他人所持的态度，这些态度一方面包括亲近人的、有同情心的、信任他人的、宽大的、心软的，另一方面包括敌对的、愤世嫉俗的、爱摆布人的、复仇心重的、无情的。这里所说的是广义的人际定向范围。宜人性代表了"爱"，对合作和人际和谐是否看重。

1. 宜人性高的人是善解人意的、友好的、慷慨大方的、乐于助人的（利他性强），愿意为了别人放弃自己的利益，对人性持乐观的态度，相信人性本善。

从心理学的观点而言，宜人性高的个体更具有获得和谐的人际关系及良性循环的团队合作助力。

而芈八子的宜人性到底如何呢？

自始至终，她忠于自己，同时不忘爱护身边的朋友、亲人、爱人。她结交友人，并非因一个人的身份地位，更多的是表现出乐于助人的高宜人性。

若然如此，她不会于闹市救助扑街潦倒落魄的张子；她也不会既为南后郑袖包扎伤口，又与魏美人患难时淡然相交，说：萍水相逢，交个朋友吧。

在初见时，她待每一个她所遇的人都是平等的、平衡的，不会势利，不会戴有色眼镜看人，除非是如芈茵、芈姝、魏夫人这般频频迫害诬陷，她才会"井水不犯河水"，泾渭分明。

高宜人性，这一点令芈月的社会关系相得益彰，在她成为宣太后这条大道上，所谓收获颇丰，成为她扶摇直上的重要助力。

高宜人性，指与周围的社会关系相处融洽，懂得与人惺惺相惜，明白和体会得到其他个体的难处，可以为他人妥善着想。要想详细了解那些高宜人性的人格特质，只需要去"最受欢迎的人格品质"的词汇中寻找前十个词汇便一目了然。

而低宜人性，显然是上述特质的反面。

2. 宜人性低的人，把自己的利益放在别人的利益之上。本质上，他们不关心别人的利益，因此也不乐意去帮助别人。有时候，他们对别人是非常多疑的，怀疑别人的动机。

所以在芈月遭遇杀人蜂事件之后，她主动到芈姝跟前提出，请求带着儿子嬴稷去巴蜀封地时，芈姝会斜睨了双目，眉头一挑，道："你当真会这么想？"芈月淡定地答道：没有比此时更真了。当时的芈八子，后宫争宠于她而言，是多么的不值一哂，她不过是想和孩儿好好静静地活着，别无他求。要说她最后为何会成为宣太后，与其说是命运安排，还不如说是芈茵、芈姝、魏夫人等人的苦苦相逼。

倘若芈月要对芈姝、芈茵、魏夫人等人一如既往的好，不计旧恶，就算是芈八子大度做得到，高神经质、低宜人性的这些"贵人"们也是难度系数太高了点吧。

你做到了真诚以待，别人未必会如你这般坚信不疑。芈姝从分封巴蜀之时就已对芈月动了杀戮之心，又如何会相信？

其三，高严谨性决定了个体具备谨慎细致、敏锐洞察力这些人格特质，还涉及一个人的责任性和勤奋努力的程度。

高严谨性，这一点与高神经质不同。高严谨性为细致敏锐，做事仔细，富有责任感，有头有尾，可以为所选择的规划勤奋努力，有所担当。而后者却仅仅是前面所言的"长耳兔"系、"波动"系、"非守恒情绪"系。

前者着眼于办事的专注力、精致品质，而后者更多着眼于个体的思维情绪过度的反应和对外攻击防御机制。

其四，高开放性，即一个人的高创造力，遇到难题，不乏解决问题突破性的能力。

开放性高的个体可以选择研究性或是与艺术有关的职业，在需要创造力的工作当中，高开放性往往可以为工作的进展加分晋级。

从芈月解开和氏璧真假谜团这一部分剧情来看，她能就"北玄武、南朱雀、左青龙、右白虎"解开镶嵌和氏璧的机关，又以"卞和的血泪"如发丝般不易为常人所觉察，已融入到和氏璧当中，以此来辨别真假和氏璧。此番才智机敏，和先天继承有关，但也与后天她自幼喜好阅读各类典籍密不可分。

其三与其四，这两点人格特质，为芈月每一次遭遇劫难能成功转危为安奠定了功勋不小的基石。

那么我们应该如何规避那些我们不能轻易改变的人格负性特质，又如何良好地建立与培养正性人格特质，让其对我们的社会关系产生正性良好的影响呢？

首先，我们都知道，人格具有稳定性，它并不轻易被改变，从一定百分比程度上它是受遗传、生理以及环境等因素决定和相互作用的影响。但它同时也因为环境的改变，个体的价值框架的接受内容具有不断发展性。

1. 多阅读优品质的书籍，吸收知识，融会贯通。

在人格特质中，若说神经质的高低与先天继承有很大的关系，或许难以改变，那么宜人性的高低、严谨性的高低以及开放性与否，在很大程度上都是可以通过后天不断的修炼、吸收知识来习得的。就如芈月要先阅读过周易八卦、奇门遁甲之术，形成了相关的知识体系，才能在解开和氏璧难题当中得以运用。

2. 多参加利人利己性的社会实践活动。

每个人的知识框架体系，会随着见闻而不断发展。多参加户外活动与社会实践，以及在专业心理咨询师的帮助下，通过个体的系统训练，可以逐渐改变和提升个体的耐受性，打开了眼界，提升了个体的价值高度，认知也自然会发生一定的变化。

就如同，10年前，某人掉了100元钱，会上蹿下跳气好几天，但10年后，同样的一个人掉了1000元钱，也不见得会再有那么多的负性情绪反应。原因极有可能是这人已经成功获得了创造自我价值的能力。试想一个每天收入比支出高出许多倍的人，还会为那一丁点儿不慎而影响个体情绪好几天吗？

3. 培养自控力，提高超我（道德水平）程度，不断自我探索。

弗洛伊德将人分为本我、自我、超我三个层面。本我代表欲望我——基本需求，自我是调节我——主管个体的需求调节和自控力，超我是道德我——个体的道德观的高低也决定了其行事作风利他性的高低，以及面对诱惑，自控力的高低。

为何在《芈月传》中，黄歇会对芈茵说，"就算没有月儿，我也不会喜欢你。"

这是无关身份、地位、财富、外貌的事，而是价值观的事，人格特质魅力的事。

试想，若芈月和芈茵即便互换身体，拥有芈月容貌的身体表现的是芈茵的言行做派，相信黄歇也一定会不喜欢芈茵版作派的"芈月"吧。

容貌未变，人格魅力不同了，自然外在社会关系与之相待的态度也会发生相应的改变。

若想提升个体的人格魅力，首先就要学会自控，提升自控力的同时，培养出良性循环的超我（即道德我）。

在此，并非就一定指超我越高的人就越高尚越可取，但不可否认的是，道德达到一定高度值的人，更容易受到社会认可。每个人都有自我的选择和生存方式，但无论个体的超我高低，以及自我调节的自控力高低，都一定有让个体感到最舒适发展的途径。但无论怎样发展，若是以频繁牺牲和伤害社会他人来达到自我满足快乐的目的，那么，其个体的社会关系发展一定会呈现抛物线向下的趋势,乃至对个体社会生活、恋爱关系、职场关系等造成负性不良反应。

美国的心理学者埃尼希·弗洛姆曾就人性善恶著书——人有两种能力:行善的能力和作恶的能力,人必须在善与恶、祝福与诅咒、生与死之间做出选择。

良善的人是为了帮助别人,不惜牺牲自我的利益;而为了自己的快乐不惜频繁伤害别人,不择手段牺牲别人的利益只为了达到自己快乐的目的,这便是邪恶。

何为善,何为恶,不同的价值框架会有不同的注解,但关键是你真的认识与了解你自己吗?与你紧密相关的社会关系人痛苦,是否真的不会对自我产生负性影响?

不管作何选择,都是个体自由的权力,只是你是否可以完全为每一个笃定的选择,从始至终笃定地担起责任?

这都是需要不断自我探索,不断完善自我身心灵的过程。

或许我们会在发现自我的这一探索道路上遭遇困难,陷入迷惘而不得出,那么建议寻求专业心理咨询,是一条越来越被社会大众接纳的明智之路。

本期(心理门)解语:人生走到最后,每个人的人生尺度不都还是由自我来衡量和把握的吗?唯有真正找到了自我,才能发现"我"这个字真正的含义,回归到内我当中,简单而平静的探索,终会明白生活的境遇要我们懂得的真谛,或许就是——淡淡一笑亦倾城。

9《美人鱼》心声：我是自恋但不狂妄

上映资料：《美人鱼》是由周星驰执导，该片于 2016 年 2 月 8 日在中国上映。

Pride makes people can't love me, prejudice makes me can't love others.

傲慢让别人无法来爱我，偏见让我无法去爱别人。

——简·奥斯汀《傲慢与偏见》

"传说在海底居住着这样一群人类，他们长着漂亮的鱼尾，柔软的长发，拥有着美丽的舞姿和动人的歌喉。小美人鱼是海的第七个女儿，她有着一条曼妙的鱼尾和海藻般浓密的金色长发……"

这个唯美的同名安徒生童话被改编成了贺岁片电影《美人鱼》，于大年初一与观众见面了。

影片主要讲述的是人类和人鱼的故事，因为年轻富少刘轩的地产计划涉及填海工程，在清水湾深海区放置了高功率声纳，致使清水湾一带的人鱼族群迫不得已蜷缩在一艘破船里艰难生存。美人鱼珊珊乔装进入人类社会，想用爱情感化轩少，拯救人鱼族群……

影片仅保留了星爷独特的幽默方式，与以往的作品相比，《美人鱼》相对弱化了喜剧的成分，更多的是在伤感与思辨当中，令人更加清晰地反思影片的主题，为发展与环保如何和谐共存，发出了响亮的宣言。

单就为环保宣言这样的正能量主题而言，都要为这部影片贴上优质的标签。

但如果从心理学的角度来分析这部影片，它在诠释的是一个怎样的影视心声呢？

"自恋"，是弗洛伊德最重要也是最有成效的发现之一。

弗洛伊德指出："一经诞生，我们就从一种绝对的自我满足的自恋朝着感知的一个变化着的外在世界迈出了一步，并开始发现各种客体。"

从精神分析层面，零自恋是最令人向往的理想状态，可在人与自然的世界里，个体倘若没有自恋，便会失去为生存而辛勤工作的动力，因为连自身生存都不关心的个体，生存意义是危险的。

所以，自恋既是生存的必需品，但同时，过度自恋对于个体而言又是生存的威胁。——也就是病态、恶性自恋。

从《美人鱼》这部影片中，我们可以找寻到许多自恋的心理语言。

邓超在影片里扮演的轩少，曾与美人鱼珊珊唱过一首《无敌》的曲目，歌词是这样的：

无敌是多么多么寂寞

无敌是多么多么空虚

独自在顶峰中冷风不断地吹过

我的寂寞谁能明白我

……

当"我是无敌的""我是全能的""我就是上帝"诸如此类的想法出现在脑际时，我们或许需要自我探索，是否有过度自恋的倾向呢？

因为全能、无敌等可以作为过度自恋的信号，自恋者会常常感觉到孤独，所以歌词里才会有"寂寞""空虚""谁能明白我"这样的字眼出现。

不难分析出，邓超饰演的轩少，在影片开篇就是一个"自恋狂人"，过度自恋打破了平衡感，令他整个人浑身是刺，"生人勿近"的言行举止诠释的是"亿万富翁的寂寞"：

从小经历过困苦，从贫民窟一路打拼白手起家，以致于成为今时今日的轩少，坚定地相信只要有钱就一定能获得尊重，期望别人羡慕自己，认为自己就配享有最好的东西，甚至会显得傲慢、目空一切，不惜一切代价达到自我发展的目的，譬如为了清水湾的填海工程放置海底声纳。

而这类"自恋狂人"多有特权感，可以为利益互相倾轧，获得的朋友也多是从利益出发，而非心灵护持的结伴。

所以，影片里，张雨绮扮演的霸道御姐若兰会曾是他的女友，因为轩少在最初和她是同一类为了利益不惜一切的自恋者。

那么，过度自恋（即恶性自恋）会对个体带来什么弊端呢？

第一，恶性自恋最可怕的结果是歪曲合理推断，对于得出的结论缺乏客观性和合理性。

自恋——个体并非把自己整个个体特征作为自恋对象，也可以是他倾注的某个方面，譬如成就、荣誉、智慧、体力、美丽的容貌等等，分为良性自恋与恶性自恋，良性自恋的关键词是"创造"，适度的自恋对个体在社会的生存具有促进作用；而恶性自恋，关键词并非"创造"，而是"占有"。

恶性自恋的对象会被自恋者认为是最有价值（好的、美的、最棒的），他通常被冠以"完美"的标签，自恋者将之理想化，但"完美"的标签并非以客观的价值来推理判断的，而是源自自恋者自恋的衍生，即"因为你是我的一部分，抑或是你就是我，这是我的"，所以才得出，"你无论如何都是完美的"这样的结论。

这是一种明显的偏见，以扭曲客观事实为代价。这也是为什么恶性自恋者常常看不到也理解不到别人的细微感情，缺乏将心比心的共感性，导致人际关系常常遭遇"滑铁卢"的原因。

第二，恶性自恋是疯狂妒忌、暴力与攻击的源泉之一。

《美人鱼》中张雨绮饰演的若兰曾如此目空一切地对轩少说："……追我的人从这里排到了法国巴黎，我拿300亿出来和你玩，你却偏偏……"

偏偏怎样？偏偏不选择她。

其实在某段关系里，谁都有权选择谁，并非你喜欢了我，我就非得选择你，这样的道理成熟独立的个体都懂，为什么《美人鱼》里的若兰不明白呢？

因为她是一个自恋狂人。

当一个正常自恋水平的人遭受到别人批评，而这一批评又是实事求是、毫无恶毒攻击意图时，我们是不会生气的。

但恶性自恋一旦遭遇到批评，他会把任何关注自恋对象的批评当作是恶毒的攻击，从而导致个体不能忍受一切批评，在情感上反映失去平衡，自恋者有两个选择，要么推翻批评者，要么推翻自身。但通常我们可以见到，"自恋狂人"是用行动来推翻那些合理化的解释与存在的。

在影片中的若兰是以对人鱼族"赶尽杀绝"来表达她不被选择的愤怒，但从更深层面分析，那些愤怒其实是源自于她对自我自恋形象濒临崩溃的深层次恐惧,她把自我的理想化状态作为自我存在的证据,过度自恋,所以她不能接受轩少的拒绝,也是不能接受自我"完美"形象的破灭这一事实。

那么,要如何才能适度自恋杜绝过度化呢?

影片里的轩少很好命,认识内心单纯的美人鱼珊珊之后,一切都在悄悄发生着改变,包括他的恶性自恋。

"正因为你不懂,所以我才会出现在你面前。"她目光如华,淡然而忧伤地对他说道。

第一,保持良性自恋,与社会群体接受的水平相平衡。前文提到过,恶性自恋者不能理解别人的细微感情,缺乏共感性。

在《心理门》前面的章节的故事里曾引用过圣经《旧约》:"要爱邻如己。"这里,谈及的爱邻,若从心理学角度来看,就是要我们尽量克服个体的过度自恋。尝试广泛地接纳除了"我"以外的人、事、物,到其中去融合,去体会,才能更好地明白"将心比心"四个字的真实含义,即"我接纳你,并非因为你喜欢我,也不是因为你是我的一部分或你是我,而仅仅是你是你,我是我,但我可以接纳你,感知你,去你去过的地方,用你的心眼看这个世界,感知这个世界。""我"接纳的是"你"不同的部分,而不是只有相同的部分。

影片中的轩少正是因为逐渐融入人鱼的世界,透过人鱼珊珊的心眼看这个世界,才会跑到科研室亲自尝试声纳,如此"将心比心",才能"痛非我之痛,爱非我之爱"。或许在他踏入科研室的那一步起,便是他成功告别旧日恶性自恋的幸福开始。

第二,擅用你的创造力,培养科学思维,而非妄想力打造现实世界。

通过不断创造,在现实中找到客观合理的证据证明自我的形象,使现实在某种程度上因为你的创造力而被改造,从而符合你的自恋形象。

比如,某人说自己是科学家,那么就需要在现实中科学界真的做出创造性的成绩,才可以被合理的客观的推论出"我是科学家"这一事实,而并非自我夸大过度的认可,毕竟"空口白话,纸上谈兵",缺乏现实客观证据,是毫无科学实证力量的。

第三,改变过度自恋的自恋对象与方向。

一切恶性的、病态的自恋，皆是因为过度化贯注能量在自恋层面上，导致爆发破坏力打破平衡。

　　倘若我们能减少个体的自恋能量，把个体自恋转向一部分到个体的家庭、个体的事业、成就，社会贡献，即形成良性自恋的话，其个体取得的成长应该是相当珍贵的。

　　儒释道的典籍中都曾有过"悟"的概念。何为"真悟"呢？其实"真悟者"即是克服了自恋的人，虽然作为社会生存的个体，为了更好地生存，我们不可能完全"零自恋"，但却能够逐渐从现实中辨清楚什么是属于"自我幻觉"与"妄境"，他的最终导向是负性还是正性，由此来慢慢培养出改变自恋对象与方向的觉知力来。

　　"当这个世界连每一口水或每一口空气都是有毒的，那么赚再多的钱又有什么用呢？"

　　在《美人鱼》影片的结尾，轩少已经从昔日的目空一切、妄自菲薄的恶性自恋中解脱出来，成功蜕变成了一个与世界发生链接的环保代言人，他接纳这个世界，也爱这个世界，并非这个世界与他相同，而是因为这个世界与他异同共存。

　　本期（心理门）解语：何为天堂，何为极乐。事实上，天堂与极乐皆是你我心中的两粒种子，今日，当你决定与这个世界温暖共存之时，那么他日，世界也会与你温暖相待。

10 《西游记》白骨夫人：善力的自由

上映资料：《西游记之孙悟空三打白骨精》是由星皓影业有限公司出品的一部3D动作奇幻电影。影片于2016年2月8日在中国大陆上映。

When you look long into an abyss,the abyss looks into you.
当你凝视深渊时，深渊也在凝视你。

——Nietzsche尼采

在没有看这部全新的影片之前，我曾一度以为《西游记》三打白骨精的故事，早已成为经典，那些经典人物形象、角色的揣摩与把握是无法超越的。

可看过之后，才发现，原来这部《西游记之孙悟空三打白骨精》仍然有令人惊艳之处。

三打白骨精的故事自不必多说，可改编过的白骨夫人的故事，还是值得我们一起去探索心灵上的那些奇妙的语言。

"我嫁到一个村子里，可不久那村子便死了人，村里人便责怪是我把不祥带入了村里，说我是妖，还把我一个人留在了山上……"

为唐三藏讲述这段故事的白骨夫人当时正幻化作人形，竭尽全力诱惑唐三藏上当，好吃掉可令她永世为妖的唐僧肉，说了那么多段谎话，骗人可以深入骨髓、至情至性，但偏偏这段故事却是真实的过往。

那是白骨夫人依旧为人之时。

她说："你们这些凡人，就是无情。"

借用一句佛经典籍中的参悟：佛的眼中众生皆是佛，菩萨眼中皆是菩萨，凡夫眼中皆是凡夫。悲观者看世界，世界是暗淡失败的；进取者看世界，世界是美丽光明的。你的世界是光明还是暗淡，取决于你的心态与智慧。

同理，无情之人，看到的唯有无情。

那么到底是什么样的心理密码铸就了如今冷酷无情、面如寒霜的白骨夫人呢？

第一，童年或曾经重要人生经历阶段的遭遇，镂刻下铭心刻骨的创伤。

花季少女满怀着待嫁的喜悦嫁入一个对她来说还是陌生的村庄为妇，可却因为村里人迷信和排外，不分是非对错，将她如花的生命结束。没有应不应该，只是她不被村里人接纳。彼时她的遭遇与内心，很是令人心疼、怜惜。

我可以想象得出，原以为心处天堂，后坠落地狱的痛苦与绝望。

就好比一个小孩从小被一根无形的界线豢养起来，身边扮演教导者的人告诉那孩子，只要你在界线圈子内，乖乖的，那么就给你糖果吃。

起初，那孩子一定会疯狂地想要越过那根界线，求温暖、求抱抱，因为，那些教导者在那里，孩子的心灵是需要和教导者发生亲密链接的，身心皆需要爱的抚慰（即精神鼓励系统）。可事实却恰恰相反，每越界一次都会遭遇严重的冲突，渐渐的，那个孩子会发现，这些她想要亲密链接的教导者并不是那么需要她，她融不进那样的教导者群体。从一个豢养者转变为一个被教导者认同的独立个体，在她生命期冀的重要阶段里，陪伴她的只有那根无形的界线，以及那个界线圈子里漂亮的"糖果"（物质鼓励系统）。

于是，心灵的创伤一旦被种植在幼小的心灵里，这样的伤口若不被看见与发现并加以修正，那个受伤的心灵就不再会痊愈。于是，孩子对这样的教导者是既深深的爱着，也同样是深深的厌恶与痛恨着。

上述这个小案例中，那个孩子想要融入与自己亲密心灵链接的团体，这与白骨夫人初为人妇时的心理需求是相同的。

在白骨夫人重要的经历里，当她被当作是妖孽遭遇她以为可以与她亲密链接的团体背叛时，在众多的"你是妖"这样的声音里，她需要在不断地自我背叛中修复或认同那些外在对自我的认知，哪怕她在最初一直都知道被曲解的外在认知不是真的。

当一个人得不到对外认同，又无法肯定自己是谁的认同时，她要么是推翻自身，要么就推翻外界，这也是诸多来访者不愿意听到任何质疑和反对声音的原因，因为，她的过往经历会扭曲一种认知模式给她。

而上述案例中的糖果，正如白骨夫人想要为妖的致命诱惑。

如此一来，这样的个体成长之后，要么是一个假装强悍，满眼冷血无情的人；要么就是一个见到一丁点儿"糖果"诱惑，便难以把持自身信念的人。

心理学上，这种现象为认同与反认同。一个人有意识的、有目的的使用自我认同或是自我反认同的方法，它的进行过程是从一个人的动力（统一）中心，将其分裂的、不协调的各个部分，综合成一个整体的、协调的及完整的有机体。

对于一个以角色或主导功能来认同自我的人，也有同等的作用，这会促使一个人在面对生命的发展或生活的过程所必须产生的"继续性"无法进行。在影片里，当白骨夫人被村里人群体认同为妖的时候，她是需要经历自我背叛的，而这与她对自我认同："我是一个人"这样的认同背道而驰。

以致于最后她已经做了杀人如麻的白骨妖了，她仍旧对唐三藏说："我最恨别人说我是妖。"

身心灵是抵御外界诱惑的能力，这种能力一减再减，以致于个体的内我变得愈来愈虚弱。

"做人痛苦，不如就做妖好了。"这是白骨夫人选择的做法。但影片中有意近距离刻画她吸人血精魄的镜头，无声无息，却全力吸纳入体内，那或许是她潜意识的愿望和声音：我是一个人或我想成为一个人。

在这种痛苦强烈冲突里，白骨夫人终于选择了自我背叛与接受诱惑，做了妖，但她仍旧放不下我想做一个人，或我是一个人的想法。当内心愿望和行为表现不一致时，个体的外在行为表现形象与自我认同是相反的，于是内心冲突就获得了越发强烈生长的温床。

个体内心长期处于激烈艰难的心理冲突当中，而自身又缺乏自我调节与导引的能力，这个时候，就需要找心理咨询。

第二，虚荣与过度自恋的结果，导致失去选择善力的能力和自由。

在我《美人鱼》那篇文字当中，曾提及自恋是分良性自恋与恶性自恋的。良性自恋可以从无到有的创造，是一种由内而外的创造性现实匹配的认可；恶性自恋则不然。

个体自身不能创造或没有发觉自我是拥有同等创造的能力的，于是就导致恶性自恋，关键词"占有"便出现了。

这就是收藏癖、恋物癖的成因之一。

譬如有些从不用铅笔写字的人，莫名其妙喜欢收藏铅笔、橡皮，这样的收藏无伤大雅，只要不害人害己就未必影响社会功能和人际关系。从这个角度分析，也能够发掘出一些名人收藏家，喜欢收集古玩玉器，不惜掷以重金，却并非用于增值投资，仅仅是因为爱好。影片里的白骨夫人，吸了人血精魄后却将自己的洞穴堆成了人骨堡垒。

其实有时候，我们会出现这样的情况：当你听说一件华美的宝藏时，你特别想要拥有它，但其实你连这宝藏的具体功用是什么，你都未能全盘了解，也不管是否适合自己，不管是否伤人伤己……

只是一心想买回来束之高阁，哪怕是今后对自己没什么用，蒙尘不被问津也无所谓。在当下这一刻，有没有思考过，那如此想要拥有的背后，隐藏的是否正被镀上了过度化自恋与虚荣的人格色彩呢？

那么，我们为什么会这样？

第三，对所有行为的反应，只源于对痛苦再现的恐惧。

白骨夫人曾说："什么叫身在地狱？"

"我就是地狱。"

当一个人遭遇重大心理恐惧之时，要么就是消灭恐惧，变得强大，要么就是索性成为恐惧，让别人来恐惧自身。

前者选择需要意志力坚韧、修行修心，在挫折与磨难中逐渐成长变得强大。

后者，则是短平快，无需自我去克服恐惧、面对恐惧了，我自己就是恐惧代言人。

白骨夫人的心灵深处同样是有深藏的恐惧的，这样的恐惧与内心的自我某种需求产生了强烈的冲突，继而滋生出更大的恐惧。

白骨夫人再也不想为人，即便唐三藏一再说要度化她，她都宁死也要作妖，因为她已经把那种不被人类认可的恐惧演化成了自我的形象或精神符号，产生了"让所有人都恐惧我，那便是我"的精神符号。

都说一个人一辈子只会真爱一个人，其他的后来者不过是那个心灵上的人的替代品或相似品。那其实也是一种对外寻求心理认同的模式，但毕竟后来者或许只是碰巧符合了个体认同模式，即被想象出来的模样，而现实一旦发现差距，就会导致此类个体陷入一种糟糕的情绪当中。因为，她接受不了这种认同模式的再一次崩溃。

所以，在影片里的白骨夫人放不下执念，一心想吃"唐僧肉"，即身为妖，又期冀着被人群认可，这样的冲突藏在她的潜意识里，以致于撕扯着她的灵识，一点一点，日积月累，吸再多的人血精魄也填不满她心理创伤的"黑洞"。

影片里的白骨夫人吸人精魄之时，只看到自己的需求，却从来都看不到别人的情绪的，诸如痛苦、无助、恐惧、疼痛……

当个体选择了靠吸食他人的幸福，观看别人的痛苦而生之时，就已经失去了选择善力的自由度。

阅读我的文字至此，会不会认为白骨夫人其实也是个可怜之人？

那么，如何用心理密码来破白骨夫人的命数呢？

1. 身心灵的自由度决定了选择善恶的能力的自由度。

A. 选择较好而不是选择较坏的决定性因素在于认知：每个个体自从出生至今，都有一套自我构成善与恶的认知体系，若是体系在成长过程中发生了扭曲，那么就需要一个专注于这个领域的人来一起工作，大家都要以发掘个体痛苦的深层原因为目标来认真负责地工作，提升认知正常平衡的百分比，才有可能使状况得以改善。

B. 认识到在何种情况下做什么决断，可以深思熟虑，但尽量避免优柔寡断：人唯有在或者成为人，或者成为妖的中间自我矛盾冲突中才会出严重心理问题，就如同白骨夫人既想要做妖来杜绝为人的恐惧，又想被人认可，强调最讨厌别人说她是妖。倘若想要做人，那就堂堂正正行人之事，言人之行；想要作妖也无不可，就堂堂正正宣称自己是一个妖，那么，极致的做自己，成为自己，只要这个决断，你担得起所言所行产生的多米诺效应，那又有何不可？其实《西游记》5个修行者，只有唐僧是人，其他的都是妖，但都恪守本分，保护唐僧西天取经，做一只极致的妖，这样明亮地修行，可以避免痛苦扭曲来撕扯灵魂与人格。

C. 能够觉察到自我行动的背后，潜意识的需求是什么，找到它、发掘它：比如个体真实的需求是自恋和虚荣的满足，而并非一定是占有一堆对自己其实没多大用途的"人骨"和"精魄"。解读了这样的需求，我们可以尝试改译它，通过别的方式来满足，比如在某个领域发挥其所长获得超乎常人的名与利，一样可以让自恋和虚荣的需求得到极大的满足，只要不伤害别人，不把自己的需求构架在他人的痛苦之上，便是重新获得善力的开始，选择的自由度也开阔了。

2. 拒绝非理性情感才能找到心路的方向。

那些被非理性情感左右抉择的人，通常会迫使人去做与自己真正自我发展格局相违背的事。当"糖果"出现时，要坚定潜意识的声音（当然前提是先学会探索与发现它）。随着时间的延长和环境的转变，往往容易逐渐改变一个人最初本真的信念，失去修行的"觉"，在各种活色生香的体验中，逐渐迷失自我，变得麻木冷酷，甚至无情。

所以，大声对自己说三遍："我现在不吃糖，因为这与我的发展规划和人生格局背道而驰。不吃糖！不吃糖！不吃糖！"渐渐的，你会发现，在你的身边有许多和你一样把身心灵更多关注于个体规划发展成长的人。而且很庆幸的是，你也是其中微渺但却坚韧、为自己梦想和行为买单的一员。

3. 全面认识行为可能导致的后果，增强意志调控力。

诚如我们先前看到的那个被糖果豢养的孩子，长大以后，他很容易一看到诸如"糖果"的诱惑便妥协，从而很容易放弃先前差点把自己都欺骗到的"初心"。本真的东西一旦迷失了，势必会沉迷于短暂满足的诱惑当中，而忽略掉所言所行的后果。这个"忽略"是很自然发生的，几乎已经从童年或过往经历中成为了一个条件反射的事件。

这就是为什么我们在下一代的儿童教育中并不提倡物质奖励大于精神奖励来鼓励孩子学习的原因之一。

当我们在面对诱惑时，灵台要有清明的神识，理性逻辑优质全面的认知系统。从长远考虑，当那颗糖果外表华丽的糖衣褪去之时，就是痛苦与追寻幸福人生规划背道而驰的开始。那么回到当下，可有灵光乍现，获得醍醐灌顶的觉悟认知——再好吃的糖果也不要。

本期（心理门）解语：良善或许是一种能力，是为内心幸福种子浇灌、助其发芽、成长、开花、结果的能力。幸福就在每个人的心灵深处，我们被人相待的态度在一定程度上取决于个体的态度。当你良善对人，就事论事看世界，那么至少这个世界大多数人也会良善地对你；你感恩际遇与磨难，那么际遇磨难就会助你成长。就看你能否发现它，抑或是发现了它，是否给予照料和负责。"一念迷是众生，一念觉则是佛。"也或许每个人的心里还住着一位白骨夫人，但度她成佛抑或是成魔，全在于心的觉悟力及时间。

11 从《盗梦空间》与伯特·海灵格谈梦境系统

上映资料：《盗梦空间》是由克里斯托弗·诺兰执导，莱昂纳多·迪卡普里奥，玛丽昂·歌迪亚等主演的电影，2010年由传奇影业出品。拍摄日期为2009年7月13日。

When you dream, what do you feel?
当你做梦时，你会感知到什么？
　　　　　——伶点金（国家二级心理咨询师原创有声书作家）

再一次看《盗梦空间》，是因为近期阅读了伯特·海灵格（Bert Hellinger）的《谁在我家海灵格家庭系统排列》一书。

伯特·海灵格是德国的心理治疗师，也是家庭系统排列（Family Constellations）方法的创始人。

在唯物主义科学辩论为主流的现代，这是一部很难得的作品。本书中谈到了大量家庭系统排列的见解，都有触及神灵、家庭系统中的灵魂等类似神话故事的话题，而这些或许与他在南非祖鲁族人那里做了16年的传教士经历有关。

他尝试把祖鲁人的音乐和仪式结合到他传教的弥撒中去，相信可以不拘一格地做更好的事情。

神圣无处不在的信念，让他不拘泥于一个点上获取他想要收集的讯息，并通过集体动力、精神分析、格式塔疗法、原始疗法以及交互分析疗法，灵活地将这些宝贵的治疗经验和讯息整合在一起。

其中，他提到了关于梦的简记，是有关一位来访者的梦境治疗记录，与2010年上映的《盗梦空间》中关于梦境的诠释有着一些共同之处。这也是我想要重温这部经典电影的原因之一。

这部由莱昂纳多·迪卡普里奥主演，克里斯托弗·诺兰的新作，用影片中男主角道姆·柯布的话来讲就是："我从事非常特殊的一项安保工作，保护人的潜意识。"

道姆·柯布（莱昂纳多·迪卡普里奥 Leonardo DiCaprio 饰）与同事阿瑟和纳什在一次针对日本能源大亨齐藤的盗梦行动中失败，反被齐藤利用。齐藤威逼利诱因遭通缉而流亡海外的柯布帮他拆分他竞争对手的公司，采取极端措施在其唯一继承人罗伯特·费希尔的深层潜意识中种下放弃家族公司、自立门户的想法。

为了重返美国，柯布被迫接下这项工作，且偷偷求助于岳父迈尔斯，吸收了年轻的梦境设计师艾里阿德妮、梦境演员艾姆斯和药剂师约瑟夫加入行动。

只是，在进入一层层递进的梦境后，柯布遭遇了费希尔潜意识的本能反抗，而且还必须直面已逝的妻子梅尔的处处破坏……

看过这部影片的老影迷们，对于电影情节，自然不必我多言，但在此，我却认为有必要结合海灵格的梦的简记提到的观点来简要诠释关于梦境治疗的看法。

盗梦这部影片中有个柯布很难面对却必须面对的人物，那就是他在现实世界已经过世的妻子梅尔在梦境中的处处破坏。

在柯布的现实世界，梅尔或许是一场现实中的噩梦，让柯布几乎不想在他的现实人生中提及，但在梦境中，他的妻子却是他的完美的心意相随。有关梅尔的破坏，梅尔的解释是，因为柯布在执行梦境任务中从主动进入最后一层LMBO（迷失域），已经转变成了无意识进入了LMBO（迷失域），而无意识进入这个公众梦境空间的人，哪怕是盗梦专家，如果不被杀或自杀是无法回到现实世界的，除非有人在现实世界通过这个人的梦来到迷失域告诉他。所以在影片最后，柯布的妻子梅尔用死亡的方式试图告知柯布，这是迷失域，希望他醒来回到现实世界。

但这里有一个梦境循环的节点，就是在柯布的现实世界，梅尔是已经死亡的人，这点，不管柯布是有意识还是无意识进入迷失域，他都是很清楚、很清晰地记得的。所以，按照这个逻辑推断，梅尔只是一个梦境中迷失域的误导。

所以，从影片的情节设置而言，是一个自相矛盾的内循环，柯布或许可以作为是梦境的平衡点。

伯特·海灵格梦的简记的观点：

一个来访者连续做一个梦，或时常想到它，在梦里总是担心一个人。

海灵格就会问那个人，在你的大家庭系统中是否有这样形象的人死去。

依照海灵格的观点，他会把一个人时常挂心的梦，与整个大家族的系统相连。

就如同，盗梦这部影片中的柯布，在层层梦境中，为什么会必须面对他的妻子梅尔，是因为在柯布的家庭系统中，妻子梅尔是一个过世的对他很重要的人，换言之，也是柯布的心魔。

通读了海灵格的这部著作，细致分析和品读之后，排除断章取义的认知态度，采用心理学上格式塔疗法、原始疗法以及交互分析疗法，抱着一个心理学者互相尊重交流的认知态度，我想谈谈海灵格说的梦境分类与家庭系统排列观点。

按照伯特·海灵格的梦境分类，在通常意义下，派生梦是为了逃避真实发生的事而对人们的梦下的定义，是人为了本能逃避一些事情，不必负责任和表示尊重的梦，是为派生梦。

其次是拥有记忆编码，没有太多戏剧性夸张的梦，叫原生梦。

还有系统梦，就是伯特·海灵格在整部作品里主要的心理分析方法：家庭系统排列。

在通常情况下，把一个总是影响来访者的梦中人物角色归纳进家庭系统排列，去寻找答案并不会产生太大问题。毕竟有因才有果，家庭系统中一个人的失去会令后来的另一个人得到，这就是海灵格家庭系统中用近乎神话故事的方式来治愈某些解不开心结的来访者的方法。

就像在盗梦影片中，柯布常常在梦境中会见到死去的妻子，那是因为他现实世界的家庭系统中她已经过世了。但因为她是柯布曾经很重要的人，所以才会梦到。

按照这种观点，分析到此都没有问题，但，伯特·海灵格忽略了一个细节，那就是柯布的心魔，在伯特的梦境观点中也曾提及过的阴影梦。

伯特·海灵格提到，这些梦让我们看到自己不想看的一面，我们甚至不愿意讲述它。

那就相当于是影片中柯布的现实中过世的梅尔，是他的心魔，造就了他的阴影梦。

而阴影梦是有可能误导来访者的系统梦境的，也就是说，来访者有时来诠释的梦境，如果只是被梦境心理治疗师按照系统梦来诠释，简单地去家庭排列中寻找答案，那么有可能就已经被阴影梦造成的误导迷惑了。

所以，在伯特·海灵格的家庭系统排列以及系统梦的分析治疗方法中，是不能忽略掉每个不同的人，以及他的家庭系统中的成员造就的阴影梦误导的情形的。

也就是我们俗称的心魔，它有可能会误导我们忽略和排除甚至是错过对自我相当重要的珍宝或珍品的时刻。

就像影片中的柯布，或许梅尔可能是他的心魔，也可能就是他的珍宝。所以，整部影片才会是以一个有点自相矛盾的内循环结束。

那么，以此影片为例，我们要如何面对和克服阴影梦对家庭系统排列中的系统梦正确治疗的影响呢？

1. 相信自我：不管那些阴影梦境要误导的是什么，但只要笃定地信任自我，同时清晰明白自己是谁，什么是对自己的将来有正向发展价值的，那便是在梦境或现实世界，都同样需要我们清醒认知的直觉。

2. 耐心等待：这一点是阅读这部伯特·海灵格的作品领悟到的一点小技巧，无论是运用在心理治疗还是在日常生活中，都可以借鉴。那就是无论我们遇到什么样的令心灵或迷惑或误导的状况，都不要被内心的迷茫和焦躁的情绪控制心神，而是应该耐心冷静地等待，以贴近自然的心态去面对所遇。那么相信在未来的某一个重要时刻，那个笃信着清晰的自我一定可以得到一个救赎的机会。

这一点在盗梦这部影片中也有诠释，柯布的妻子或曾经迫切想要回到现实世界的柯布，或者他的同伴，在未完全搞清楚状况的前提下，过早想要强行揭示答案的代价，或许就是错过救赎的机会而迷失。就像那些不知自我就被迫进入了迷失域梦境层的人们，不正是影片对这样的含义最好的诠释吗？

3. 珍惜生命特殊的价值：伯特·海灵格在他的治疗笔记中曾提到过一种圆形治疗。他这样设置的初衷是为了让每一个参加动力性精神治疗小组的成员，避免在个体人格不是很强硬与牢固的基础上被集体防御攻击。

所以，他美好的治疗初衷，希望在没有人会被攻击，没有人会被责备或赞扬的氛围中，获得完美的疗愈。

只是，他忽略了一个看上去微妙但其实很有可能稍有不慎就摧毁整个动力治疗的因素，也就是类似盗梦影片中提到的变数。在表面祥和的安宁下，潜伏着要么就是容易引发极大波澜的困难挫折的变数，要么就是极度幸运令祥和回归的变数，譬如柯布一开始盗梦失败遭遇到的齐藤，又或者是提示柯布迷失域的妻子梅尔。

结合伯特·海灵格的这部奇特的作品和盗梦这部奇妙的电影，对于这位海灵格家庭系统排列心理治疗学者提出的圆形疗法，在面对那些人格中真实不强硬的来访者而言，这样的设置并无不好，只是，在这样的祥和安宁的治疗团体中，每一个认真从事疗愈心灵的心理工作治疗者都必须要考虑预备较为强硬的应急防御攻击的戒尺。若是把圆形治疗比喻为祥和的话，那么，刚性的戒尺同时也是可以起到捍卫整个家庭排列系统治疗有序长久稳定进行的有效措施。

在这样刚柔并济的紧密相连作用下,才可以在面对不同来访者的治疗时,发现不同的特殊的生命价值,同时也珍惜同等的生命的原始动力。

本期(心理门)解语:唯有在这样的系统治疗当中,来访者才可以更清晰地珍惜自我,即便是遇到误导或迷惑的状况,才会把生命的关注力更多地放在清晰认知自我的所为上,而不是因为或恐惧,或焦躁,或愤怒,或指责,或逃避等负面情绪,有可能诱发的破坏力上。毕竟,珍惜自我,珍惜生命的价值才是更应该关注的课题——人生随处是修行!

12 从《魔法老师》识别善良的智慧

上映资料:《魔法老师》是由特瑞·琼斯执导的科幻喜剧电影,由西蒙·佩吉、凯特·贝金赛尔联袂主演。2015年8月14日(英国)、2016年9月9日(中国)在中国大陆上映。

Control his anger and forsake his wrath.Don't be unfair,So that they do evil.

应当控制住怒气,离弃忿怒。不要心怀不平,以致作恶。——《旧·诗》37:8

根据银河议会授予的权力，默默无闻的单身中学老师尼尔（西蒙·佩吉 Simon Pegg 饰）无意被选中，并成了外星人随机挑选中的例行考验对象，并被赋予了很强的超级能量。在这个过程中发生了一系列啼笑皆非的故事，外星人希望能在这个小人物的身上看到其可以识别善恶的能力，并用超级能量做一些惩恶扬善的事情。

　　尼尔从一觉醒来，忽然发现自己拥有了单只是把愿望说出来、单手一挥，就能让所有梦想成真的奇妙超能力，包括那些从前他想都不敢想的事，包括与他的梦中情人凯瑟琳约会、共进晚餐……

　　从毫不通晓到随后的机械勉强运用，尼尔这个小人物开始无比崇尚这样的超能力，并愈发地把自己当作是无所不能的人，犹如神一般的存在。他太需要这样的感觉，这一点从他帮助他的好友雷，让原本雷追求的姑娘疯狂地崇拜他，可以洞悉出一些影片中想要传递出的基本的心理密码。

　　很显然，一个小人物在突然天降的幸运里，并没有真正妥善地运用这样的能力。首先，他最初并没有真正识别善恶的清晰辨识力，却把能力大多滥用在满足个人私欲上。从一个教师的角度看，他最初的愿望，随口一出，就是灭掉自己的班级。心理分析技术可以看出，他并不真正热爱他的工作，身为师者起初还没有意识到"教师"这两个字的责任，他的灵魂深处似乎有着矛盾的冲突。所以，在一系列失去以后，他又会想方设法去弥补，感到无比内疚。

　　这让我想到了现实中的一个案例，有一个喜欢做梦的少女，她常常会梦到自己是一个少年，而在现实中，她其实是一个依赖性很重的人。她做过太多的梦，还喜欢和梦中的少年做一对形影不离的好友，甚至幻想是伴侣。时间一长，她开始记不清楚梦中发生的事情，也渐渐出现了一些问题，那就是会容易把梦中出现的一些不太好的事情，当作是真实世界发生在她身上的事。

　　那些梦境中的感受，让她感到难以启齿，甚至是羞耻。那种很深的羞耻感不断地吞噬着她的心智，已经对她的正常生活造成了某种影响。一直到我发现了这样的她，鉴于她身上发生的现象，我理智地提出建议，为她做必要的心理治疗与疏导。

　　就如同《魔法老师》这部影片后半段，魔法老师滥用的能力，导致了一系列不良的后果。譬如，他的好友雷不再喜欢他，因为他自以为幽默却把唯一的好友，从一个普通教职员工变成好姑娘眼中非凡的"圣人"，又到最后变得惹人厌恶。那使得雷从一开始的欣喜若狂、受宠若惊，到因为恐惧而惊慌失措、夺路狂奔，再到最后，如闻一声旱雷炸开，从云端被打下地，犹如做了一个极其荒唐的梦。可端视现实，却更加残酷，爱情似乎于他而言，突然变得了然无趣，唯留下满脸的怅然。

再譬如，尼尔最期望的凯瑟琳，也因为他为了脱离他的情敌的控制，居然在最后一个愿望时，选择暂时丢弃口口声声的最爱，而愤然而去。可事后，他又内疚万分。逃避责任的人格特质再一次在尼尔身上体现，这一点在影片开头他炸掉他的班级就已经有所显示。而这一次，居然是想要选择轻生来逃避一切，而并非利用他的超能力来妥善修复过失。

影片中尼尔的人格特征，就好比那个常把自己的梦境感受当作是真实的少女。尼尔的处境，恰如梦境，是现实生活中没有的事。可惜很多小人物都太想要满足那些想要成为大人物的奢望，从而选择用各种行为模式来逃避现实中应该担负的责任。就如同，尼尔在充满对友情的愧疚、对爱情的绝望中，宁可选择跳桥，也不要尝试弥补过失。从综上的人格特征表现，我结合交互分析疗法，还看到了尼尔和那个少女极其细微的一个人格特征，那就是完美主义倾向。

只有完美主义倾向人格的个体，才会无法容忍自己犯错。他们通常表现得谦和有礼，各方面都常让人感觉到非常好。可惜，这些表象都只是为了维护他们不能达到的完美。他们期冀完美，可现实告诉他们，他们达不到。于是，他们不能接受这一步理应需要觉悟自省才触发的痛苦心灵感受，才会变得消极，甚至出现短暂性轻生念头。

就影片中的尼尔犯的错所生的觉悟为例，恰好可以解开我那位少女的难题与疑惑：

第一，有善良还要有足够的智慧，这样才能有适当区分出善良与邪恶真伪的能力。

第二，具备基本的迎击邪恶的恰当力度与分寸，这一点也体现在行为自我控制的分寸把握上，如此才能打出一个漂亮的全垒打。既不是后知后觉，伤人伤己，也不算手段激烈，一片混打，伤及无辜，过犹不及。

第三，尊重过去，把握现在，才会有更好的未来。就好比我为其做过心理治疗的那位少女，经过心理治疗与疏导，她变得敢于直面那些羞耻感、内疚感，并明辨了那不过是梦境中的一些虚假演绎，只为了让她难受而已。

如今的她，已经彻底放下了那些羞耻与内疚。回忆起因为梦境中的景象而曾有过短暂轻生念头的自己，她总算愿意释然。因为抓住过去不放，就是不放过自己。所以，她在我的催眠疗法中用了一个特别奇妙的方式，对那个梦境中的少年说，再见，就是永远不见。

治疗结束后一个多月，我无意中再次见到了她。她在一家大型超市卖场上班，脸上的五官变得更为秀丽，整个人焕发着如沐春风的神采。只是，她当时热衷于超市理货的工作，并没有注意到我。

在我心底，由衷欣慰。

唯有如同《魔法老师》影片中曾被贪婪的敌人抓住，利用到淋漓尽致，如同下过地狱、曾不敢面对过去的自己、倍感羞愧内疚、跳过大桥，却又因为连不会游泳的忠犬都敢于勇救主人，才可以从过去的经历中获得转生的灵觉。

本期（心理门）解语：放下过去，获得新生。

心理门·倾听儿童

　　A：教育者培养孩子的定力，是让他们从各种外界讯息的误导中，专注于自我——此时此刻"我是谁"以及自我应该做什么，而不是把自我的注意力放在"我哪里对了，哪里错了"。祝孩子们快乐。

　　B：在慢慢的发现中获得成长，需要蜕变。这样的过程可能会有一些成长期的正常情绪表露，甚至错过一些愉快学习的时间，还可能错怪本就关心自己的伙伴。一直到在自我反省与审思中，找到精准的答案，然后铭记那些让我们成长的懂得。到最后，会发现，其实值得儿童成长珍惜与关注的，一点都没错过。

　　C：在同等环境与际遇中，懂得让迫切的愿望得到一份自我的安宁与平静的等待，该见的总能见到。但作为教导者或父母，抑或是在大家庭氛围中，对于孩子的小小滑头，要更多地区分出他们是同样需要更多的关注，还是有其他更深层次的原因。但我始终相信，所有的问题都会得到一个圆满的答案。

D：大概在 2016 年 9 月 27 日左右，我收到了一部很好的绘本《花知道，风来过》。昨晚精心拜读，讲述了一个小傻瓜四处找一朵梦中花的故事。无论遇到什么情况，他都可以沉静以对，无论什么挫折都不能将他的信仰磨灭，因为他要找的花一直在陪伴着他。

E：也不知多少年月之前，貌似是好久好久（long long ago）。朦胧的记忆中，有一位金色头发的男孩子，他曾对我说："我好喜欢和你在一起的感觉啊。"套用一句俗话，就是"和你在一起我才是谁"。可我依稀记得，仿佛是在 2013 年底的时候，我才又收到他的短信。手机壳很冰，短信的字里行间透着熟悉，可写的内容，还是这一句"和你在一起我才是谁"。陌生，熟悉，再陌生，可还零星残余着些许的熟悉……

我问："你是谁啊？"

他言："我是……我是一个你对我说过一句这样的话的人，你知道。"

……

"好孩子，你还是错了，关键不是你和我在一起是谁，而是你随时都应该知道，你自己是谁，将来会成为什么样的人才对。"

……

嗯……依稀间，我可能是有说过这句话，还是那种感觉，是自己说过的，可又不是，是吗？或许若那个金发孩子真的和我说过话，我有 92% 的可能会说吧。通常这种情况，我总会说一些这样的话，而且还会镇静自若、淡然坦荡如常地看着那个小孩子，却又吓坏了他。我嘴快……也许我还会换种说法。

"那姐姐说你是猪，你是猪吗？"

那依稀寥寥残存的记忆深处，那个金发小男孩说："不猪。"

也许他也会气鼓鼓地鼓着腮帮子，回我一句："你猪。"

……

1 因材施教才是最合理的教育理念

　　相信大家都还记得赵薇和佟大为饰演的《虎妈猫爸》电视剧，相信很多观众看过之后，对剧中家长的教育理念都产生了不小的共鸣。

　　五岁的小公主罗茜茜，先由奶奶爷爷带，俗话说，"宝贝隔代亲"，强调在自由环境下培养孩子气质的奶奶，给予了孩子充分的尊重和选择权，却少了规矩，让孩子养成了不能吃苦、嫌贫爱富、娇生惯养的诸多坏毛病。

　　"虎妈"毕胜男意识到这样下去，孩子就会毁在没有规矩的溺爱里，于是将孩子接回家自己带。可从小接受了"必胜决"教育的她，继承了父亲的强迫教育方式。过多的保护欲，演绎出强悍的控制欲，几乎不容旁人辩驳半分：她不准孩子参加课外活动，认为郊游写生只是在浪费学习时间；晚上已经上床且倦意浓浓的孩子会被她从床上拉起来，只为了告诫孩子"今日事今日毕"的道理；她甚至还偷看孩子日记……这样的爱，多了规矩，却因为少了尊重，造成了孩子与母亲之间真实交流的隔阂。

其实，三到五岁是孩子自我意识的萌芽阶段，也是可塑性最强的年纪。孩子这时候的行为模式，往往更多的是与家长脸上的情绪在发生互动，而不是深入意识中的价值对与错的取向认同。

五岁的孩子，处于价值自我评价阶段，他还并不明白什么是对，什么是错。（再说，这个世界，也并非仅仅由非黑即白就可以完全诠释清楚。）比如，剧中爷爷奶奶常常和罗茜茜玩"小公主和奴仆"的游戏，大人小孩都开心，以致于孩子从成年人脸上的笑容反馈的信息就是，"哈，我这样做，他们开心，我也开心。"然后就以为这样的互动继续下去，并没有什么对错之分。而后来毕胜男作为母亲，强势地阅读和修改茜茜的日记，而忽略了五岁的孩子其实也有自身价值观念的初始状态，也有选择权利和隐私的权利。只是，她在家庭关系中处于至关重要的母亲角色，而且强势施压，振振有词地规定，让孩子从自身不舒服的情绪中产生了疑惑和探究，"是否我不喜欢妈妈看我日记，这样的想法就是不正确的，因为妈妈会生气？"

如此继续演变下去，高压与强势的教育下，孩子会逐步被剥夺自我的选择权、创造力、自我快乐以及兴趣的自由发展都会被抑制。这样的孩子，会变得缺乏主见、怯懦，做什么事都想关注身边人的情绪才会去做，而越来越忽略掉自身的需要与感受。或者也有可能完全成长为更加强势的反面，比长辈更过之而无不及。

而从母亲的角度来诠释这样的教育理念，其实更多的是来源于毕胜男的父亲。因为从小虎妈就是在同等高压的教育环境下成长起来的，虽然她一直对父亲的教育方式有阴影，也本能地表示反对，可自然而然却在自己的教育行为和理念中复刻从长辈那里得到的教育模式。虽然在虎妈身上，"必胜决"的高压强势教育在她自己身上颇见成效，但却忽视了教育客体的个性。

到目前为止，都还没有一种固定的教育理念或模式可以适用于所有不同个性的孩子。这不比选衣服，教育上，没有"百搭款"，只有适合与否。

在这个世界上，但凡正常的家庭，没有不爱自己孩子的父母，都想把自己的真爱传递给孩子，并收到合理同等的反馈。

尊重＋规矩＝真爱。真爱里的爱的感觉是流动的，不是封闭与缄默的。

因为和谐的交流、理解，用与对方平等的方式去看这个世界，才让我们的爱得以流淌。有爱的温暖与接纳，就像妈妈温暖的怀抱，在温暖我们幼小的自尊时，也教会了我们如何在别人的心眼里，认识自己的影子是否有残缺，是否完美，检视自己的处事方式，然后慢慢地成长，一步又一步，直到……当我们可以自己一个人独立地好好行走，独立地面对风风雨雨，在内心深处形成明晰的是非三观理念，并通过我们的不同经历归纳总结，慢慢使之完善。这样，我们才将真爱融入接纳与尊重，可以用自己的心眼看世界，也可以用别人的心眼看世界，用真正懂得自爱与爱人的新的方式，将爱传承，让我们的血脉生命找到新的适应的方式生存。

剧中的"虎妈"毕胜男，由缺乏经验盲从教育到摸索，最后自成一派，明白了"因材施教"的教育理念。在这样的转变过程中，其实父母与孩子都在一起摸索成长，彼此适应，最终找到最和谐的真爱的传递方式。而假如迷信任何固定模式的教育理念，生搬硬套用到孩子身上，就如浇灌养育一棵小树苗，施与和养育成型的机会只有一次，一旦成型，想再重来，已经是不可能了。若非"因材施教"，或会种下苦果，这才是我们与孩子成长路上最担心的事。

2 尝试采用区别增加来管住你的小嘴巴

"你这间心理咨询室太 TMD 棒了。"这是慧荣刚来我心理工作室所说的第一句话。虽然语气中带着讨好的成分，却也有骂人的脏字。

她是个才 7 岁的小孩子。可每每说话，话语间都有一大堆脏字在那里储备着，随时随地都能爆出粗口。

"你这支笔不错，太 TMD 炫了，真是亮瞎眼。"

"你这沙发太 TMD 不错了，舒服！"

"这杯果汁太 TMD 好喝了，我正好渴了……"

不错，慧荣是个三句话不离 TMD 问候语的小孩子。为此，她的父母无计可施，托了朋友关系，辗转找到我这里，前来求助。

慧荣的父母很宠溺孩子，他们不希望老师在学校为此过度批评慧荣，免得慧荣没面子，也不希望老师为此惩罚她。所以慧荣的这个毛病愈演愈烈，她也在成长的道路上愈发自我发展，毫不顾忌，还真是应了那句，小孩子说话"百无禁忌"。

可慧荣的父母都是知识分子，每每带慧荣出门做客，慧荣三两句就爆粗口，有些还是成年人都闻所未闻的脏字（此处不再赘述）。旁人问起，令慧荣父母无地自容，他们知道再不管管慧荣，这孩子怕是要毁了。

我了解了大致情况，对慧荣道："你为什么喜欢每一句都带脏字呢？"

"这还不简单，因为这样显得我成熟呀。"慧荣耸耸肩膀，一屁股坐在我咨询室的布艺沙发上，翘起了二郎腿，"这样同学们都会怕我，也不敢惹我！"

这个年龄段的孩子心智还不够成熟，却渴望得到成人般的关注，故而慧荣会有这样的现象。

"我们不妨采用区别增强策略来管住她的小嘴巴。"我这样建议道。

我首先做的是让我为慧荣做一周的心理咨询。在此期间，让我成为慧荣的"大榕树"，我有一个大大的树洞，可以随便让慧荣肆无忌惮地倾诉自己的想法。

起初，慧荣对我毫不限制她说话带脏字这一点感觉很开心。我这个树洞也起到了最优质的倾听与接纳作用。其实我也正在从关心慧荣的角度，在观察她骂脏字的次数。

经过一周的评估，我们了解到慧荣平均每天骂人带脏字超过15次。于是，我开始找慧荣交谈："你知道吗？其实骂脏字并不能表示你的成熟，真正的成熟是我们遇到事情之后处理的方式和能力的体现。同学们不是怕你，而是因为你骂人而远离你。这样下去你会没人愿意和你玩。骂脏字除了能表现出你行为不良，还会把你从一个不错的女孩儿变成一个不太好的孩子。这样你也乐意吗？"

慧荣愣了愣，怼我："我TMD还就喜欢这样说，怎么办？我改不了。"

我拿起一沓《斗罗大陆》的小舞贴纸，冲她扬了扬："从即日起，但凡你一天骂人次数未达6次，我就送你一张这种贴纸，你第一次来说过喜欢的。"

她伸出手想要抢过我手里的贴纸，被我阻止，藏在身后。

她缩回手，揉了揉鼻子："好，6次而已，我TM……没什么做不到的。"

"相反，如果你做不到，那就要罚你帮你妈妈倒垃圾。"

于是，我们约定每天下午四点到我的咨询室和她母亲一起做评估和奖惩的实施。

经过一段时日的实施，果然，慧荣从每天骂脏字6-8次，到后来的每天5-6次，再后来的3-4次，最后约定为1-2次。

一个月后，慧荣从最初的15次每天的标准，逐渐减为7次、5次、3次、2次、1次，到最后的0次，她彻底改掉了骂人的习惯。

我的小舞贴纸也正好送完了："这样的你，更像斗罗里的小舞了，不错哦。"

这个案例分析一下，不难发现，对慧荣骂脏字已成习惯的辅导，我们的基本原则并不期望她一下子就完全改善，而是采用渐进的方式。只要减少了不良行为的出现频率，就给予正向增强，奖励她小舞贴纸，用她喜欢的物件进行强化并使其循序渐进地改善，然后再逐步减低频率标准，终于达到改善的目标。

根据研究，富有攻击性的儿童，遇到挫折，容易乱发脾气，好争辩，以骂人和打架来解决冲突，忽视了他人的权利和期望。对这类儿童我们可以采用区别增强策略来辅导。

3 如何做一个情商高的父母

发脾气会摧毁一个孩子的灵性，但不发脾气又憋得难受，那我们该怎么办？

相信我们当中不少人都带过孩子，在意识当中，我们都想成为一个绝佳的父母，可带孩子这事儿吧，大多数人总不能做到始终保持心平气和。这是一个大问题吗？我们的情绪是否会影响到孩子呢？

首先，其实从孩子的心理层面来看，每次我们发脾气的时候，孩子眼神中总能捕捉到一些害怕的情绪。我们不知道的是，孩子真正害怕的并不是我们发脾气这件事，而是害怕自此之后，我们和他们再也不是朋友，他们也再也不能获得父母的爱了。

这种不再被爱的感受，比挨骂挨打更加让孩子感到恐慌。

第二，既然你说孩子这么害怕我们发脾气，那我隐藏起我的怒火，努力克制自己不再对孩子发脾气，这样总行了吧？

不，这样也是不可取的。因为我们是有血有肉的人，是个人都会有发脾气的时候，有爆发情绪的时候，不发脾气的人几乎是没有的。除非是"行尸走肉"。

而我们每次想冲着熊孩子们发脾气的时候，我们反而强忍克制住脾气，这种处理负面情绪的不良方式，会被孩子敏感而幼小的心灵捕捉到，他们已经可以从成人克制的语气、腔调、举止、神态等诸多方面，感受到一个强烈的讯息："这会儿别惹我，否则我就要发飙了，我发飙了，你这熊孩子可没有好果子吃。滚一边去，哪儿凉快，哪儿待着去！"

正因为孩子可以感受得到我们克制的情绪，所以，他们很可能会在长期这样的处理方式下，也学会这样的处理负面情绪的方式，最大的问题就是，以后，他们在外面遇到了什么事儿，都不告诉你，而是选择闷在心里。情绪得不到正向的流动，长此以往，这样对孩子的心理成长是极其不利的。

那么，你说，发脾气孩子会害怕失去爱，不发脾气又不利于孩子的心理成长，那么我们是正常的有血有肉的人，当我们有负面情绪时，又要和孩子交流，那么我们应该怎样互动呢？

1. 我们在遇到熊孩子捣乱时，比如打烂了你心爱的瓷器；或者毁了你的工作文档；或者在家里墙壁上乱涂乱画；或者和邻居家熊孩子打架……诸如此类，熊孩子惹得父母心中燃起熊熊怒火的时刻，不胜枚举。那么这个时候，**我们作为教导者，就应该选择"对事不对人"的处理方式**，好好地讲道理，针对熊孩子所犯的这件事儿上来摆道理，引导其理解到自己犯下了错误，是怎样的错误，下次如果遇到同等情况，又当如何操作等等。

2. 当负面情绪来临前，作为父母，我们应该尽量在情绪失控前，向孩子做出必要的预警。比如对孩子说，"我心情不太好，现在我必须要一个人待一会儿，你的事儿过一会儿再聊。"这样在情绪来临前和孩子互相处于一个冷静的状态，等情绪过去后再去呼唤熊孩子。

3. 冷静下来之后，如果我们有对孩子恶言相向，那一定要第一步跟孩子讲讲，我们为什么会发脾气，讲讲我们发脾气时的心理感受，让孩子能够在你快要爆发时，理解你的难处。

发脾气之后的关系重建才是真爱的关键。

有的父母从来不跟孩子认错，他们会认为天底下哪有父母向孩子认错的道理？由来已久就只有孩子向父母认错的道理呀。其实，这样的想法是有点偏颇的，也不利于家庭里情绪的正向流动。毕竟这世上人无完人，哪有人从来不会犯错误。如果有，那才是天底下最大的笑话。

那么如何重建与孩子的良好关系呢？

1. 如果我们冲孩子发了脾气，伤害了孩子的自尊心，那么我们一定要在情绪平复时，第一时间找孩子认错，说一声"对不起"，这样偶尔放低姿态的教养方式，才张弛有度，并且让孩子明白，我们冲他发了脾气，但并不是说我们就不爱他了，我们依然很爱他。

2. 跟孩子谈谈心事，我们为什么会突然发火？比如："妈妈，今天工作上不太顺心"，抑或者"我今天不小心犯了错被别人骂了"……这样开诚布公地和孩子交心，让孩子的心目中明白，原来他的父母也是和他一样的，是普通人，所以会有怒火。而同时我们也要告诉孩子，当他心情不佳时，也是可以发脾气的，并不是说孩子一旦闹腾，就是铁定孩子不乖不听话了，所以不要制止孩子哭泣或倾诉或宣泄。

这样围追堵截的教养方式，是"双标"，也是不利于孩子成长的。他要拥有一颗健康的、具有一定抗压能力的良好心理，就得允许孩子对自己的情绪有清晰的认知，并教导孩子如何正向地处理负面情绪。

3.跟孩子一番畅聊之后，又彼此回归心灵，问问他我们是否和好了呀？当确认了这一点后，再给彼此一个温暖的拥抱吧。

在一个良好的家庭里，必定有一个或一对情商很高的父母，这样开怀畅谈的处理方式，能让负面情绪得到很好的宣泄，也能使这个家庭的情绪正向流动起来，慢一点，一点一点，不能急躁，总会引导孩子活得恣意痛快，又坚强，又自信，且快乐健康。

4如何让你的孩子拥有强大的内心？

如何让你的孩子拥有强大的内心？这恐怕是许多父母对孩子的期望，但要如何操作呢？

简言之，**就是请你多多夸奖他。**

我们常说，让一个孩子自卑其实很容易，只要不断打击和否定他就可以了，不断地打击，或不断地将他跟别人家的孩子相比，不认可他身上独特的优点，否定他的所言所行……作为父母，您只需要这样一通操作，就可以轻而易举地让孩子的自信心受到强而有力的打击，久而久之，变成一个自卑感极重，或脆弱玻璃心的孩子。

而相反，我们想要树立一个孩子的强大内心却很不容易，尤其是要树立一个内心很自卑的孩子的自信心，就根本不是一件简单的事。

这就好比我们做成一件坏事很容易，但要做好一件好事却很困难。

那么我们要如何夸奖一个受到了批评后自我怀疑的孩子呢？如何让一个孩子面对外界质疑的声音时，仍可以坚定地喜爱自己，相信自己呢？

您不会夸孩子，到底是什么原因呢？

1. 有的家长认为，如果从小不对孩子进行挫折教育，那么将来上社会工作了，会经不起别人的指责，或一丁点儿挫折就选择轻生的道路。有的家长还认为：有些孩子一夸就上天，最后反而一事无成。

可实际上，每个孩子的内心深处，不管我们有没有受到外界的批评或质疑，我们都是需要获得许许多多来自家人的夸奖的。只有获得了这些夸奖，才有助于孩子在形成独立的人格时，让孩子意识到自己身上有这些或那些的闪光点，而这些闪光点是能让孩子逐渐点亮自己的人性之光，逐渐形成正常健康的三观，照亮自我个性当中懦弱的部分，然后驱散它。唯有如此，在不断肯定声音中成长的孩子，才更加有足够的自信经得起风雨的洗礼。

2. 从小不太被父母夸奖的孩子，内心其实很自卑，一辈子都在证明"我其实很棒"这回事。

小A从小不被父母夸奖，都是在父母的一片打压声中长大，骨子里他认为自己不够好，没有别人做得棒。长大成年后，也因此与父母的关系很疏离。后来，成立了小家庭后，另一半却经常夸赞自己，一丁点小事，小到哪怕只是自己为爱人削了个水果，摆在果盘里，也会被爱人称赞"有艺术气息，有天赋。"渐渐的，小A生活中也能看到自己很不错的这些优点了。他开始变得逐渐有勇气，认清自己的优缺点，逐渐开始为自己能实现的梦想努力了。他笑言，是他的另一半给了他第二次自我成长的机会。

所以说，夸赞对于一个孩子的成长历程来说，是何等的重要。它能帮孩子逐渐建立起自我能力认知的边界，知道何所为何所不为。他能够很清晰地明了自己的自我能力的边界在哪里？既不会好高骛远，也不会自怨自艾地轻易放弃。

那些不夸奖孩子的父母内心是怎么想的呢？

1. 父母从小也是在批评和打压的挫折中长大的，这样的成长历程自然而然就复刻到了自己孩子的身上，童年的记忆就是："我也是这样在苦痛中成长起来的，你是我的孩子，也应当在这样的苦痛中长大"。

这样拿出来分析，并不是要我们做父母的，不让孩子吃点苦头，而是在孩子吃了苦头，或遭遇了挫折时，我们是不是能够适时地为孩子打气，鼓励，加油，一句"我看好你哦"，那么孩子就真的能独自一个人坚强地走过挫折的风雨，逐渐阳光地成长起来。

2. 父母把内心的担忧和焦虑，通过不断的批评辱骂，反映到了孩子身上。

父母自身没有处理负面情绪的能力，于是通过发泄在孩子身上排解，久而久之，居然养成了习惯。但凡情绪不佳，行事不顺，就拿孩子当你的"情绪垃圾桶"。

殊不知，孩子的心理承受能力已经达到了一定的峰值。渐渐地，孩子也通过打骂其他的同学，来宣泄自我的不良情绪，于是"校园霸凌"类似的问题就产生了。还有一种，就是当孩子遭遇到这样的情绪暴力之后，无法对外人表达，于是就采取自残、自虐等对内攻击的方式来宣泄心中压抑的不满情绪，于是，我们偶尔也会看到孩子身上有一道两道被刀片切割出来的伤口。

这类孩子是在自我的疼痛中寻找那些许的快乐与释放啊。

3. 父母的权威过于维护。

这一类父母，他们不懂得与孩子如何做朋友，只知道利用家长的权威来压制，用不断鞭策与挑剔的话语来表达爱与权威，最后孩子成年之后，也会可能与父母的关系越来越生硬，亲情越来越远。

那么我们如何夸奖孩子才算正确的呢？

1. **尽量认清孩子真实的优点来夸奖**。不要不切实际，夸大化的夸赞，那样只会让孩子内心感觉你是在敷衍他，而不是真的觉得他很不错。

2. **适时及时地夸赞孩子的长处**。当我们发现了孩子的优点之后，我们应当给予他适时及时的夸奖，这样在孩子的记忆中才会留下深刻的印象，从而形成"我在这方面可以表现得很好"的认知。

3. 有的家长不善言辞，不知道该怎么夸赞孩子。那就请你在发现孩子的优点之后，**如果实在不知道怎么做，就给他一个温暖的抱抱吧**，拥抱能加深彼此的亲情链接。

那么，怎样才是一个内心强大的人呢？

1. **认可自身存在的价值**。

2. **对自我的能力有清晰的边界意识**：什么是我能做到的，什么是我目前为止还不能做到的呢。

3. **能够自己掌握自我控制力**：不会因为外界不良的评价就轻易阻碍自我行动的脚步，该做什么，还是依然做什么。

4. **能够快速地从挫折中恢复**：也就是我们俗称的，抗打压能力强。

5 走出逝去的阴霾，从抽动中解脱

小C刚来我的咨询室求助时，只有独自一人，而他还未成年。

幼小的年纪，生活就给予了他异于常人的痛苦与经历。他见到我的时候，说话间有止不住的挤眉弄眼的举止，以及轻微的耸肩。他告诉我，在一年前他发作此症状时，更加厉害，还会不住地点头。那个时候，人人看到他就像面对一个怪物，为此，他旧伤未愈又添新伤，还增加了病耻感。

小C的病症，叫抽动障碍，即小儿抽动秽语综合征。这是起病于儿童和青少年时期的一类神经精神障碍，患儿会反复出现多个部位运动性抽动伴发声性抽动，一般伴有强迫障碍、注意缺陷以及多动障碍等并发症。

由于小助理的疏忽，在我第一次准备咨询医案时，被告知是多动症，故而我的咨询医案是按照多动症来进行心理辅导咨询的。而面对小C，我该如何着手咨询呢？

"你是什么时候开始发现自己患了这样的病症的？"我想了想，对他提出第一个问题。小C在我面前，一开始显得很拘谨，虽然年纪小，却很懂事。从他的描述中，我了解到，他最初的发病是因为身边最亲的人永远地离开了他。

我观察着他叙述中又有不住的抽动和挤眼睛的举止，根据过往的咨询经验，我立即在心中有了全新的咨询方案。

"你这一年多以来，可有用药治疗？"我知道一般这种涉及神经精神的障碍是需要用药治疗，并同时配合心理咨询治疗辅助进展的。

"有，之前用一种口服药，服用后，我头晕脑胀，根本无法学习，也无法集中精力，后来，就改用了另外一种贴在后背肩胛骨处的药了。"小C努力回忆着。我注意到，他在我面前尽量控制着自己的言行，或许是担心不自觉的行为会吓到我。

"你可以在我面前尽量放松与释放自己，不用那么刻意。"我提示他，好的咨询师就像摇篮，可以给来访者提供温暖安全的港湾。

鉴于小C的抽动症主要的诱因是亲人离世对他的强烈刺激导致的，而如今，时隔一年，他依旧沉浸在悲伤中无法自拔。

但书本上传递的这方面的知识表明，**小儿抽动秽语综合征的病因和发病机制尚未完全明确，或许跟遗传因素、神经生理、心理因素和环境因素等诸多方面有关系。**

就这一情况，我适时调整了对小C的咨询方案：

首先，在循序渐进的咨询治疗过程中，我不断地告诉他，这个病症是可以治疗改善的，以逐渐消除他的病耻感，增强他的治疗康复的信心。

同时，我问及了**他在学校与人相处的情况，这可以判断他的病症是否有损他的社会功能，尤其是与人相处的方面。**

很庆幸的是，小C的同学中没有嘲笑讥讽他的人，老师对他也很关爱，这让小C感到很温暖。

"我喜欢上学。"他一提及学校，脸上就露出了难得的有点开心的表情。

"嗯，这很好。"如果小C在患病的过程中，能得到环境上社会面的诸多支持，是有助于他建立起康复的信心的。

其次，我打算在后续的咨询中，对小C提供支持性的指导和行为疗法，以帮助他合理安排患儿的正常生活。

因为这样的抽动症，大部分的患儿可以在进入青春期后期，其症状会**逐渐好转**，虽然也有部分患儿会带着这样的症状持续到老年，但不影响智商和寿命。

第三，因为小C还对一年多前亲人的离世无法释怀，根据这一特征，据以往经验，是需要对他进行哀伤辅导咨询的。

要让长久沉浸在丧失哀伤中的来访者明白，哀伤只是生活的一部分，它不能代替全部，这个时候，我们需要做的就是整合哀伤。

1. 增强来访者对丧失事实的现实感，增加失落的现实感，即接纳这个事实。

2. 帮助来访者处理情感和行为上的痛苦，协助当事人处理表达或潜在的情感情绪，把哀伤表达出来。

有些没有经验的养育者，可能会在这个时候提出质疑，患儿在悲伤，这个时候，他们更倾向于帮助患儿将这个哀伤的伤口藏起来，而且久而久之藏得很深。他们以为这样做，患儿就好像不会再哀伤与悲恸，有的养育者甚至固执地认为，"只要看不到他哭，就是好的。"

其实这样做，一点都不利于患儿走出哀伤，伤口就是要暴露在阳光下，一旦见了光，才能正视它，才有利于伤口的痊愈与结痂。

只是鉴于如小C这种抽动症患儿的情况，在咨询室处理哀伤辅导时，应该遵循不过度刺激的原则。

但这并不是说，不帮助其认清现实，处理哀伤。

3. 鼓励当事人向逝者告别，以及以健康的方式坦然地重新将情感投注到全新的关系当中。就小C而言，我鼓励他与同学多交往，与其中的一两个交上朋友，在家里与现在的养育者处理好亲情关系，多拥抱，多倾诉心事，多靠近，允许建立新的依赖关系。

4. 为来访者介绍并让其了解正念疗法，即不带批判地观察当下的自我及他人，以佛教的理念疗愈自身。

哀伤辅导的总体原则是：去者善终，留者善别，能者善生。

最后，但愿每一个受伤的灵魂都能有所依赖，能得到抚慰，从悲伤中重新站起，勇敢地淌过黑暗之路，走向光明的人生。

Ps：鉴于咨询保密原则，本文中的案例分析皆为虚构，仅提及抽动症，希望对大家有帮助。

心理门·我们的情绪

1 为自己做一个"转移计划随身带"

Whoever of you loves life and desires to see many good days, keep your tongue from evil and your lips from speaking lies.

有何人喜好存活,爱慕长寿,得享美福,就要禁止舌头不出恶言,嘴唇不说诡诈的话。——《旧·诗》34:12、13

他拎着一个破烂不堪的塑料袋,袋子里空空如也,满脸怒气冲冲出现在咨询室门口。他是今天的来访者,叫巧南。

"你是需要帮助吗?"我看着这位年轻的来访者,语气柔和地问。

"不知道！"他的回答依旧藏着很多怒气，眼珠子似乎在看我，似乎又在我注视他的时候，不好意思地别开看向别处。

我意识到，他的愤怒情绪依旧还在，但很显然，这怒火并非针对坐在咨询室里等待来访者的我。于是，我从沙发里直起身来，放下我的书，很自然地倒了一杯白开水，也为他倒了一杯，然后递到他面前。

他愣住了，站在那里，不知道是接还是不接，眼神瞄了瞄我依旧微笑的脸，恍惚间出现了几分尴尬。我招呼他进来坐下，他喝了一口水，有些悻悻然垂下头，"你怎么都不生气？"

"你认为，我应该生气吗？"我在揣摩他的逻辑。难道在他的世界里，有人伤害了他，他是那种一定会十倍奉还的人？那么这愤怒又从何而来？

"你不该生气？"他像看怪物似的看着我，但很快又颓然道，"我想，我的确需要帮助——我的问题是，我……我时常会控制不住我的脾气，然后，常常为我的愤怒买单。"

"那你是如何看待那个时候的自己的？"我问道。

"以往，我总认为，我的身边的人，都应该理解我，所以，那些情绪，既然理解，就该承受，但后来，随着时间的流逝，一些经历，让我逐渐意识到不应该，没有人生来就该为我的坏脾气买单。可我不发出来，我感觉我快要炸了，您了解吗？"

"但肆意发泄，你又感觉不妥当了，是吗？"

我的话音刚落，他就点点头，然后告诉我他来此之前，本来手里提着一袋苹果，可因为接了朋友的一个电话，对方并没有按照他期待的安排来配合他的合作计划，他就控制不住地想要乱发脾气，而对方也为此挂了他的电话，让他简直怒不可遏了，猛地把手机摔在了地上，还不分时间地点地叫骂一通。他实在是太气愤了，横冲直撞地行走，把塑料袋勾破了，苹果撒了一地，那一刻，他感到这个世界上所有人都在嘲笑他……

"你原本是期望怎样的发展？"

"我期望，我的朋友一打电话过来，我就能收到好消息，我们的合作计划顺利实施了，我不希望有任何耽误。"

"你不期望你的思考规划里有任何改变或打破你的期许，是这样吗？"

他拼命点头，斩钉截铁道，"是的，很不喜欢，我就喜欢什么都顺顺利利的。"

"可实际上,那只是你的思想,不是现实,现实里也是不会有改变吗?"

他想了想,"不是。其实我知道,现实是真实存在的,它不会随着我的思想而改变,我无法用我的思想控制现实的变化性。"跟着,他脸上的挫败感更深了一层。

"对,其实你明白这个道理,但你的主要问题是控制不住脾气而已。"

"那我需要怎么做?"

我笑起来,"你需要建立一个转移计划小便条随身带着。"

转移计划小便条,即针对那些容易控制不住脾气的人专门定制。这需要当事人选择在平静的时候,为自己创立一个转移注意力的行动小便条,上面可以写出自己想要尝试的一些事情。这种转移与自我抚慰的办法可以有效将自己从愤怒几乎快要失态的情况中拉出来。在感觉有一点愤怒在心中激荡时,就赶紧拿出来看看,然后选中其中一项来实施。

下面列举几种常用的"让坏脾气消失的法宝":

——尽快回忆过去一些难忘又愉悦的经历。尽可能想得仔细一点,譬如当时吸引住你目光的美好的细节和瞬间,那些"吸引力"事物都有什么颜色、气味、触感?当时曾给予你什么样的感受?

——如果在街上或公共场合,就赶紧抬眼看看四周或窗外,在远处能否找到美丽的人事物并观察他们。如果找到了并开始专注于其上,那么思考一下,他正处于什么状态,那或许有什么背后的小故事呢?

——保留一份你最喜欢或最崇敬的人的名人名言。想愤怒的时候,就拿出来看看,读读,想象一下,如果你总有一日,也能站到他那样的高度,成为他那样的人,他在这个时候,会怎么做?会简单粗暴把自己和周围的环境变成原始丛林吗?嘿,不会是吧?你又不是傻子,所以闭上眼,想象这个时候,头顶出现一处祥瑞的光芒,开始照耀你,抚慰你,把你周身的不痛快能量都照耀得无影无踪了,你会越来越完好。

——是否很久没有新的兴趣开发了?没有吗?就去想一个,一个就好,哪怕是类似把花盆里的土翻一翻的小事。

——做家务,譬如把一大堆家里人的衣服都洗了,晾在阳台上。

——洗个热水澡,顺便把头发也洗了,吹干。

——把你的皮鞋擦得锃亮。

——如果被困在一个小环境里,就数数,数你的呼吸,听你的呼吸声,静静的,然后感觉你身边的气息。

——调动你的嗅觉和味觉,闻一些安神香薰或干脆去你钟意的美食店闻一闻那里的食物香气,顺便猜一猜这道菜都有哪些食材和香料,然后大快朵颐吧,只要不怕胖:)

——调动你的听觉,听纯音乐,可以听类似班得瑞的亲近大自然音乐,想象你在那样优美的环境里自由徜徉。

——调动你的触觉,放一块玉石在裤袋里,轻轻抚摸那顺滑的质感,去感应玉石的内部天然的构成,谦谦君子如玉。或做做自我抚慰的按摩,按摩你的手掌,手臂,肩头,甚至是抱抱自己。

……

如果你已经阅读过我的转移小便条,那不妨回家制作你自己的吧。然后在以后还想发脾气的时候,拿出来,选中一个,在上面用铅笔打一勾,立即去实施,你会发现,坏脾气不翼而飞了。

巧南离开的时候,顺便借走了我的小便条,他打算选择去喝一大杯热巧克力这类放松性饮料,在他情绪平复之后,再找个时机给朋友打电话,问一下可否修改合作计划。

"下一期您讲承受痛苦的高级技巧的时候,我能来听吗?"

"Of course." 我保持着淡淡的笑意,和他一道,迎着阳光走出门去。

本期【心理门】解语:我们的人生,或许幸福就在我们身边,倘若对

生活赏赐的痛苦加以抱怨，就难以宁心静气地感受到它赐予的快乐。认真地工作，积极调试自我的身心，简单便是富足幸福。

2您是否能全盘接受这样的自己？

Has no slander on his tongue,who does his neighbor no wrong and casts no slur on his fellowman.

不以舌头谗谤人，不恶待朋友，也不随伙毁谤邻里。——《旧·诗》15：3

千百打来电话，告诉我：他想伤害自己，还想一把火把现在住的房子都烧掉。

我当时正在听舒缓的音乐，我并没有立刻问他为什么，而是说："你能告诉我你最喜欢的音乐是什么？"

他余怒未消，气呼呼地说："没有。什么都没有！"

"那最喜欢看的影片是什么？"我又问。

"没有，别人看着发笑的电影，我通常都不笑的，不觉得好笑。"

"那动画片呢？"我继续。

"谁看那种小孩子看的东西？您该不会告诉我您会喜欢看这类幼稚片吧？"他的语气已经没有先前那么气急败坏。

"我如果诚实地告诉你，我有时候的确会看看动画片的，然后像个孩子似的傻笑，你会鄙视我这样的心理工作者吗？"

"不。"他回答得很快，像一只担心被人踩住尾巴的猴子。

"我们之前签订的契约有规定，来访者必须对心理师提供真实的情绪反应。"我说。

他沉吟了一会儿，缓缓道，"唔，好吧，有一点。"

"现在，你在哪里呢？"

"我当然是在来你临床咨询中心的路上。"

我放下了电话，估摸着再过15分钟，他或许就该到了，很显然，他已经忘了刚才想放火烧房子的事情。

这样的危机干预，对于一个心理师来说，再常见不过。其实或许我的朋友们已经注意到了，**在处理痛苦时，可用的策略只需要三点：转移、转化放松以及应对。**

无论我们当下遇到什么事情，或许我们都可能会产生愤怒、焦虑、暴躁、伤心、疼痛、心塞、抑郁、胆怯、自我封闭、言语攻击，甚至是侮辱性言语、自残或伤人等情绪或行为。这个时候，常人通常的处理方式，是与之对抗。

因为无法接受眼前突兀的现实，尤其是有完美主义倾向的人，或许在规律控制被打破之后，可能更加难以接受。

就以上案例，我们来谈谈痛苦承受的高级技能——全面接受。

全面接受一件事，并不是意味着你让步，完全被动接受任何不好的事情在你身上发生。比如你遭受了不公正的侮辱和攻击。但抛开那些情况，仍然有一些情况，值得我们去思考，它发生的时候，我们应该在与他人人际关系交往中承担哪些因为处理不当而导致关系失衡的这部分责任。

怒火、自残、焦虑、暴躁等负面情绪的传导，伤害自己也伤害别人。 而全面接受，是相当于开启了我们多方位的视角去观察这段关系。我们不得不承认，当下的现实，是过去一连串的事情以及我们和其他互动的人所作决定产生的结果。

每一个选择，都有一定的导向性。

所以，我们需要为这个结果承担起全面接受它的责任。

就以上案例，我们可以具体细化，来分析几个方面：

首先，是什么事情导致千百的现状？

因为和同住宿舍的几个同学闹了矛盾，他感觉自己一直受到排挤。而今天，他忘了带宿舍钥匙，午休的时候回去敲门，居然没有一个同学为他开门。

形成现在的局面，千百该负什么责任？（不要不理性地断定千百没有责任，那一屋子同学全疯了。事情的起因一定有曲折，对吧？）

很明显，千百最初想要处理问题的方式是伤害自己以及扩大伤害的影响力，由攻击朝内转向攻击朝外——处理情绪的方式不对。

再次，如果遭遇同住的同学无理相待，确有不公正之处，那么仔细思考一下，为什么他们可以这样对待你？而是否有同样的事情发生在别人身上？在这段人际关系中，千百在平衡同学间和谐相处的问题上，是过于强硬对抗，还是过于卑微，一副好欺负的样子……等等，他到底在同学中展示了一个怎样的自我形象，才导致同学们会这样漠视他的感受，这些问题，都是值得我们思考的。懂得向内探索，思考产生的原因，才能获得思考的价值。

对这件事，那些同学又该负什么责任？

的确在这件事上，那些同学有漠视千百需求的现象出现。如果仅仅是以"熟睡不知"为理由，那么如果在外敲门的不是千百，而是老师或学生会纪检干部，他们还能用这样的借口搪塞吗？又或者，门外敲门的真的是千百，可他的要求不是"请开门"，而是"着火了""地震了""对面有人撒钱跳艳舞了——"……诸如此类的理由真的发生，那么那紧闭的房门还真的会如此纹丝不动吗？

答案很明显，不是。

目前的情况，什么是千百可以把握的？

千百着急愤怒的原因，是因为想回宿舍，而恰好在午休时间。而他想回宿舍的原因不是午休，而是在教室自习的时候发现自己没有带国家六级英语测试题典，只有生词本。按照原计划，他是需要每天先背诵200个单词，再做题典的。可当他背诵完之后，就发现没有带题典，返回宿舍去拿，就遇到这种事。

那么，他可以掌握的部分是什么呢？如果非要进宿舍，可以叫宿舍管理员拿钥匙开门。如果没有钥匙，又非要开门，可以有很多折中又好用的办法，这里就不赘述，建议心理咨询的时候，我可以告诉你。

或者，他灵活地改变当天的计划，就背诵400个单词，等过了午休时间，再回宿舍去拿题典就好。没必要为了这样的小事，就和长期大学四年朝夕相处的同学闹得每天不愉快，大眼瞪小眼，让自己长期处于负面的情绪环境中，对自我良好的身心成长是不妥的。

目前的情况，千百不能把握的是什么？

如果千百仅仅只是因为性格内向、沉闷、压抑性情绪而导致同学们如此相待，那么在做好真实的自己之后，他仍旧不能把握的是同学们对他的短期态度和看法。这个是需要长期的自我改善、主动的沟通、善意的交流、互相尊重与互相帮助等等一系列稳定善意的行为言谈，才能逐渐改变。所以，就目前的情况来看，千百短期内是不能改变同学们对他的看法的，除非是他深刻地自我探索、完善自我、获得成长，才能逐渐改善旁人对待他的态度。

就目前状况，千百的最初反应是如何影响这件事的后果的？

千百在门外午休时间大吵大闹，破口大骂，不仅让午休的同学更加不喜欢他的所为，而且对他的态度更加恶劣了。千百自己无形中为自己织就了一张满是倒钩的人际关系网，害人害己，更影响正常的学习功能，建议做心理咨询或大学心理辅导。

千百应该怎样改变现状处理方式，以减少他和宿舍同学的痛苦？

他本可以选择很多良好方法来处理解决烦恼和怒火，全面接受这样的情况，多角度考虑问题，重新审视现状的可能走向，是可以得到不同结果的。最下下策的方式，还可以更换宿舍。虽然这样得到的成长不是最大化，但至少可以保护千百不再长期浸泡在负面情绪关系网中，备受煎熬，影响学习。

假设千百在处理"不开门"这件事上全面接受，事情会怎样？

如果在千百应门不开的情况下，他很敏锐地觉察到了自己受到不公正待遇的怒气，那么，他也许可以选择去找宿舍管理员开门，或重新回到教室，拿上词典，选一个环境优美安静的小草地上再背诵200个单词，等午休过后，再回到宿舍，并且并不把这件事放在心上，但可以委婉向舍长提出，自己应过门没有开这件事，为此表示遗憾。有时候我们或许可能很难向别人拒绝我们不喜欢他们对待我们的方式，但学会跨出第一步，而不是一味地压抑情绪，那就是一种勇敢的成长。没有了压抑，学会正确地委婉地表达自己的感受，注意，只是表达感受，给出建议，并不是要你评判。采用这样折中的方式表达自我，不失为一种明智之举。

"以后我们继续来谈谈自我肯定的陈述。"

"时间过得真快，反正您要下班了，不如让我顺道送你回家，你在路上给我讲讲也可以啊？"千百脸上洋溢出快乐的情绪，提出要求。

我看了看他,挑挑眉,温和地婉谢,"不行哦,你知道我所做的一切都是每天帮助预订时间内的来访者,这是工作,仅此而已。"

"好吧,我知道你又要说心理师守则。"千百理解地表示出不勉强,"我们下周见。"

本期【心理门】解语:古人说:"妇人之仁"这句话的意思,是要人们的慈悲不要走小路线,要发大慈悲,具大仁大爱,所以才用"妇人之仁",而并非偏颇地指一些一惊一乍的尖声惊叫的"仁"。——摘自《南怀瑾》

3释梦——一个心理师的梦境分析

It is not only the old who are wise,not only the aged who understand what is right.

尊贵的不都有智慧。寿高的不都能明白公平。——《旧·伯》32:9

"咨询了一段时间，我认为我应该静下来。"一位男性心理师朋友"理智的 Rose"跟我交谈的时候，忽然真的停了下来。原因是他看到了一幅画，它正好就放在我给他看的一篇微博文字里。

那是一幅一只威严的狮子俯在一只纯白小羊羔旁边，脸上的神色很温和。

"你怎么了？"我注意到他的异样。

"很和谐，这幅画。可……狮子真的可以吃素吗？"他开始向我解释，他的异样是源于他做过的一个梦。

"那是怎样的梦呢？"

"重复性，连续性。"

他开始娓娓道来：以前有一段时间我时常坠入相同的一个梦境，梦里有一只黑色的猎豹在铁丝网前来回逡巡着，不安地走来走去，它深邃的目光只是注视着一片光明的天际，淡蓝的晴空。而我站在铁丝网的另一边，端视着它。一个心底的声音在轻问我：

你可以让一只豹子不吃肉吗？一只黑豹。

你可以吗？

……

梦醒，我感觉肩上好沉重，似乎背负的使命更让我时常大汗淋漓，负重吃痛，可我不能卸下担子，两袖清风。

梦的分析：

梦的材料，从某种程度而言，都来源于现实中生活的体验，或许在某一刻某一时，或某一段时间被特殊强化后，就容易形成梦反复的主题。而关于梦的重复性、连续性，是因为那些潜藏在深处的材料被大脑多次加工过。然后，梦的内容要直接地与现实生活经验找到合适的比对，那是需要仔细琢磨的。

而我的那位男性的心理咨询师朋友"理智的 Rose"的梦境，在某段时期反复出现，应该是与他的现实经历有关。那时，他的心理师工作经过至少 6 年以上的淬炼，心理行业从一个小规模的发展状态朝着一个更好的规划方向发展。只是，他可能面临了一些事情，让他身心疲惫或者焦虑。他说他每天几乎需要面对那些带着不同问题来的来访者，虽然有预约，可各方面的心理工作加在一起，这或许是他疲惫与焦虑的缘故。只是，身为一个身经百战的资深心理咨询师，他依旧无法解释清楚自己那个梦境材料的来源——黑色的豹子以及那一片光明的天际到底是什么。

以弗洛伊德为代表的精神分析观点认为，梦是具有显著心理特征的，而且梦代表着我们不被察觉的记忆。它或许在现实清醒状态下，被遗忘在某个记忆的碎片空间里，但在梦里会以不同的方式再现，从而以某种特殊的表现形式，让我们回忆起来。

过去就曾有过一个画家，在清醒状态下，他毫无灵感，不能作画，或者作出的画很糟糕。可偏偏在梦境中，他却能获得美妙的灵感，在催眠或梦境状态下，提笔作画，便能绘出美轮美奂的色彩构图。有人戏称他是梦中的天才，而现实生活中他却一无是处。

其实从心理学精神分析观点来看，这种说法是谬论。因为即便是梦，也是来源于现实的生活体验。这个人，或许是在清醒的时候，游历四方，然后将那些美妙的色彩记在了脑海中。而到了一定时期，就通过梦的主题，被强化出来。

这个人就是美国密执安州有一位叫库尔迪斯·瓦坚斯的画家，他在梦中创作了一幅幅优秀的作品，而且他在梦中是用双手作画的，但清醒状态时，他的左手并不会作画。我们都知道的事实是梦容易被遗忘，可被遗忘的原因，也可能是它产生的来源。

感觉知觉是否微弱或伴随我们在梦里的兴奋点薄弱与否，其实并不是能否被记住的原因。倘若梦中的材料，是在生活经验中常常被重复或心理强化，并在感知、意识中形成了适当的联系和归类的，就更容易被记住，留在梦的记忆中。

梦的确有不能被解释的空间，但精神分析的观点认为，梦是有情绪和感情色彩的。譬如"理智的Rose"的梦，黑豹、逡巡、注视，这些或许是平日来访者带来的负性情绪残留在了他的意识里，在梦境中显现出来。而"黑色"代表着严肃、谨慎、沉寂的含义；而猎豹的逡巡，意味着"理智的Rose"的某种焦虑情绪，或许是对自己心理咨询工作的把握性以及未来规划的某种未知造成的些许不安。而有些人甚至拥有具备用梦中的意志指导梦朝向的能力，即，梦境在表达出很强烈的情绪色彩时，睡眠的愿望为另一个前意识的愿望所替代了。

那么，就"理智的Rose"的梦境而言，那道铁丝网，以及他注视的光明的天际，也是他对自我的一种正向暗示与催眠。铁丝网，或许是意味着理智，也代表着某种界线。铁丝的感觉是冰冷的，坚硬的，那不是一般的动物可以轻易破坏的，也代表着某种刚性特征。但铁丝的弯曲结网构成的安全界线，又意味着某种柔韧性。他梦境中注视的光明，也意味着他的意识可以感知到，他未来的方向和发展前景。

梦境分析到这里，其实不难看出，"理智的Rose"已经是作为一个观察者，在梦中观察自己的梦，而且让它具有一定的可控性。当一个人开始有这种梦境的感知力时，那么他醒来后，那个梦反而更容易被清晰地记得。

梦境代表着潜意识的愿望，外加白天的遗留物，借助潜意识的协助，由前意识努力冲向意识。这里就不得不提及精神分析中梦境的凝缩和置换作用。每个人的意识都具有稽查制度，即相当于我们可以在清醒状态下感知的层面，就如同是"理智的Rose"梦中的那道铁丝网，代表着理智。

当梦境遇到稽查制度时，就会被歪曲，借助近期的生活体验或材料发生转移，跟着梦的程序开始后退，在此过程中梦才取得了表现形式，即凝缩。

而一个人每晚至少会做5-6个梦，之所以未被察觉，是因为我们在梦里的记忆，普遍噩梦比好梦更容易被记住。而"理智的Rose"在这个梦中惊醒，尽管他的意志可以将这个梦导向一定的可控性，可这样的梦，以及梦里蕴含的负性情绪，带给他的反应，很显然，就一个具有综合分析与灵活经验的心理咨询师而言，最佳的处理方法，就是帮助"理智的Rose"，我这位男性心理咨询师朋友提取与关注正向、正念、积极向上的自我精神，并保持对内良性的平衡指数。

心理门

  本期【心理门】解语：诚如我们每一个称职的心理咨询师，所面对的各种问题的来访者，或许在从事这一行的初期，都有过遇到过这样的梦中黑色猎豹所代表的潜藏的些许对未知的或恐惧或徘徊或疑惑。可或许在这样的沉浮当中，我们是否也曾努力抱紧我们的双肩，好好问过我们自己，你可以凭什么让一只黑色的猎豹不吃肉呢？这很显然是我们急于想要解决来访者的问题导致的焦虑。但时间一长，大都不会这样想了。与其一味着急地想要去给某个人的梦境一个"That's right."的答案，还不如给予一定的适度的建议。在心理咨询"释梦"的基础上，"理智的Rose"会在某段时期的等待中，自我探索与自我领悟生出适合他的生存法则，带着问题中的痛苦一路前行。或许，某一天时，就会明白——

  "当上帝为你关上一扇门，同时也会为我们打开一扇窗。"这句话的真实含义是什么。

  毕竟无论我们曾遇到过什么，也不能失去让自己稳稳快乐幸福的能力。

4 重识自我的价值

The healthy man does not torture others.Generally it is the tortured who turn into torturers.

健康的人不会折磨他人,往往是那些曾受折磨的人转而成为折磨他人者。

——Carl Jung荣格

提到"价值"这个词,我们首先可能会想到的是黄金、珍宝、股票、期货、投资、房产别墅等实体概念。可若一定要从心理科普的角度,为"价值"加一个注解,那么从认知层面来说,是指客体能够满足主体需要的效应关系,是主客体的相互联系。

"老师,您看我有用吗?"这名叫Ben的来访者,在咨询中,常常问我这样类似的问题。

"有用"等于"价值"。可这样的问话,等同于自我认可的物化性、功能性。而且……但凡提出这类问题的来访者,的确是过度看重别人眼中的自己的人,具有自卑特质,强调自我对外在客体关系的功能,即他用价值。

"那要看,你指的是哪一方面了。毕竟它涵盖着伦理、原则、理想、标准或道德这些范畴。每个人都会有不同的人生价值观,你这样问是遭遇了什么问题吗?"

"是的,我最近在人生的低谷期。"Ben低下头,"我女友常常认为我没用。我好像什么都不会。"

"是什么让你这样思考呢?你说她认为,她是明确这样说了吗?"我注意到Ben的措辞——"认为"。

Ben低下头,思索了一下,不做声。忽然又道:"就算没有,但我知道她是这样想的。"

"一切事物的认知,都是有据可循,也就是说,你的伴侣并没有这样说过,但你却有这样的认为,是这样吗?"

"是的,我常常这样觉得。"

Ben 来咨询，是要我找到 Ben 的价值所在。

一个人的人生价值观可以决定一个人在面临困境时的选择和处理方式的走向。所以，探究自我的价值，是人生相当重要的课题。

在这里，可以提供几个科普的方法来重识价值，请注意是"重识"，而不是"重拾"。前者是你可能在很长一段时间内忽略掉它的存在，或者你从没有认识到自我的价值方向，这是自我价值感低的其中一个原因。而后者是明确自我价值，或在遭遇重大挫折或变故后，调整自我，重新拾起来，重建的机制。

那么要如何重新认识你的价值呢？

第一，做一个问卷测试，清晰人生目标偏好。

在 willson,2002;wilson&Murrell,2004 人生价值调查问卷中，可以看到人生十个方向清晰的自我价值探索程度：

1. 家庭（不包括恋爱关系和父母情）

2. 恋爱（婚姻、终身伴侣、约会等）

3. 父母情

4. 朋友和社交生活

5. 工作

6. 教育和培训

7. 娱乐休闲

8. 精神和宗教

9. 公民和社区

10. 自我照顾（锻炼、饮食、休养、爱好等自我稳定与自我升值）

以上 10 点，按照级别划分，0-3 分是"一点不重要"、4-7 分是"比较重要"、8-10 分是"极为重要"。

据上表做一个自我测试，不难发现，你看重的部分是哪一部分。例如，Ben 更看重恋爱和工作，那么下一步，我们就应该在这两点上完善一个目标——即，在我们看重的人生方向赋予一个让我们人生更完善的目标。

Ben 在恋爱方面制定的是和伴侣和谐美满的长期相处；在工作方面，是制定了新的目标和高度，去达到一个新的认可，譬如为了掌握某一项新技术去参加一个精英班的学习，以为获得新晋职位增加砝码。

第二，将目标准确性具体化、行动化，拒绝空想。

"那么最后你要为这些目标，采取什么行动呢?"我问 Ben。

Ben 想了一下，打算把上述人生的目标具体化、行动化。他甚至立即填报了一个课程报名表，将之赋予行动。

当我们的人生被具体的目标和行动填充完满后，心灵也会发生一些明显的改变。

"那你现在还认为你的价值感 lower 吗?"

Ben 看到那张问卷上自己填上的目标和人生关注的方向，忽然舒了一口气，"好像有点用了。"

我们可以用这样的方法，针对一个或多个目标，问自己，"我认为我有价值的人生部分是什么?""我针对目标制定了什么行动去达到它?""那么，我具体是怎么做的?"把这三个问题借助 willson,2002;wilson&Murrell,2004 人生价值调查问卷确定下来，反复思考，并付诸行动，不难找到生命的意义。

如果说第一步做问卷的目的是找到我们偏好的人生方向目标，那么第二步就是把行动力建立起来，这件事不能他人代劳，只能通过自己的手、眼、身、心、灵的感知。这样做至少从自我认可上，你会发现，你是有方向的，有目标的。

第三，就是建立个人成绩∣目标的笔记本，确定你的内感报酬和外加报酬。

把达到的目标或成绩分成几个层级，具体由个人情况和目标难易程度来制定。比如一个人想做商业精英为自己赚得一桶金，那起码得制定步骤，分层级来完成，而非一步登天。越是最终目标奖励机制效应大的，越需要详细划分奖励等级，依次渐进。这样避免了实现目标毫无套路章法，也科学顺应了皮格马利翁效应的作用。

皮格马利翁效应（Pygmalion Effect）指人们基于对某种情境的知觉而形成的期望或预言，会使该情境产生适应这一期望或预言的效应。该理论提出者心理学家罗森塔尔认为，你期望什么，你就会得到什么。你得到的不是你想要的，而是你期待的。只要充满自信的期待，只要真的相信事情会顺利进行，事情一定会顺利进行。相反地说，如果你相信事情不断地受到阻力，这些阻力就会产生。成功的人都会培养出充满自信的态度，相信好的事情一定会发生。这就是心理学上所说的皮格马利翁效应。

　　当这三部分都完成后，你会发现，你的自信心在随着你自我价值感的建立逐渐增加。而且这样建立的价值感，是由你自己建立起来的，而并非通过外在客体找到的"点赞"或"认可"。那么在自我建立价值和自我恒定形象越来越清晰这两点上，我们相辅相成的环节可以获得良好整合。

　　那么找到人生的价值，生命的意义，还有什么难度呢？

　　本期【心理门】解语：套用一句老话，"不慕他师，塑造自身"。在人生的道路上必然会有为我们点赞的人、为我们贬损的人、为我们不相干的人……五花八门等等出现。或许在某一时刻，我们的情绪会因为被人贬低或被人吹捧受到影响，而内心的历练随行。慢慢地，我们就会发现，唯有学会自己为自己点赞，知道自己的目标，制定规划，去填充行动力去完满它。那么一切或吹捧或崇拜，或贬损或鄙夷，或麻木不仁，别人的情绪和看法，在自我价值得到良好建立的时候，就不再能够影响我们的情绪了。所以古语才有，"宠辱不惊，看花开花落；去留随意，任云卷云舒"。内心的修炼，是伴随我们的自我觉察和修行延展的——原来，智者，都是习得了为自己的真实技能点赞的人。只要是真实的，就算起初不尽如人意，但一点点从那真实根基上修缮而起的人生舞台，才会奏出世间唯美的音符，完满自身和他人。

5 致心灵书

There is a mine for silver and a place where gold is refined. Iron is taken from the earth,and copper is smelted from ore.

银子有矿，炼金有方。铁从地里挖出，铜从石中溶化。——《旧·伯》28：1、2

考完心理咨询师证书，你以为可以如同想象中把博士帽、硕士帽扬空一抛，那么洒脱，然后像个大侠似的仗剑闯江湖赚大钱去了，那你就大错特错了。

你可问过自己的心，"你准备好了吗？"然后听见它淡然、肯定、自信地答：是的，我准备好了。

走上这条路，一旦选择，对于每一个充分经历过的心理师，我想都会对这句话深有体会：——这是一条"少有人走的路"。

1. **当你遭遇负性情绪**：在承受得住那些负性能量感染与传递的同时，你得用咨询师的技术，在陪伴的同时，让眼前的来访者感染到你真实由内而发的灵魂能量——平稳祥和。他不会强迫你改变，或急于指责你的异同差异，而是如所有的存在般无条件接纳你。保持中立、共情，极少直接表达评价，除非是迫不得已的紧急或特殊状态。

2. **神经症与你我同行**：如果来访者烦恼、紧张、焦虑、抑郁、恐惧、强迫、疑病症状、分离症状、转换症状或神经衰弱，处于痛苦的自我折磨与挣扎之中，或犹若置身于泥沼，或濒临崩溃的边缘，来访者带着负性情绪，带着症状而来，身为一名称职的心理师，你要怎么做？

首先你需要大量学习各流派的治疗技术，不同的心理学流派对神经症发生机制有不同的解释和治疗方法。然而，经过国外100多年，国内短短几十年的实践和发展，心理治疗技术逐渐通过整合、折中、合作，融合成较广泛、综合和实用的模式。选用哪一种治疗方式才是目前较为有效的治疗，这个是我们将之所学变为助人助己的"功法"，但却也不可以强加给患者。

就像我们常常听到父母对我们的选择方式的剥夺以及侵入，仅仅以一句"我是为了你好"如此解释，相信已经不能被成熟的个体接受，更何况还是住在成人躯壳里的小孩子呢？

在短短50分钟的治疗时间里，我们或许是他们退行后的父亲、母亲、理想化的亲密守护者，但在共情的同时，仍然不要忘记守则和心理师的职责与身份，时刻铭记，我是一名心理咨询师，是去掉所有权威与华丽光环之后，包裹着技术功力的50分钟心理陪伴倾听者。

3. 人格障碍不是我之能选，为所当为：人格（personality）或称个性（character），是一个人固定的行为模式及在日常活动中待人处事的习惯方式，是全部心理特征的综合。人格的形成与先天的生理特征及后天的生活环境均有较密切的关系。

这部分来访者，明显偏离正常且根深蒂固的行为方式，具有适应不良的性质，其人格在内容上、质上或整个人格方面异常，由于这个原因，病人遭受痛苦和/或使他人遭受痛苦，或给个人或社会带来不良影响。人格的异常妨碍了他们的情感和意志活动，破坏了其行为的目的性和统一性，给人以与众不同的特异感觉，在待人接物方面表现尤为突出。

这样的特征，通常是开始于童年、青少年或成年早期，若是非要下一个定义，那么这属于终生症状。

但为什么还要心理咨询？

对于这类来访者，作为心理咨询师要做的并不是带着来访者一并走入祛除症状、祛除障碍，回归正常的地带的误区，也不是告诉他，"你不好，你错了。"

而是站在来访者的角度，甚至是把自我的精神领悟力与来访者链接共情，从那些症状与困难重重的生活方式中，帮助他找到一条创造美好的路。

在这个世界上，生命是以各式各样的形式存在的。

这里，我想套用森田疗法的基本治疗原则："顺其自然、为所当为"。不强求，做我们能做的。倘若我们不能选择自我的人格障碍，但至少我们可以掌握的，可以选择的，是让我们尽量避开那些躺在我们开发生命之光道路上的阴暗巨石，找到一条独辟小径，哪怕它真的很狭窄，但只要我们好好运用，也一样能借助这样的小径，通往人生意义的彼岸，实现自我价值。

到了那个时候，我们甚至可以带着症状走完我们漫长的一生，然后回顾过往种种，可以对当下的自我说，我又比过去的自己成长了许多。

那么你爱当下的自己吗？

如果答案是肯定的、淡然的，那么，我们的成长就是值得的，也是有价值的，不管我们是否有症状，是否异于常人，是否艰难困顿、自卑自贱如蝼蚁，但仍然可以感到生命之平等与可贵，可以安然对自己说，哪怕是蝼蚁，哪怕我没有别人寻常的幸福，但对于过去的自己与当下的自己相比，我已经做到了。那便是远胜于常人的意志力与追求幸福的能力。

以上所述的三类人，皆是有症状的人，其中一些甚至徘徊在精神病性的边界处，那么作为心理治疗师，我们能做什么来缓解他的症状，如何帮助他学会成长与获得幸福的技巧。

这些功力都绝非"一日之寒"。

常常看到有很多喜爱心理学的心理人，对这条路充满憧憬与迷惘，可到底要如何在此路上行走，如何阅读与学习，都是值得仔细规划与考虑的现实。

这里可以探讨的是，心理学博大精深，不同的流派或许在分界的时候，就是一种对知识的偏颇划分。真正的心理学专家，到最后是整合性的，但同时也是具有精确的专业性的，像父母，像医生。

要如何能做到这两点，还需要结合你自己的优点和长处来做。

第一，寻找你喜欢的心理话题，然后顺藤摸瓜去找它属于什么学派，然后研究它，读懂它，同时结合实用性来考虑。这样你会在长久的专注学习中感到有兴趣，并获得持之以恒想要学好它的强大内驱力。

第二，建议拜真正很好的名师来获得指导，注意，我想强调的是，真正好的，而不能仅仅图一个华丽的"名气"。有时候，不难发现，真正的高手，或许是有名气的，也或许是低调的，并不是一定要多张证书和华丽的名气才可以表明那是"专家""名家"。

"证书"的偏见，是值得每一个心理师个人成长道路上需要去探索的，证书的背后，意味着什么？你想要获得的到底是什么呢？

诚如，是不是大学生一定比高中生知识多，一定对社会、对周围的人实现的个人价值与社会价值颇高，远的，看看农民皇帝朱元璋，近的看看没念完大学的比尔·盖茨……这里就不谈远了，主要是想说，真正好的，展示的是实力以及身为一名心理咨询师灵魂的高度，即超我（良知）与成熟的自我肯定价值、自我观念的确立。

老师好不好，其实通过交谈就能感觉到。

以前曾读过一篇大部头的名著《理智与情感》，用这5个字来形容这个职业的特点之一也不为过：他是否满足了你共情良好的需求，是否同时又谨守优秀心理师的准则，坚定地理性用智慧来分析你的冲突？他是否承得住你突然怒气冲冲的怒火与非理性中伤？是否依然秉持一颗身为心理师正直而热爱每一个生命的初心，渡己渡人。

最后一点，除了好，还要找到适合你的发展的，适合你自身的特点来发展的。有了一个好老师的指导，想要学好这一门就不难了。但好的老师真的不好找，太有名气的老师，又非常贵。譬如精神分析我们都知道的曾奇峰老师，如果让他做督导案例，你除了要注意对内分析你的自我与他是否合适，还需要准备好至少三年的好多钱，你的收支是否能平衡？这些都是必须考虑的，长远考虑。

本期【心理门】解语：一名合格并优秀心理咨询师的语言应类似禅音，就是把一切的音声当作美妙的音声，把辱骂的声音转为慈悲与接纳，为诽谤诋毁者祝福祈祷，用技术和心灵真实地陪伴——做得到这些之后，同时还不要忘了，你自己也需要个人体验与成长，因为，我们也是人。

谨以此文，送给每一位心理人，祝愿走出一条适合自己的心理人之路，完成整合，将所学用于自我成长，完善自身的同时再帮助合适的来访者吧！

6 优质标签的背后——还原别人眼里"万能"的我

For she is more profitable than silver and yields better returns than gold.

因为得智慧胜过得银子，其利益强如精金。——《旧·箴》3：14

导语：我们当中有一部分人，自小从学生时代起，就因为出类拔萃而被赋予了"精英""优质""金牌"少男少女的标签，可脱去这些漂亮价值标签的"糖衣"，少男少女们真实的模样应该如何还原呢？

案例：高三的学生正杰，从小学、初中、高中都是第一名，这个第一，不仅仅表现在学习的课本成绩上，连很多同学不能过关的2500米长跑，他也是第一名，甚至在省级以上数学、物理竞赛中也有获奖，无论是德智体美劳，他始终都处于第一的位置。

"如果我不做第一名，我会感觉我的生命没有意义。"他来咨询室时这样说。

现阶段高三很快就要进入最后的备考期，虽然现在的教育新政策，以各地考生的实际情况为基础，更加讲究适应性和公平性，想上一所好一些的大学，已经不算特别难的事，但对于始终想保持"第一名"的正杰同学来说，却成了他越来越困扰的事。

他开始紧张，时时处处感到焦虑，甚至时常身体肌肉紧绷，以致于时常做一个相同的噩梦：

梦里，他恍惚间看到了一头像驴子，背上压着沉重的货物，正一步步艰难地往山上走，而长年在山林石阶跋涉，已经让那驴子的背部伤痕累累，它喘不上气。它刚想停下来喘息一下，而周围丛林里就会出现一双双黑漆漆的眼睛，死死地盯着它，这种感觉，令它很想逃离，可脚下的路一直延伸着仿若没有尽头。

每次醒来，他都觉得腰酸背痛，就好像那些东西是他驮的，而不是那只梦里的驴子。

这样的梦一直断断续续持续了一个月，因为晚上休息不好，白天上课精力也无法集中，成绩虽然暂时没有受到多大的波动影响，但他却常常担心，总有一天，他的成绩会一落千丈，然后再也不能和"第一名"这个优质标签挂钩，终于有一天，他居然上学迟到了。

面对父母、老师对他信任、包容、殷切期盼的笑脸，他愈发陷入了无比的苦恼中，他几乎不能原谅自己，更加不能接受自己迟到的行为——"你居然迟到了，你不再是第一了！"这样的声音居然反复出现在他的脑海里，眼看高考将至，他根本看不进书，忍受着几乎难以言说的痛苦和折磨。

他感觉，那一次迟到的经历，令他无地自容，整个人都快要崩溃了。

【分析】

按照弗洛伊德精神分析的观点，梦的素材来源于现实生活，表达着潜意识的需求，但这些现实的材料在经过意识、前意识、潜意识的环节时，经过加工，已经被置换与扭曲了。从正杰的梦境里，不难看出，他的内心正承受着巨大的压力，梦境里那头驴子背负的重物，或许反映的正是他这样优秀的学生从小一直背负到大的元素：譬如，个体的优秀、父母的期盼、同学的羡慕与关注、老师的喜爱……等等，而这些也在无形中化为了正杰梦中那一双双"黑漆漆"的眼睛，让他想要逃离，却又不得不前行。而在这些元素的背后，反映的是我们当下社会信奉的文化。

第一，核心信念会影响行为，情境不过是诱因。

我们信奉的是什么文化，往往最终就会导向什么体系框架下的行为反应。当下的社会，被"精英文化""金牌得主"这样的价值文化充斥着，这样的价值框架在常态下是带着鲜明的、积极向上的正能量，也深入到我们的生活、工作，甚至是学生当中。正杰这样的高三学生，信奉的正是这样的文化，也正受着这种文化的深刻影响。

在正常情况下，良好的核心信念，对于一个人，乃至一个社会积极向上的人生观、价值观是大有裨益的，因为它促使人力争上游。但是，这样的核心理念会带给人持续不断增值的低变量的压力，而且是在不知不觉间逐渐完成原始积累。

所谓"温水煮青蛙"，正杰的案例正彰显出这个道理。他的积极上进，同时也带来了一定程度的焦虑和压力，它们平素慢慢地积累在体内，并不是那么容易被身体感知到。

经历了类似"高三迟到"的情境体验之后，便将他日积月累的压力蓄积提升到了峰值，从而通过肌体调节失常显露了出来，导致他的压力调节机制濒临瓦解。

"你居然迟到了，你不再是第一了！"这样的声音居然反复出现在他的脑海里，在正杰看来，是迟到这样尴尬的情境让他变得消极负面，但实际上，真正给他带来压力的是他过度信奉的"精英文化"。

存在主义说："生命并不需要意义，存在本身就是唯一的意义。"当"精英文化"的核心理念和"基本存在"这样的生存理念发生碰撞时，便会丧失它被创造出的优质价值与意义。因为这已经不是"华山论剑争天下第一"的问题，而是关于一个人首先需要如何安好存在的主题。

我们每个人都有不同的信仰，从心理学观点出发，信仰本身没有对错之分。如正杰的案例，由于从小到大他都是在父母、老师、同学的关注下，给自己牢牢贴上了"优质""第一名"的标签，且不断给自我这样的暗示，于是在他的核心理念中，他永远就是要和"第一名"这样的佼佼者标签画上等号的，而这样的核心理念也导致了他不断取得优异成绩的行为，从而更加被加深笃定，从而得以强化。

《论语·先进》曰："过犹不及，事缓则圆。"当我们过度崇信某种信仰时，有可能会导致我们焦虑、羞愧、强迫、压力过度等严重困扰，甚至是造成"存在危机"，那么这样的核心信念被崇信的程度或方向就需要被适当的调整，使之合理化。

第二，爱美之心人皆有之，骑虎难下容易忽略学生本身的需要：崇尚美好是人的天性。在人群当中，最出类拔萃的那一类人其实更加容易吸引大众的关注，大到商业精英、能人新秀，小到生活中跳广场舞的领舞大妈。若落脚于学生的层面，老师批改的作业本上，字迹最漂亮、择词精美、逻辑合理、构思巧妙、解答精巧的那一个学生，也是更容易获得老师的青睐。

正杰的梦境里，那一双双眼睛的注视，让那头原本已经万分辛苦的驴子又迈开了脚步，不能停下。由于从小到大都是优异的佼佼者，在这样的外在过分期许与关注下，容易让学生不会适度调整自我休息与学习的方式，一再忽略身体疲劳不堪的基本需要。而身体健康，却才是所有发展成长的最基本需要。

第三，争当第一的内驱力是需要被关注的诉求。高三学生家长关注的点和老师关注的方向依然有区别：

"如果我不做第一名，我会感觉我的生命没有意义。"从正杰的这句话，其实也反映出了他内心潜藏着需要被众人关注的需求。从更深的心理学层面来看，需要被关注的内心需求，也有可能与学生所处的家庭亲密关系有关。作为高三学生的家长，是否过度在意孩子的成绩而常常忽略孩子的内心需求呢？是否以孩子的成绩作为德智体全面发展的衡量唯一标准？学校的老师，因为社会角色的局限性，很可能容易通过关注学生的课堂表现、测验成绩来判断学生的发展状态；但家长却不能仅仅用这样的方式来完成对孩子的互动。因为监护人如父母，不仅仅是孩子的老师，更是以身作则的父母。因此，仅仅是通过学业成绩来表达对孩子的关注，那很容易就忽略掉了父亲母亲与孩子之间心灵互动的需求。而这后者，恰恰是学校的老师不可能去胜任的关注。

【对策】

古人说："能者安邦定国，无能者独善其身。"这两者的存在具有同等重要性。

诚如法老的金字塔，留在金字塔顶端的最后一块石砖，为这一世界的伟大奇迹画上了完美的句号，可与金字塔数级向下层的那些千千万万的石砖相比，其构成实质都是一样的，都是砖，也都是修建金字塔的工具。如果没有逐级向下的石砖积累排列组合，那么最顶层金字塔的石砖存在也不会有任何意义。

这种比喻，无论放到我们所接触的任何一个群体中，都展现着同样的道理。高中三年级的学生们，也形同一个社会小群体，每个人就如同金字塔的石砖，其本质具有相通性——首先，我们是学生。其次，是高三竞争较激烈的学生，最后，才是学生个体的特质。也就是说，我们首先得明确我们的存在感，才能在这样的基础上，发展自我的特性。

1. 拒绝过度信念，生命的存在才是万事俱备之本：

每一种精神信念都有其局限性，就如同适合A同学的学习理念，不一定对B同学管用；过去对A同学管用的学习理念，不一定现在和将来都对A同学管用。人是一个不断学习、接纳和吸收的个体，认知的核心理念也应该随着个体的适用性而做出适当调整，才能顺应身心灵的发展。正杰正是这种情况，"一定要做第一名"，他曾经把始终做"第一名"这样的核心信念作为他学习的信仰，可因为过度坚信不疑，导致他身体在长期的压力机制下，出现了失眠、强迫、羞愧等一系列负面情绪反应。心理治疗师的建议是，拒绝负面误导与暗示。"你居然迟到了，你不再是第一了！"正杰这样的学生，面临考试将至的迟到，或许既有焦虑感又有羞愧感，从而将这样的负面认知扩大化，在不知不觉间已经将它篡改为衡量作为学生价值的唯一标准。

这是人自动思维的篡改模式，也是大多数人拥有过的自我防御体验。只是，什么是现实？什么是我们夸大过的想象？这些不能只听从内心的声音来判断，而需要依靠感性思维、理性思维、逻辑因果、学习生活中的体验以及是非观念来为我们做出明确、清晰、精准的判断，合理我们的认知。

2. 世界上没有完全相同的两片叶子：每个学生一定都有各自的特点，而这样的特点就是我们的爱好与擅长的方向所指。 在这个世界上，再没有比自己更了解自己的人了。我们的爱好可以是多样的，但却不会是全面的，即便有，那也只是短期投入。因为人作为一个生命体征的存在，其精力是有限的，如果以100分值来计算，假设我们会用40分来满足衣食住行，那么剩下的60分精力应该如何分配才妥当科学？像正杰这样的学生，力争上游的精神动力是值得褒奖的，但却不能忽略，我们能用的只有60分精力而已。从精神分析的理论分析，如果过度消耗有限的精力，人更容易患上各种神经症，身体也会在日积月累的"负资产"精力的情况下，出现各类负面症状，从而影响我们的发展。更科学合理的建议是，把自己的精力用在自己的优势方向，科学合理地规划，在一般情况下，只要找对了法门，想要付出和收获成正比，并非难事。所以，与其拥有"万能"标签，不如独树一帜，发展自我优势。

有的学生或许会认为自己没有优势，毫无特长，其实，不是没有，而是你还没有发现而已，人的潜能是强大而深远的。古语有云："天生我材必有用。"发掘出自我独特的优势，提升学习，就能事半功倍。

3. 学会认输，接纳丧失感，拥抱自己的不完美。 曾经有一部影片《人生遥控器》，主要讲述的是一名建筑师，拥有一个三口之家和一份稳定的工作。就如同美国众多中产阶层一样，日子过得相当普通。但面临中年危机的男主角不甘于这样的生活，他想要升职，获得年薪百万的工作，想要做总裁，想要妻子少一点唠叨，想要女儿很快就长大成人，不再拖累他日渐疲累的身心。这些愿望，居然在他无意间获得的一个小小遥控器时，全都一瞬间实现了。他终于获得了他想要的一切，似乎所有的收获都是他梦寐以求的完美，只是，只要他按下了开始的按钮，快进之后就不能重来。很快，男主角厌倦了这样的获得与拥有，因为他所有的获得都没有过程。

既感觉不到辛苦，不会有失去，不会有挫折，不会有竞争者，也就没有收获后的万分雀跃。他似乎得到了游戏的作弊密码，生活依然在继续，可一切求索的原动力和经历感受却被整个跳过了。

就像喝一杯水一样，我们渴了，我们会去找水喝，然后烧水、等待、调配到合适的温度，再端起杯子，慢慢喝下去，感觉水分子通过我们的味蕾，滑下我们的食道……也许在整个过程中，我们还会感觉水太凉或太热，需要重新调配，直到它合适，最后满足我们口渴的需求。

这个过程就是经历，倘若我们跳过找水和喝水的过程，那么我们的所有获得就只能被改译为简单的字符，毫无生机。

唯有尝过挫折，才能认识到缺陷，才会想法弥补与改善；尝过苦的滋味，才能更珍惜美好的甜果。若然人生一路从未输过，如若不是你被过度保护得太好，那么，就很可能永远生活在立于不败之地的幻想世界里，只是，那不是现实，更不是完整的人生。

如果我们认定我们从不会出错，也不可能出错，那是"圣人"，不是现实生活中的人。接纳你的普通寻常的那一面，接纳丧失感，拥抱得起自己的不完美，这样的人才更接近于完美。

4. 从行为放松开始：考试焦虑是一种情绪反应，不仅影响学生的学业成绩，也同时影响学习效率，严重情况下，还会极大影响学生的心理健康。

人的机体是天生的吸纳体，它会一点一滴地吸纳掉平素生活、工作、学习中遭遇的压力，但当它达到峰值时，就会出现身体不适应反应。同样的道理，如果先放松身体，适当休息，每天坚持一定时间和次数的放松训练，从肌肉放松开始，反其道而行之，通过身体肌肉的放松，也能缓解积累的压力，达到缓解学习应考备考焦虑的目的。要明白，我们崇尚的信念能刻画给我们过得更好的模板，因为它能引导我们的日常行为去完成自我实现的目标，可这些信仰都是建立在生存的基础上，才有价值和意义，所以，首先我们要学会觉察我们机体的基本需求的适度满足，才能去追求更上一层楼的精神动力。不尊重生命自然进程的求学者，到头来，得到的很容易会比失去的更多。

5. 家长的适度关注与关心才是孩子的坚强后盾。

俗话说"家家都有难念的经，人人都有难唱的曲"。即便是再风光美满的家庭，都会有一些难以言表的矛盾和不愉快。作为监护人（父母），在我们遭遇一些不愉快的情绪体验时，不要把这些负面的感受转嫁给孩子来承受。作为一名成年人，一个高三的学生家长，更应该负责任地担当并处理好自己的不良情绪。只有家长先照顾好自己的焦虑、愤怒、抑郁等不良情绪，才能更好地担起关心孩子身心灵的监护人角色。高考，作为学生而言是人生的转折点，作为一个家庭整体而言，又何尝不是家庭未来的转折点呢？

作为家长，需要明确的是，片面地关注孩子的成绩作为"关心""关爱"孩子的代名词，这样的做法并不可取。曾有心理学家做过一个实验，相同智商的两组学生，一组老师家长采取鼓励为主的教育策略，一组不鼓励，一段时期后，测验结果较高的是受到鼓励最多的一组。而鼓励也不能被偏颇地解读为物质鼓励，精神鼓励需要大于物质鼓励，显然更科学。

毕竟，家虽然是最不需要讲理的地方，同时也是最暖人心的港湾，也是父母与孩子一同陪伴成长的"伊甸园"。

本期【心理门】解语：

杨绛先生百岁感言曾这样说过：上苍不会让所有幸福集中到某个人身上，得到了这样多一些，其他的必定会少一些，保持知足常乐的心态才是淬炼心智、净化心灵的最佳途径。

一个人经过不同程度的锻炼，就获得不同程度的修养、不同程度的效益。好比香料，捣得愈碎，磨得愈细，香得愈浓烈。我们曾如此渴望命运的波澜，到最后才发现：人生最曼妙的风景，竟是内心的淡定与从容……我们曾如此期盼外界的认可，到最后才知道：世界是自己的，与他人毫无关系。

（此段杨绛先生的话语，仅为她作为一位智慧老者的自我感悟，至于如何领悟我们眼中所见的人事物，个中智善知识与认知，仁者见仁智者见智，还是允许我们自己去参悟吧。）

7 由重庆两幼童坠亡案引发的思考

The lamp of the wicked is snuffed out;the flame of his fire stops burning.

恶人的亮光必要熄灭。他的火焰必不照耀。——《旧·伯》18：5

2020年11月2日下午3时30分许，嫌疑人张波趁母亲刘维华外出不在家之际，将正在卧室玩耍的张某甲、张某乙双腿抱住，将二人一起从次卧室飘窗窗户处扔到楼下，致使张某甲当场死亡，张某乙被送医院抢救无效死亡。两条鲜活的小生命就以如此惨烈的方式离开了人世……

而邻居报案后，张波还坐在小区楼下的地上嚎啕大哭，他的内心此时正为所有人上演了一出大戏。

张波是在2017年8月17日与陈美霖结婚的，婚后分别于2018年3月生下女儿张某甲、2019年1月生下儿子张某乙。2019年4月左右，张波开始隐瞒自己已婚有子女的身份追求网络恋人叶诚尘。同年底，叶诚尘得知张波有子女，仍继续与张波来往。

2020年2月，张波才与发妻陈美霖协议离婚，双方约定女儿张某甲归妻子抚养，儿子张某乙在六岁前归张波抚养，六岁后归妻子陈美霖抚养。

于是，张波在离婚后带着儿子张某乙与母亲刘维华一道生活在一起。这起惨绝人寰的两幼童坠亡案就发生在这时。

一切都要从叶诚尘这个网络恋人说起。自她认识张波后，叶诚尘曾多次表示自己和父母不能接受张波有小孩的事实。两人自2020年2月左右，在长寿区见面时便共谋杀害张波小孩。随后，叶诚尘还通过与张波多次面谈、微信聊天等方式共谋杀害两个小孩的方法，并商定采用意外高坠的方式杀害张某甲及张某乙。同年6月，叶诚尘还多次通过微信催促张波作案。同年10月，张波、叶诚尘商定以给张某甲买衣服为由，将张某甲接至家中预谋杀害，计划因为陈美霖一直在场而被阻断，而这个杀人计划在2020年11月2日被精准实施了……

这起案件背后不得不引发我们从理性心理分析层面的沉思，人人都说虎毒不食子，那么到底是什么原因导致了张波身为人父如此丧心病狂的作案呢？

从与叶诚尘这个女人的交流中，我们不难从检察院给出的案件资料中发现，她曾多次通过面谈、微信等方式催促张波动手作案，不难分析出，其实在这些谈话交流过程中，张波是面临了不少压力的。每个人只要在社会上生存，都或多或少会面临压力，**那么设想当一个人承受压力巨大时，他会暴露出各种各样的问题，压力会在我们被完全控制毫无还手之力之时，吞噬掉我们的理性与智慧，精彩地扮演一个生命中的"杀手"。**

我们每个人都应该有正确的排解压力的方式，把它当作负能量从身体里排出去，但若是一个没有这样压力感受的人呢？那无疑是一场致命的自我毁灭。

在这里，浅谈压力对人们的影响，仅仅从心理与情感层面，也不是在为张波这样一个丧心病狂的父亲辩护，我们都知道，尽管受到了叶诚尘的怂恿与催促，**但他是一个有完全行为能力的人，他的恶行受犯罪心理支配着，操控着，这是一种有意识犯罪，理应受到法律最公正、最严厉的审判与制裁。**

但这样的人，通常都采用暴力犯罪的手段来排解内心巨大的压力，这是一种最愚蠢的排解压力的方法。

那么，压力到底影响了我们什么呢？

从情感和心理迹象上看，当我们遭遇压力时，我们会生气、手心出汗、失眠、容易哭泣、焦虑、神经过敏、容易心烦、急躁、保持清晰的思维有困难、健忘、记忆力丧失、无法做出决策、持续的担心、丧失对幽默的敏感度等等。

那么我们如何正确地应对压力呢？

1. **认识自己**：古语有云，"人贵有自知之明"。压力管理的第一原则就是"认识自己"。我是一个怎样的人？我的个性是如何的？我是压力易感个性吗？

已有研究表明，个性和压力之间存在着密切相关的联系。**个性是压力应对的重要组成部分，有些人偏向于属于压力易感个性；其次，压力易感个性者，通常最容易被暗示。**这就是仅仅凭叶诚尘大半年时间的怂恿和催促，就令张波将杀子计划进行得如此顺利的原因之一。

而这一类人，或有严重心理问题的人，容易产生犯罪心理。这一类人的心理健康受着极大的折磨，他们的身心灵里没有可以观照自我行为的光芒，于是，要么继续对内折磨自己，要么就滋生出恶念，转而朝外攻击。荣格说过，"健康的人不会折磨他人，往往是那些曾受折磨的人转而成为折磨他人者。"

如果这一类人有一点哪怕是一点自我觉察的能力，比如张波，觉察到自己这段时间沉浸在网络恋人怂恿杀子的压力中，开启一段科学的心理咨询之旅，我认为，这样的惨剧有80%的可能不会发生。

可惜这一类人，通常在犯罪心理支配他以前，什么都不会做。而压力易感个性者的犯罪攻击性通常和焦虑有关。攻击和实施计划是这一类压力易感者表达自身焦虑的主要方式。

他们的内心深处常常会有一个小人儿，在告知他们时间的紧迫性，为了更有效率，他们制定计划、目标和标准、最后期限，来自内心的压力一直迫使他们达到最终目的为止。

2. **懂得承受生活的考验和磨难**。不得不说，张波的人生在遇到叶诚尘之前都是普通人当中幸福的，尽管这份内心的淡然与富足，他不一定感受到过。毕竟是和前妻2年就生了2个孩子，难道这样的家庭中就没有爱了吗？答案是肯定的，只是我们的人生总是要随着时间的沉淀，才能如同香料一般越磨越香，随着这份沉淀，品出一个完满的"好"字来。只可惜，这些认知，像张波这样的压力易感者都未能体会到。

比如，他与陈美霖的离婚，那么离婚了一切都要重新开始，我以后会幸福吗？如果没有遇到叶诚尘这样毫无底线的同样有犯罪心理的人，而是另外一位温柔娴雅的女性，他和陈美霖两人都可以"一别两宽，各自安好"。

又比如，我和老婆又吵架了，我真是厌倦了这样无休止的争吵，那么我该怎么做？

……

这些思考，他似乎从来答案都是朝着负面情绪去的。

而其实，我们是明白，尽管我们一次次面对生活的挑战与改变，挫折或磨难，或许可能有时我们会变得无所适从，但大多数时候，我们不会马上放弃对生活的憧憬和渴望。于是，我们会积极调整我们的内心能量，做出一些乐观和积极的假设：

如果我的生活方式能改变一些……

如果我能与爱人亲密无间，我多帮他做一些家务……

如果我有时间，我就能休息放松一下了。

……

上述这些假设，是我们应当珍惜的想法，因为这是承受生活考验和磨难的良药。

3. 通过锻炼来减少焦虑。我们应该都了解锻炼的价值，在体育锻炼后所体验到的积极情感能量比只是观看运动要更加强烈，更加增加心理状态的正能量，身体也更放松了。

4. 改变认知，发挥认知潜能：这里不得不提到由美国心理学家埃利斯创建的情绪 ABC 理论，他认为激发事件 A 只是引发情绪和行为后果 C 的间接原因，而引起 C 的直接原因是个体对激发事件 A 的认知和评价而产生的信念 B。这里也称错误信念或非理性信念。只要改变了认知信念，才能有效避免 C 的发生。

最后，呼吸，放松，冥想，可以开发认知的潜能，让我们身心灵的光芒照亮自我。

本期【心理门】解语：真爱最好的试金石无非是，哪怕是困顿苦厄、哪怕是疾苦哀鸣、哪怕是跌落低谷、哪怕是身心灵遭受重创，我都可以无条件的爱着你，但……请记得，亲爱的，我修的是无条件的爱，但不是无底线的爱。所以，这份爱，你得珍惜、珍重，因为……它是如此厚重、沉稳、强大、包容、滋养着我们，成为了我们魂灵中生发出灵魂之力源源不绝的真爱之泉。

8 有时候我们要学会哀悼哀伤

I will speak out in the anguish of my spirit, I will complain in the bitterness of my soul.

我灵愁苦，要发出言语。我心苦恼，要吐露哀情。——《旧·伯》7：11

"据初步统计，7月16日以来，截至25日12时，此轮强降雨造成河南全省63人因灾死亡、5人失踪……"

"小南的弟弟买好了饭菜，再有两站，姐姐就能吃上热乎乎的晚饭；丈夫特意为小月送来一双绿胶鞋，因为暴雨，妻子提前下班；路面雨太大，阿娣嘱咐丈夫'别开车'，自己搭上了晚高峰的地铁……"

他们都同时搭上了0501号地铁，然而这辆遭遇洪水侵袭的地铁没有终点。

胡和刚来咨询室的时候，拒绝我询问任何有关他妻子去世消息的问题。

"那天到底发生了什么？你能谈谈吗？"

他显得异常愤怒，"不知道，我什么都不知道，你别问我！"

我们沉默了半晌，我任由这种沉默发生着，然后我轻声问，"……你能告诉我，那件事对于你意味着什么吗？"

他过了半晌才缓缓道，"自从那件事后，我每晚都要手里抓住点什么东西才能入睡。这几天我过得很苦，像没有了灵魂……"俗话说，男儿有泪不轻弹，可说到这里，他还是呜咽着哭了。

"如果那天我开车去接她，她兴许就不会上那辆地铁了……"

"我彻底失去她了吗，老师？"

我为他递上一杯暖茶，点了点头。

创伤后应激障碍（PTSD）是指个体经历、目睹或遭遇到一个或多个涉及自身或他人的实际死亡，或受到死亡的威胁，或严重的受伤，或躯体完整性受到威胁后，所导致的个体延迟出现和持续存在的精神障碍。

通常引起创伤后应激障碍（PTSD）的原因可以归为三类：（a）自然灾害，例如洪水、火灾、地震、飓风以及龙卷风；（b）意外事件，例如撞车、爆炸，或是枪击；（c）人为事件，例如强奸、抢劫、袭击、诱拐，或是虐待。

在创伤事件发生后，个体会出现对即时环境刺激反应下降的情况，并伴有精神麻木或是情感淡漠。

"其实，我们很多时候都在经历着丧失，譬如这一次的洪水，新冠病毒疫情的肆虐，2008年的汶川地震等等，"我缓缓道，"一切都会随着时间而改变，但这样的改变需要花费点时间。"

"我还没有告诉孩子，他的妈妈已经不在了……因为不知道该怎么说？"

"你有这些诸如麻木回避、焦虑、难以入睡等症状都是PTSD的正常症状，我很同情你，你现在这种悲伤的情绪我很能理解。那能谈谈那天你的妻子她是怎么去工作的吗?"

"可以……明明是多么寻常的一天，没想到早晨的再见就是再也不见。"

PTSD的核心症状有三组，即创伤性再体验症状、回避和麻木类症状、警觉性增高症状。但儿童与成人的临床表现不完全相同，且有些症状是儿童所特有的。

我们可以使用很多方法来帮助来访者寻回记忆，处理哀伤，包括梦、联想、幻想、图片以及旧的医疗记忆。

那么我们应该如何来处理哀伤呢?

接受丧失的现实，并面对这个人已经过世的事实；用丧失取代最初的否认和逃避。

体验哀伤的痛苦。 承认并走出这种痛苦是必须的，否则他会通过自我挫败的行为来证明自己的存在。

适应亡者已经不在的环境。 幸存者必须要面对原来生活中由亡故者扮演的众多角色已经不存在的现实。

从亡故者的情感中摆脱出来，并投入另一个关系之中。 失去亲人的最初本能反应可能会使一个人觉得自己再也不会去爱其他人了，但幸存者必须对新的关系或是机会持开放的心态。

在处理与亡故者有关的记忆时，要接受失去亲人的痛苦。

要公开地表达懊悔、敌意及内疚，并能够公开地哀悼。

要能够理解失去亲人的强烈哀伤。 例如，如案例中，意识到这些症状，如焦虑、坐立难安、难以置信——这些可能会暂时影响其开始或维持正常行为模式的能力。

能够忍受针对死者、自己或是其他人的愤怒情绪；重新定位自己的责任，不要认为自己在某种程度上应该可以阻止死亡。

"胡先生，要知道，生命是无常的。在生命面前，我们都是脆弱而无助的。因为我们是人，而不是神，在生死面前，我们得允许我们这般的无助。"

"是的，我现在最想的就是如何跟孩子说这件事?"

那么如何帮助孩子顺利完成哀悼的这个过程呢?

第一，父母应该告诉他到底发生了什么事? 给出"案例中妈妈去哪里了"

的真实准确的信息，允许他哭泣或提出各种问题，让孩子参与到家庭中的哀悼仪式中来。

第二，幸存者稳稳地陪伴孩子。对于幸存者来说，有时候没有在意自己的情绪，更没有及时调整好自己的状态，而让孩子承担起照顾父或母的责任，这是最不应当的。所以，对幸存者而言，最应该的是调整好自己的状态和情绪，能心理咨询的就积极心理咨询，让自己成为一个很好的容器，能承载得了孩子哭闹等情绪，稳稳地陪伴，这一点很重要。

本期【心理门】解语：

人生在世，只要活着，就会有喜怒哀乐，悲欢离合，可以说，我们从出生起，最不缺的就是遭遇丧失，体验哀伤，它会让我们悲伤难以言表，甚至失去某一部分社会功能，有时候，我们会为此倍感孤独，觉得在这个世界上无依无靠，无处依偎，但只要这种悲伤与哀情被表达，被看见，那么浓浓的温暖，一定会为我们内心点亮疗愈之光，驱走我们的寒冷与孤寂，让我们不再惧怕哀伤。

因为，我和宇宙爱着你。

（因为涉及保密原则，文中案例均为虚拟模拟）

9 为什么有的人难以与人建立亲密关系？

Surely no one lays a hand on a broken man when he cries for help in his distress.

一个受伤的人在急难中呼救，没有人伸手搭救他。——《旧·伯》30：24

有的人生来就有"社交牛逼症"，交一大堆朋友都不是什么难事；可有的人在现实中交友却寸步难行。

这一群人，他们或许对即将发展的关系感到恐惧，或许是没办法在人前释放自我；再不然就是不知人与人之间有边界意识这回事，自我的边界意识极差，在人群中喜欢过度暴露自我隐私，引发众人的不适；又或许不知如何和喜欢的人发展亲密关系……

以上种种情形，我们姑且归因为两种：

1.有些人不敢与人亲近，没办法在人前释放自我，完全是因为潜意识中，对可能会在这段关系中受到的伤害产生无比严重的焦虑和不安。因为严重的焦虑或不安全感，使得他们没办法在人与人之间发展亲密关系，这种人我们俗称为"社恐"。有的人甚至会因为这种即将与他人相交的恐惧，而产生手抖、身体发抖、心跳加速或头痛、胃痛、心口痛，抑或是莫名其妙地浑身起疹子、食欲不振等等身体不适的症状，但奇怪的是，到医院去检查，各项身体指标又是正常的。

但一接近人群，或将要与人发展一段稍微亲密点的关系，就会出现上述这些类似的症状。

弗兰克·维克多曾写过一本《生命的探问》一书，书中总结道：人的痛苦有两种。

一种是你已经受伤了，你却毫不知情。你没有体验到你正经历的是一些可以令人痛苦的感受，这种表现，往往是一种自我感觉良好的状态，问他，"你工作关系怎么样啊？"他说，"没问题啊。"再问他，"你最近过得怎样啊？有没有遇到不顺心的事情啊？"他又说，"我神经大条，没什么特别的事。"这一类人，在其实遭遇了痛苦的经历之后，在他的意识层面，是没什么痛苦反应的。但在他的身体上却能出现类似上述的讯号，比如头疼脑热、心跳加速的……

这类人在生活中是"憨憨"，自评是"神经大条"，以为什么事在他眼前过都不算是事儿。可其实，他不知道的是，他所经历的一切，已经对他的心理造成了伤害，而且一般是极大的，才会通过身体的讯号传递出来。这种状况，我们叫"身心一体"，是你的身体在帮你做情绪上的代谢，代谢或表达一些东西，心理学上把这种叫作躯体化。

比如，小A在洪灾中失去了父母兄弟，全家只剩下他一人，这段失去亲人的日子，他照样还是该上班上班，该回家回家，该吃饭吃饭。别人对他的遭遇报以同情吧，他却"呵呵"一笑，说"没事儿"。他认为自己很坚强，至少能吃能喝能睡。可等到过了一段时间，他遇上了一个他喜欢的女孩子，想要跟人家表白的时候，他总会犯头疼或胃痛。以至于耽误了去表白的时机。可说来也怪，只要一想到今天可以不表白了，他的身体上的毛病就立即消失了。到医院检查，依旧没有毛病，身体一切正常。

小A这种情况，是我们的身体靠疼痛来让我们自己感受不到情绪上的痛苦，因为即将与女孩发展的亲密关系，建立起的良性互动，会激发小A潜意识深处一夕之间失去所有亲人的痛苦。只是这种痛苦，小A这类人平**时是感觉不到的，因为这叫作隐性创伤。**

弗兰克提到的第二种，就是显性创伤。就是你能感觉到你在这段关系中受伤了，你被冒犯了，又譬如你被诬陷了，你被背叛了……诸如此类，这些你可以感受得到。这种显性创伤，相较于前一种隐性创伤，要更好处理一些。

而隐性创伤呢？它所造成的痛苦往往远远超过了人机体的承受能力。这种痛苦就变成了你潜意识中不能被碰触的伤痛，变成了你人格中隐藏着的"魔鬼"，从而造成一些人格障碍，甚至是精神失常。

以上都是在谈不敢尝试一段关系的建立的情况，追根究底，其实是我们害怕受到伤害，比如受伤后无地方疗伤，无足够的社会支持系统依靠等等原因造成的。

那么在一段关系中，我们再来谈谈另外一种情况：
2. 我们敢于去尝试，虽然我们害怕恐惧，但我们还是愿意走出那一步。

就比如我们想开启一段新的关系，但最坏的设想就是我们被欺骗、被污蔑、被打击等等，我们受到了伤害，但这一类人，往往有足够的社会支持系统疗伤，也不会感到无助或孤苦无依。

现在，我们来谈谈如何疗伤呢？

在生活中，我们都有非常重要的人际关系要维系。**一个健康正常的人，在一段健康良性循环的关系中，是既要有付出，也要有收获的**。任何关系，你不能想当然地认为我只要付出，或我只要收获。那是失衡的关系，不健康的关系，也必然不会持久。当我们在一段关系中，既有付出也有收获时，我们是能感受到这种平衡的，在你遭遇显性痛苦的时刻，就请把痛苦交给这段关系来承担，让这段关系来帮助你，帮你镜映，帮你吐故纳新，让你被聆听。

但如果你有隐性的创伤时，你有身体上的感觉，身体出现莫名其妙的疼痛或不适，有些疼痛甚至会失控或出现躯体状态异常，或者你做了许多事，却常常力不从心，你感觉自己好像总不能坦然洒脱地活着。

那么，这个时候，就需要找一名有经验的心理咨询师，来陪伴你做咨询了。如此这样，才能让你敞开心扉，让你把那些陈年的隐性创伤，已经遗忘在潜意识里的创伤激活，你才能无惧它们，走到阳光底下，代谢出那些创伤在你心理上留下的东西，得到真正的疗愈。

本期【心理门】解语：
唯有拥有一面照见灵魂深处的镜子，你才能正衣冠，才能真正的认识

自己,看清楚自己,明白自己是谁,能成为谁,对于任何一段关系,你才能在一段关系中明白自己的真实需求,也懂得别人的需求,从而变得更无畏,才能身心完整地享受一段关系中的温暖,迎来心灵上的春天。

10绘画疗法真的能治愈受伤的心灵吗?

有时,在做心理咨询时,心理咨询师会碰上一些小来访者或表达上有障碍的来访者,他们不能准确地表达出他们内心深处想要表达的意思。

这时,有经验的心理咨询师通常就会采用绘画疗法来进行会谈。

通过绘画来代替一部分语言的表达,从作画中表达出或担心,或恐惧,或焦虑不安,或心如死灰等等不良情绪,是常态。

将作画或欣赏画作作为一种情绪的宣泄口。

据研究表明,欣赏世界名画,能有效地改变我们的脑波。我们可以从绘画中找到与身心灵完美契合的规律,释放自我。

本文以过往的咨询经验,一起来欣赏分析以下几幅世界名画,希望能以此带给各位不一样的感受。

第一幅名画:

画中是以一个普通花瓶中静态的向日葵的呈现。画作中的向日葵繁盛地盛开在瓶中，在温暖的阳光下，摇曳着各式各样的姿态，整个画面给人一种温暖又积极向上的感觉。

试想在繁忙的一天中，我们要经历许许多多的事情，一颗心很难有安宁下来的那一刻，等到拖着疲惫不堪的躯体回到家中时，若是能找到心灵上的一处安静之所，是不是很令人惬意舒心呢？

在向日葵静默开放的时光中，下午斜斜的阳光照耀在身上，那浅淡的花香中，似乎经历了纷纷扰扰的身心灵也能在那一刻得到疗愈。内心某处的创伤，似乎也被这阳光照耀着，渐渐愈合。

所以整幅画多采用了阳光的颜色，给人以温暖，给人以祥和。

第二幅名画：

这是一个荡着秋千的少女，她活泼可爱地翘起了一只脚，踢飞了鞋子，她的顽皮从整幅画面中不自觉地洋溢出来。她在花枝间微笑，飞舞的裙裾写满了她的欢快，她的身下右边是两个小天使，舞动着小翅膀，围绕着她。

这就好像寓意着这世间一切好运和美好都降福于她一般。

画面为了凸显少女的活泼，于是她的长裙选取了粉橘的亮色。

能注意到前一幅画与这幅画的颜色主色调给我们情绪上带来的变化吗？

不同的颜色,给人的情绪会带来不同的影响,那画中亮丽的粉橘色是不是也让你的情绪跟着想要雀跃起来呢?这就是这幅画带给我们的能量流动。

荷兰阿姆斯特丹大学医学院的实验表明,一模一样的精神治疗药物,用红色糖衣包裹起来能使人兴奋,而用蓝色或绿色糖衣包裹却能让人产生镇静的效果。

这说明,红色调的确能带给人"振奋""向上"的效果。

这是有科学依据的,人的眼睛接收到光线,通过对视网膜的刺激使肾上腺素分泌,由此又加速了血液循环,提升我们的体温和血压,从而刺激神经组织。

这就是为什么大部分的抗抑郁症治疗药物特别喜欢用红色糖衣包裹的缘故。

心情低落或疲惫不堪时,除了保证充足的睡眠之外,再多欣赏欣赏红色调的名家画作,也是很有效果的。

第三幅名画:

画作中是一两只动物与小女孩的互动,他们的身后是一片宽阔的草坡,一两处幽居的小房舍,一位少妇在房舍边悠闲地走着……

这样的构图，是不是很能让人放松下来呢？

当你从白日里一片"厮杀声"中解救了自我，打算放空自己的时候，欣赏这样一幅心情闲散的画作，是不是格外让人解压呢？

动物与人是大自然的一部分，很多研究表明，常常和动物相处的人，不容易患上抑郁症、焦虑症或孤独症。与动物相处的过程中，那是一种无比惬意的无言的表达，但又充满了爱的流动。

不良的情绪和诸多的烦恼，仿佛在那一刻都消失无踪了。

最后，结合现实的案例，从欣赏名画谈到真正意义上的绘画疗法，我曾对多位5-6岁的孩童采用过绘画疗法。因为这个年龄段的孩子，他们的语言功能不足以表达出他们的经历和遭遇，而绘画疗法的运用，在此时此刻的确取得了很好的疗效。

孩子们可以通过作画，来描绘出他们曾经经历过什么样的糟糕事件，以至于过去很久了，这样的经历事件依旧在他们的小脑袋瓜里留下了深刻的印象，当然，这些事件在他们的心理上也造成了不小的伤害。

但在绘画的过程中，他们的不安、恐惧、无助等等不良情绪都得到了很好的支持和呵护，我们由此建立起了更好的更牢固的工作同盟。

那么，**在心情压抑或烦闷，又不足以向外人道时，就不妨试着欣赏一幅世界名画或绘制一幅色彩鲜明的画作吧**，用各种你想用的颜色把它填满，你会发现，你的自我得到了更好的释放，由此你获得了身心灵的平静。

11怎样的亲密关系才叫高质量的关系呢？

人与人之间的交往有很多种，有亲有疏，不同的关系，就会出现不同的社交距离，无论怎样，我们内心深处还是最渴望建立良好甚至优质的亲密关系。

那么，怎样的亲密关系才算是高质量的亲密关系呢？

1.意识与意识是可以交流的关系。

两个人也好，三个人也罢，抑或多人的团体关系，在这些人的交往中，我们可以各自抒发各自的意见。这些意见有与我们意识层面相同的观点，也有不同的观点。但这些交流是允许求同存异的。他们可以独树一帜，也可以团结统一。因此，这样的交流可以算作是正向流动的，不会在交流中形成阻滞。而这样团体中的这些人的认知，对整个世界的看法，或人生经验与道理，甚至是购买一件商品需要花费多少钱才划算等等观点，都是可以相得益彰的。他们在一个区域内可以形成共振。也就是说，这些人分享出来的认知可以五花八门，但总会在一个统一的认知区间内产生统一的共鸣。

2. 彼此间的情绪是可以被倾听、被看到的。

比如，小A刚刚失去了自己心爱的小狗，他很伤心，但当他将这件事对小B讲的时候，小B愿意倾听，也能看到小A的悲伤，并可以让小A通过自己关切的眼神、语言以及表情看到这样为小狗的逝去悲伤的自己。小A与小B之间，情绪在此能得到很好的映照与容纳。

3. 彼此之间不仅能分享快乐的事，也能分享悲伤的事。

就像上面这个例子，当小A的痛苦悲伤被倾听、被看见、被容纳之时，小B内心也会涌现出同样类似的伤痛过往并愿意分享出来。小A与小B一起愿意面对彼此的痛苦、悲伤、无助，甚至是绝望的感觉。

而反之，倘若小A分享出自己的悲伤与痛苦，他在向小B提起这件事时，其实是希望能在小B这里得到温暖的回应的，而小B若是丝毫不能承受住小A的这些伤口疼痛的感受，回避、逃开，甚至是恶言相向："你去找别人说去，别跟我说这种事。"

他以为，这些伤口只要不提及，小A内心的痛苦就能不药而愈了？

归根结底，出现这样的情况，主要是小B不敢面对自己内心同样的创口，一旦外面接收的讯息在产生痛苦、悲伤、绝望等情绪时，小B就会回避着把自己包裹起来，他不知道该如何处理自己内心的这些伤口，所以就会在小A向他诉说时，采取回避甚至恶言相向的态度来回避自己内心的陈年伤口。

换句话说，其实是小B不太会处理自己的负面情绪，他无法面对一个陷入无助、脆弱的自己。

小A遇上这样的情况，是没办法很好地倾诉的。

一个良好的倾诉对象，他需要是一个可以承得住你所有不良情绪的容器，你需要被看见，被温暖，被映照，被包容，被接纳。

在朋友团体之间高质量的互动是需要达到以上三点要求的。

那么，在家庭当中夫妻之间、亲子之间需要怎样高质量的交往呢？除了要达到前三种，还需要达到第四种：

那就是肢体与肢体的接触。

比如，一个温暖的拥抱、牵牵手、拍拍头或肩背等等，这样的肢体接触能给人温暖与鼓励，这样的亲密接触也是一个家庭当中高质量的关系自然而然的需要。

12 愿我拥有蒲公英一般的人生

为何我总是反复思考个不停？

"每日在睡前，我几乎都会做这样的推理：如果眼睛看着眼睛会怎样呢？我们为了能入睡，一定要合上眼睑。可万一没有了眼睑呢？

如果是那样，即便是不情愿，眼睛也是不得不看东西的吧。但瞳孔又为什么不能看着眼睑呢？否则，虽然自己闭上了眼睑，仍能看到自己的眼睑内层的呀，即使不想看也得看，那可怎么办啊……"

每每想到这些有的没的，我感到自己已经无路可走了。因此我陷入了漫长的失眠中。我们当中有的人，可能会经常性地将自己带入以上类似的推理或已经发生过的痛苦经历，抑或是根本还未发生过的幻想当中，反复地思考，一分钟又一分钟，一个小时又一个小时……反反复复，周而复始。

然而这些思考，对于我们当下的生活是毫无意义的，但我们又控制不住地偏偏要去想这些问题，白白耗费了许多生命的长度。虽然明知是如此，但依旧会抑制不住地想，反复地想，连自己都忍不住。这是怎么回事呢？这是强迫症中的一种，穷思竭虑。

那么，强迫观念是如何形成的呢？

1. 迄今为止，有关的叙述认为："强迫观念是其本人感到不快的一种观念，在内心深处强迫性呈现。"

很多有强迫观念的人，执着地认定，这些突然窜入脑子里的想法是思想的异物，想要千方百计将之排出体外，就像是排泄物一般。可越是这样想，反而问题越发严重。这是患有强迫症的人自我的防卫观念，尤其是我们被症状完全控制住时，这恐怕令我们身在其中，反而完全看不到其背后的问题，一旦就医，就始终要求医生治疗这些症状。

但其实真正想要缓解强迫症的症状，应把治疗的焦点放在打破"被束缚"的机制上，患者被症状束缚实际上是强烈的生的欲望的表现。

关键点是如何向患者传达这种微妙的"内心感受"。

2. 强迫观念绝非思想的异物，而是把平常生活中谁都会产生的不悦情绪，误认为病态或者异常。这是一种试图将恐怖、担心等心理消除掉而拼命挣扎所引起的痛苦。

比如，小A常常为自己的眼睛会瞥到自己的鼻尖而感到痛苦不已，他也不想这么想，可越是不想，越容易看到自己的鼻尖，他也变得越发焦躁，不能安静下来学习或工作，最后连正常的生活、工作都停止了下来，一天到晚就专注于如何不让自己看到自己鼻尖这样的问题上。

又或者，小B常常上课紧张而导致字句不认识，他就常常告诫自己不要紧张，结果反而越注意不紧张的问题，就越紧张，到后来，老师课堂提问，他连简单的字句都说不出来了。这样的状况越发严重，以致于后来休学在家，不能正常学习了。

……

古人云：灯笼不知脚下黑。

3. 森田疗法中认为神经症发病的真正原因是个体的疑病素质。

即是外人看得很清楚，可患了强迫症的人自己整天纠缠在自己的症状中，作茧自缚，痛苦不堪。如果让患者意识到自己发病的真正原因，相当一部分患者会恍然大悟。

这就好比，有的人将自己的影子当作了"魔鬼"，恐惧害怕，一旦知道影子是谁都有的，没什么危害，恐惧自然就消失了。

再者，我们从精神分析上来看强迫症中的穷思竭虑这个症状：有的人，因为反复思考一些没有现实意义的问题，一直想一直想，直到把自己想糊涂了。

从潜意识上，就是要把自己思想堆得满满当当，想到不能再想，那就不能够再想了。

其实是在逃避问题形成的实质。

他为何会这样对待自己呢？

因为如果还能思考的话，他能清楚地感受到自己不被现实允许的许多欲望与冲动、关系、自恋等等因素，所以才逃避。

另外一种可能就是，他不能面对自己失控的局面，所以以一种阿Q精神或事后诸葛亮的幻想沉浸其中，才能逃离现实中被攻击的痛苦与悲伤等不良情绪。精神分析的精髓是症状是潜意识的冲突，如果将其意识化，痛苦自然减轻甚至消失。

那么，如果患上了强迫症，我们该怎么办呢？

强迫症的患者，常常为自己某一观念或生理反应而痛苦。

行为疗法认为，人的心理和行为是在后天环境中通过条件反射式的学习形成的，同理，病态的思维和不良行为也是通过条件反射形成的。

这就是为什么有的强迫症患者明明了解了自己的病因，道理也明白了，但还是会反复、停滞不前的原因了。

这里强调必须通过阳性强化法强化健康行为，厌恶疗法淡化抑制病态行为，有时带着必死的勇气进行暴露疗法和脱敏疗法。

行为疗法揭示了强迫症顽固的根源。

森田疗法则要强调"顺其自然，为所当为"，但同时也强调"重在实践""忍受痛苦，带着症状去生活""日日是好日"，并认为目的本位、行为本位是打破精神交互作用的关键所在，强调"不问症状"。

在森田疗法的传统治疗方法中，除了第一周是卧床，其他时间基本上都是各种作业与生活体验。

所以，从严格意义上讲，注重行为实践，制定计划，让我们动起来，才是缓解强迫症的一大良方吧。

其实有时候简单想想，我们何不像一根蒲公英一样，随风而起，随风而落，随遇而安地生活呢？

本文只是简单地描述了患了强迫症应当如何治疗的方法概要，倘若真的患上了强迫症，"冰冻三尺非一日之寒"，又岂能是这简单一篇文字就能说得清楚的，建议还是要谨遵医嘱，愿所有患强迫症的患者，早日遇见健康的自己，鼓足勇气，过上弥足珍贵的健康且洒脱的人生。

13 咨询笔记之咨询师如何在咨询中克服选择冲突

案例：小A是一个入行不久的心理咨询师，他虽是新手，但好在他足够热情且善于探索，这让他即便面对一些很困难的咨询过程时，都能很好地共情和接纳。

在遇到小B来访之前，他并未感觉从事这一行吃力。

这天，小B带着问题来访，并出现了一些焦虑的症状。他迫切地想要小A立即、马上回答他的提问，从而对他无奈的人生进行指导。

望着小B期待的目光，小A是想要马上共情他的苦恼，并积极做出回应的。但他马上又想到某本教科书上明确讲过，不能立即给出指导，咨询师应该在咨询过程中遵守节制原则，应该引导来访者自我觉察、自我认知，从而获得真实生活中的改善。

于是，小A陷入了究竟是该选择立即给出回应，还是应当遵守节制原则的漫长思考当中，而小B的反复追问以及他的焦虑情绪逼迫着小A进入了一个进退两难的境地。

他不知该如何选择了。这次的咨询也因此合作失败，小A感到了从未有过的无力感，他甚至开始怀疑自己是否真的适合这一行。

当一名咨询师无法自由地选择到底是应该给来访者及时的回应，还是遵守节制原则的时候，这就是冲突的发生了。

从上述案例中可以清晰地感受到，小A在进行这次咨询时，陷入了选择的不自由当中，他的一个冲突也就出现了。这是很多新手咨询师都容易遇到的一个问题。

首先，我们不是应该让导师来告诉你该如何选择，是该选择及时地对来访者做出回应，还是应该遵守节制原则，而是应该从更深的一层去分析，你为什么会出现这样的状况？为什么我在当时的状况下无法给出回应或无法遵守节制原则。

这里，通过导师的笔记整理，我总结出以下两种解释：

其一，也许这并不是你在这两个场景中间的冲突，比如说给出回应或是节制。而是你内心里面有一个冲突并没有得到整合：

即是，我到底是根据来访者的实际情况来及时做出回应，去共情他呢？还是根据教科书上或某位导师的反复叮嘱，应该遵守节制原则。

这样的冲突，不仅仅在这一件事上，可能还涉及其他出现冲突的地方。

比如：当小A在给来访者小B及时做出回应与解释时，面临着一个新的冲突，那就是到底是解释移情呢，还是解释早年的关系对现在的影响。因为移情是当下发生的，那就是解释你和他之间的关系呢，还是解释他跟他养育者之间的关系呢？

这显然是两个咨询师小A可能面临的全新的冲突，之后的咨询过程中，还可能再产生第三个、第四个、第五个……乃至更多的冲突。只要涉及A或B的选择时，这些不自由的徘徊就会出现在心头，让你不知该选择哪个好。

这第一个解释就是，这种情况的发生跟这两个冲突没有关系，而是你内心的某个冲突投射到了这两件事情上。

其二，也许在表面上看是事件选择在冲突，实际上却是人与人之间的冲突。

比如，有位导师教你是让你能够越灵活地处理每一个案例的具体情况越好，当来访者需要你及时做出回应时，教科书上让你遵守的节制原则就可以抛诸脑后了。

但同时，随着时间的推移，你继续心理咨询的学习，另外几位导师又告诉你，在心理咨询工作中，有一些心理治疗的基本设置还是要遵守的。

于是，外面的不管是教科书上所说的，还是导师教授的知识，这样的冲突被你内化成了自己的冲突。从而使咨询师在具体操作时，困难重重，不知该怎么办？

这些情况，尤其是遇到一些有选择困难症的新手咨询师会变得更加困扰。

那么，我们应该如何正确地处理这种选择冲突的情况呢？

第一，不管选择哪一种，都先尽量降低自己的焦虑情绪。

倘若你是一位已经入行有十年咨询功底的咨询师，那你就会明白，在某一个特定的时候，你是应该保持缄默，还是应该及时给出合理的解释与回应。有前辈的操作在前，这样依据具体实际情况而定的处理方式，可以极大地缓解新手咨询师的焦虑，从而更好地在会谈联盟中工作。

第二，不回应具体的问题，但可以换一种说法来回应，以表达某种程度上的共情。

比如，小A遭遇到小B连番的追问之下，已经明确地感受到了小B的焦虑和急躁情绪了，对他做出一些回应已经显得尤为必要时，我们可以这样说："我知道你很想知道我的回应，但我想和你沟通一下，因为我对你的表述情况还不是很了解，我不知道我该为你反馈什么。所以最好的办法是，你再多跟我说一些关于你的事。我相信在我对你有了更多的了解之后，我就自然知道要与你反馈什么了。"

第三，认真记好咨询笔记，分析每一个需要你注意的细节，包括情绪反应、来访者诉求、产生当下问题的诱因等。

保持良好的记录咨询笔记的习惯，可以更好地清晰分析你从来访者那里得到的讯息，从而在必要给出回应时，你可以言之有物，也能让来访者感受到被尊重，缓解他的焦虑情绪。

另外，保持做咨询笔记的习惯，可以让来访者看到你认真对待这次会谈联盟的态度，从而更有利于建立良好的工作同盟关系，让新手咨询师在咨询过程中更加充满自信力。

本期【心理门】解语：

务实开放真诚的态度，耐心的倾听，以及穿入穿出各个来访者人生剧本的高级深度共情之力，你才能以一颗通透、清醒、理性、大智慧的道心，打开你魂灵中的照见之镜，去看到每一个不一样的灵魂，不一样的需求，他们发出着什么样的声音。

14 如何走出焦虑的心境？

安来访时，显得惶惶不安，整个人都没有能安稳下来的状态。除此之外，她还双眼发青，无精打采，双手不住地颤抖，冲着我说："帮帮我，快点做点什么？让它停下来……"

虽然已经有了不少的咨询经验，但我面对她的症状时，依旧感到了一股无力感。然后我说："好的，你先躺在我们的沙发上，谈谈到底是怎么一回事？"

兴许是我有条不紊的语调、平和的心态，让安意识到了什么，她忽然放声大哭，落下泪来，好半天才说："我……我只想像您一样，可以平静地生活和工作。"

安不能平静地生活和工作吗？

我随着她的讲述，慢慢进入了沉思。

距离安来访，已经有一段时日了，她常常夜不能寐，一颗心纷乱地怦怦乱跳着，像是不听使唤似的想要蹦出来。

我问她，她晚上不睡觉，是在想些什么。

她说，她会常常因为一些芝麻绿豆的小事睡不着觉：比如窗户关没关严？煤气有没有检查过？厨房里有滴水的声音，应该是水龙头没有关好。

身边的伴侣发出细微均匀的鼾声，她却羡慕他能睡得如此香甜，可她却睁着双眼一直翻来覆去想着前面所述的那些芝麻大小的事情，睡不着觉。

我告诉她，你这已经是持续的焦虑和失眠的症状了。

她感到无所适从。我接着问她，你现在最想干什么，才能让自己变得好受一点？她毫不迟疑地回答，睡觉。

于是我允许她在咨询室的沙发上小憩片刻，只要这样能让她感到好一些。

可她依旧睁着疲倦不堪的双眼，沙哑着嗓子絮絮叨叨地讲述着，她还是睡不着。

"我要怎样才能结束这一切？我要怎样才能停止担心这些我不得不做的事情？更糟糕的是，这些毫无意义的事情不是已经脱离了我的掌控，就是还没有发生。"

"既然知道是毫无意义的事情，那为什么还要想掌控它？"我问她。

"因为我想要控制自己的思想。"这是她的回答，"我想要变得更加放松和自信，就像老师一样……"

我为她尝试性地做了催眠放松治疗。我让她想象自己来到了一片美丽的海边，海风微微地吹拂着她的发丝，海鸥在天边翱翔，海水轻轻起伏、潮涨潮退的声音，一次又一次传进耳畔……

然后，我告诉她，你想让自己从不断反复的焦虑状况中解脱，想要停止午夜梦回时，在床上不断臆想的那些循环魔咒，想要清晨一睁开眼，就轻松惬意地收获一天的美好，不再会被那些令人消沉的可能性和即将到来的阻碍所带来的恐惧与不安困扰……

"你需要勇敢地迈出第一步。是充满希望的一步。"

首先，我们来了解焦虑思维是如何工作的。

通常情况下，我们都知道，当我们面对状况时，大脑是先焦虑，然后才思考。

我们往往会先察看环境，确定是否存在危险，哪怕是遇到了友好的人，或处于安全的状态里。

我们的大脑倾向于先察觉威胁，相比正面信息，它对负面信息的反应反而更加强烈。

事实上，我们给予负面情绪的关注更多，因为我们往往会过度查找所谓的"FUD因素"：恐惧、不确定性和怀疑。

而这就是我们大脑的"负面倾向"。如果承受长时间的负面压力，大脑就无法达到静息状态，所以，就很难得到放松，进入深度睡眠，你就更加不可能恢复平静的情绪状态。你身体紧绷，困在反刍思维里，会觉得心情很糟糕。

在这种状态下，大脑重新形成新的神经通路，规划新的路线图，通向未来的观点、情感、思想、知觉和行为会受到目前精神状态的影响，但路线图却是在目前很糟糕的精神状态下绘制的。

你的大脑开始将大大小小的生活冲击编织成一种关于生活信念和规则的限制性模式。

这种模式会引发焦虑的、恐惧的和情绪化的思维，干扰你的思路，阻碍你坚持到底的毅力、破坏你的信心和满足感。

你的自卫习惯只会让你的人际关系更差，健康受损，工作不顺，情感麻木。

其次，焦虑往往会让你困在对现实或幻想的担忧和不确定里，武断地做出消极判断，无法中途暂停，对现实进行反思。

这样的躁动，使你不停地想要解决问题，寻求出路，却未想到过寻找轻松和解脱。

如果你身处焦虑状态，你可能就会发现自己一直在试图寻找所有可能会变糟糕的事情,这样你就可以做好准备去迎接它们了。可事实是,这样的思维方式,只会让人挣扎在困扰中,不得解脱。

那么,身处焦虑的我们,要如何做才能让我们重获平静呢?要想缓解焦虑,我们需要运用干预手段使大脑平静下来。

1. 通过练习,你可以重新疏通大脑。这种过程叫作自我导向型的神经可塑性。

你的情绪、行为模式、态度和观点全都和你的精神状态有关。

如何以及何处放置你的注意力决定着你大部分时间里的精神状态。

唯有转移注意力,你才能改变你目前的精神状态。

2. 通过自我调节和对信念、感受和行为的控制,你就可以做出改变,并能在长时间内保持更加快乐的精神状态。

备受焦虑的困扰,是因为你的大脑里一直播放着"我的未来最糟糕"的电影,会让你陷入危机风波当中。

唯有当你学会有意识地控制自己并进行自我调节,你就能更清晰地认识世界,更加合理地对待你的经历。

就比如来访中的安,若她将夜不能寐的所有不安的思维放置在一边,抱着豁达的态度去看待这些芝麻绿豆的问题,那么这些问题,在她眼中就不值得一提了,也就不能困扰她了。

3. 你的身体状态反映你的精神状态。

你非常清楚,焦虑会导致你肠胃不适或头痛。你的精神状态每时每刻都会反映你的身体状况,它在发送那些会引导你行为的无意识思想和情感。

当你不自觉地将平静的思想带入你的大脑,不管怎样,你都能够在你的神经系统里制造出惊人的变化。你确实可以通过重新疏通大脑来改变你的精神状态,重组你的思维来改变你的身体状况。

卓别林在《当我开始爱自己》一诗中曾写道:

我只活在当下

进入正在发生的一切事物中

我充分活在每一日

如此日复一日

而我懂得

这就是完美

本期【心理门】解语：

每一段关系，无论多么美好，都有告别的一天，或许早一点，或许晚一点，但并不是说，我们知道这段关系注定会结束，那就不去选择开始，相反每一段关系，都会带了不同的任务和使命而来，他们总能够以不同的形式，让我们从中学会什么，比如……看到我们残存在灵魂中的创伤，抑或是助我们成长……

所以，心怀感恩，去全然的打开接受每一次奇妙的际遇，去充分体验它，从而发现我们爱别人的能力，也同时看到，感知到，我们也正在被别人深深的爱着。

Psychological Door · Guarding Happiness

1 The Ones Who Disappear in Love

A good feeling of song...

It can prove that truth. We live so truely. Correcting the mistake again and again.Because our knowledge is existent in our brain ,our blood and our soul forever.

Love your neighbor as yourself. ——Old Li 19:18

She can't eat, can't sleep, and needs someone to accompany her with everything. Just as you left for a while, she hummed and hawed, but just looked around for people with her eyes

What's wrong with her

When Nini first visited, she was brought by two best friends, with a numb expression and almost no response to external stimuli. Due to her heartbreak, she was unable to work or live normally, and even regressed to the state of a baby walking, eating, and sleeping, exhausting her girlfriends.

There is a type of person in intimate relationships called a 'parasite'.

Excessive dependence, fear of abandonment, disgust, and abandonment; So they tightly cling to each other, taking everything they have as their full or partial spiritual support, giving up social life, alone time, spiritual thinking and practice, and even their originally positive preferences and values for each other. This type of person is called a "disappeared person" or "parasite" in romantic relationships or other intimate relationships.

And for this group of people, although there are also men among them, due to the vastly different ways of thinking between men and women, the "disappeared people" mentioned here are mostly women.

American psychologist Beverly Ingle also discusses in her book "Love Him, Love Yourself" why "disappearing women" sacrifice their subjectivity and self-esteem, and miss opportunities to pursue personal growth?

Once there is a problem with intimate dependence, such forced withdrawal is almost unacceptable to this type of 'parasite'. Some people are unable to return to their previous lives, and even revert to a state of infancy in terms of clothing, food, housing, and transportation. They feel depressed, haggard, have no taste for food, cannot sleep at night, suffer from sensory disorders, self blame, insomnia anxiety, and even depression, leading to significant impairment of some social functions.

After waking up a little bit, Nini began to vent her emotions crazily, not even realizing that she had unknowingly become a resentful woman.

He told me not to go to my best friend's birthday party, so I didn't go; he told me not to wear short skirts, so I threw away all the short skirts at home; he told me not to talk to strangers, so I didn't speak; he told me to uninstall WeChat and QQ chat tools, so I uninstalled them; he told me to read more books, so I read more books, and I had to read the books he chose for me, even though I never liked reading or studying; he didn't even allow me to watch comedy movies like "Pancake Man" and "Diaosi Man", saying that I was stupid enough and that watching them might make me even less intelligent... I have already done this, what else does he want

After venting her emotions, her energy was depleted and she fell into depression, accompanied by symptoms of physical pain and weakness.

Nini met the male protagonist of this relationship through the shaking function of WeChat. As soon as they met, Nini was deeply attracted by the male protagonist's charming appearance, humorous and witty sense of humor, attention to small details, and high salary.

She almost sighed in her heart, 'Oh my God, besides him, I've never met such a good man again!'

Perhaps this kind of thinking gave her the hint of 'hold on tight and don't let go' from the beginning, and the two quickly fell in love, from chatting happily to developing into an intimate relationship in just one month.

From then on, Nini went from being forced to accept the male protagonist's transformation, to actively cooperating with the transformation, and even to the final "obsessive-compulsive attachment".

Now, the 'male protagonist' in this relationship has suddenly disappeared without even saying 'goodbye'. He was ruthless and heartless, while Nini suddenly felt a huge void in her heart. The shoulders she used to rely on suddenly disappeared, and her soul had nowhere to rely on. She fell to the ground with a loud bang, and her behavior was normal to regress.

Why did you never refuse his forced change at that time? "I asked her.

She blinked her tears and asked a seemingly comical question, 'Can I... can I?'

This is a bit like a 5-year-old child pulling his mother's clothes at home and asking if he can go to the bathroom, which is both funny and funny.

You know, on a psychological level, parasites are usually classified into three types, "I said as I looked into Nini's eyes.

Can you tell me, what type of person am I

What kind of parasite does Nini belong to?

Psychological Gate: Guarding Happiness 1- The People Who Disappear in Love

When we only focus on the cruelty of reality and the difficulties of life, we will not pay more attention to how to actively face them, whether to wait for others to give us alms or to think about how to create beauty and protect happiness? After all, every trauma is a form of maturity.

2 Love Halo

To shun evil is understanding.——Old Uncle "28:28

In the previous episode, we mentioned that in a romantic relationship, Nini regressed into a "giant baby" due to heartbreak. I told her that this is a type of 'parasite', so which type of 'parasite' does she belong to?

We analyze the causes from the perspectives of psychology, social relationships, and biology:

Firstly, the dependent personality disorder type 'parasite' has almost no sense of personal existence and value, and can only obtain a sense of existence by attaching to external objects. They have strong dependence and are quite afraid of withdrawal and abandonment. This type of personality disorder requires the establishment of long-term counseling relationships, which consumes a great deal of effort from psychologists in order to improve. But overall, if such personality disorders are related to innate genetics, the chances of being completely cured are quite low. But there are also cases where senior psychologists have successfully cured such personality disorders through sand table games or hypnotherapy.

Do you belong to this category? "I asked Nini.

Nini thought for a moment and shook her head. 'Before I met him, my independence wasn't particularly strong, but it wasn't the kind mentioned above either.'

You're lucky that you don't have a congenital personality disorder, "I said," because in that case, it would be a bit difficult to improve

Ah, is there anything else for the day after tomorrow? "Nini asked.

This is the analysis of social relationship environment and psychological aspects that we will focus on next, "I nodded.

Given Nini's statement that 'I will never find such a good person again', it is a form of 'halo effect' misleading in psychology. It is precisely this halo effect that leads two people to enter into an intimate relationship before fully understanding each other, developing into a "fast food love" with high opening and low closing.

So what is the 'halo effect'?

The halo effect, also known as the "halo effect," refers to the tendency of a cognitive person to infer other aspects of a person's characteristics based on a positive or negative impression of a certain feature. Essentially, it is a cognitive bias of generalizing from one perspective to another. Just like how we often come to the conclusion that 'a person with a bright appearance must be a person with a beautiful heart', but in reality?

This effect will affect our organization, decision-making, and judgment at the cognitive level, whether in friendships or romantic relationships, resulting in the consequence of 'poor friend selection'. Being confused by external elements such as appearance, the other person's identity, status, superior material conditions, etc., but neglecting to carefully examine each other's inner world, whether the spiritual level is suitable, whether the three values are compatible, and whether the two people on the spiritual level can accept each other?

Instead of waiting until two people quickly fall in love and realize that they are not suitable for each other, it is inevitable that one party will desperately try to control themselves, causing separation anxiety. Such a relationship will have no happiness and will only suffocate people.

Have you been affected like this? "I looked at her calmly.

Oh, this damn halo effect, I seem to have a bit of a crush on people like that, "Nini said, looking down at her finger." But I think I'm still a little sad

You mean pessimistic and emotional, right? "I corrected her concept.

Easy to become pessimistic and emotional. Women like Nini care too much about how others perceive them and are afraid of being rejected or disliked for refusing to change. As Nini said, 'I'm worried that if I don't change, I'll give him a stubborn image.' But in reality, it reflects our own inner rejection and uncertainty of ourselves. Our inner self doesn't have enough confidence to support it, so how can we get constant affirmation of our self values from external evaluations?

I still don't quite understand, "Nini asked me.

I don't understand, let me give you an example. For example, if someone says you're overweight, would you mind

After my faint voice, there was Nini's laughter.

Because she is very slim, she knows it herself.

There's no other way, this is what my ex boyfriend asked for. He said that if I became fat, he wouldn't want me. But I'm still slim now, and he still doesn't want me

At the same time, inferiority complex, sensitivity, and excessive thinking are also one of the causes of the "parasite" personality. I won't go into detail here.

I noticed her frustration and joked with her, 'Look, this was also a clear benefit from our previous relationship. Of course, there are still many benefits now, all related to growth. Sometimes we have to go through pain to truly trigger thinking and gradually mature.'

However, in situations like Nini's, how can we prevent the occurrence of the "parasite" phenomenon?

Psychological Gate: Guarding Happiness 2: Love Halo

Many times, what we believe is actually just what we are willing to believe. So, what is true when both appearance and essence appear at the same time?

3 Am I a parasite of love?

Man does not comprehend its worth. ——Old Uncle 28:13

In the previous article, Nini became a parasite of love due to heartbreak, and factors such as dependent personality disorder, halo effect, pessimistic emotions, inferiority complex, sensitivity, and overthinking are all causes of this phenomenon.

We all want to achieve perfect love, warmth, reliability, and a constant sense of security from intimate relationships. No one wants to be a parasite during sex, so how can we prevent ourselves from becoming a parasite in intimate relationships?

1. Extend the time when love is intense.

In today's vibrant and colorful world, be a serious and objective observer, disregarding the glamorous external conditions of your lover, including identity, status, wealth, sense of humor, sweet words, and even some considerate small details; To understand such a person from the perspective of ideology and spirit, what kind of person is he? Only in this way can we get to know the real other person, and is this the kind of person who is suitable for us to have a less heart wrenching but worth your careful effort to go through the details. This method, I believe, is also a trump card to overcome the "halo effect" in romantic relationships.

2. Be true to yourself and honestly express genuine thoughts.

Don't hide your true self just because he doesn't like you. Over time, even if he's with you, he doesn't love the real you, but the person you pretend to be; It's never you, so what other precious meaning does this love have besides each taking what they need? So, if two people are truly in love, then I can take care of your feelings, but I cannot lose my original self because of loving you. Accepting each other's true selves and being honest with each other is a good way to open up an intimate relationship within equality and authenticity, rather than hiding from each other. I remember Liu Ruoying once said, 'When you find a partner who doesn't have to worry about needing to tighten your belly in front of him, it proves that your' true love 'or' heavenly daughter 'has appeared.'. A true hit person has a common trait of being able to get along with others freely.

3. Have your own independent life, work, hobbies, and profession, those... besides the elegant crush, there are also things worth celebrating or being proud of.

Some women are good at cooking, flower arrangement, coffee tasting, painting, carving, writing, music, and so on... These can be considered hobbies. With a little cultivation and dedication, these hobbies can be turned into bone ash level professions, achieving the best level in the industry and turning it into money. Then use money to advance to higher dreams and constantly improve yourself. Even if one day your crush runs away with another girl, you won't be as miserable as Nini in the case, making yourself feel like a resentful woman or a "giant baby". The profession discussed here is related to dreams, which will be specifically discussed in future dating and emotional programs on how to take responsibility for the dreams we choose. But this should be considered a skill in ancient times. However, in this era, the notion that 'a woman without talent is virtuous' is no longer highly respected.

4. Cherish your 'shadow personality'. What is Shadow Personality?

Psychologically, everyone has a personality trait with a shadow side, just like an introverted person who actually prefers outgoing and lively colors deep down; And a person who is not good at words is full of longing for social experts who are eloquent and strategic in their hearts.

People with a 'shadow personality' can make up for the other side of our shadow personality, and social relationship psychologists believe that if we find such a shadow personality, our personality can be continuously learned through the principle of similarity and complementarity in our interactions, and we can successfully fill the gaps and deficiencies in our hearts, thus growing into a perfect personality.

The most difficult thing for humans to change is the innate inherited personality traits, but perhaps even more difficult to change is our fragile human nature when faced with desires, and the "shadow personality" can precisely perfect this part of us to a certain extent, gradually becoming perfect.

However, many people, after encountering a "shadow personality" that suits them, unconsciously start to try to change the other person and transform them into the person they want, based on their familiarity. If the other person always forces you to change, it means that they may not truly love you. They only love the person deep in their heart, which is why they force the person in front of them to constantly change into that person's appearance in real life, rather than loving the real you.

Just like when Nini met someone good, everyone else was just a passerby, a "teacher" who came to teach her or a "student" who needed to teach her. Before meeting her own "Mr. Right", she worked hard to become an independent subject. Even if she was alone, she could arrange her life freely, freely, and happily until she met someone as independent and happy as you, someone who perfected her personality.

In this way, "Nini" and "Hao Hao" can meet and become a simple and peaceful yet truly fitting sentence - "Hello".

Finally, please approach love with a peaceful attitude, while also paying attention to the beauty of inner cultivation, upholding a mind that is both internal and external, insisting on beauty, and being unique in this world.

Nobel Prize winner George Bernard Shaw once said, "At this moment on Earth, there are about 20000 people who are suitable to be your life partner, it depends on which one you meet first. If you have developed a deep relationship of mutual understanding, appreciation, and trust with the previous person before the second ideal partner appears, the latter will become your good friend. But if you have not cultivated a deep relationship with the previous person, your feelings are easily shaken and changed, until you have a stable deep affection with one of these ideal partner candidates, which is the beginning of happiness and the end of drifting

High level love is a great love that can transcend desires and cravings, and is a true practice of giving, spiritual communication, and emotional flow of love.

Regardless of which one it is, if it is true - please cherish what you already have and strive to do well in the present for a better version of yourself in the future.

Psychological Gate: Guarding Happiness 3- Am I a Parasite of Love?

In this issue of 'Psychological Gate', it is said in Buddhist scriptures that the reason why people suffer is because they are pursuing dreams that may not be suitable for themselves. Their hearts are blinded, but one day they will find the answer because there are happy factors guiding them.

4 Love's' Fury Madness'

Resentment kills a fool, and envy slays the simple.

——Old Uncle 5:2

British biologist Darwin once said, "To get angry is to take a step back on the ladder of human progress." Impatience is a bad personality trait. When things don't go smoothly, do you become impatient? Do you not calm your inner self, or do you allow it to easily control you?

When I first met Nini, she was wearing a white floral dress with flowing long hair, fair skin, and delicate features that exuded a clever aura.

She came to me with only one question keyword: 'irritable'.

She and Haohao are very in love. They have been together for more than six years, with normal values and similar yet complementary personalities. The only contradiction is that she often speaks ill of things the size of a sesame seed, and even throws things out of control.

At first, she thought it was just a small temper caused by women. After making noise, she doted on her consistently, but recently, she gradually realized that her small temper had escalated unconsciously. Not long ago, there was an argument still over a trivial matter of oil, salt, sauce, vinegar, and tea. She slammed the door hard, but accidentally crushed her good finger, causing the consequence of broken finger bones.

Nini feels very guilty about this matter, deeply understanding her own mistakes, and being tolerant makes her hope for improvement even more. In fact, Nini is not like this in the office environment, nor is she like this in daily interpersonal communication. At most, she is a little rough, but it does not affect her normal interpersonal relationships.

I just want to be his wild girlfriend occasionally, not a hot tempered person who everyone hates

The visitor Nini in the above case is a patient with irritable psychological problems, but she has a strong desire to improve.

Being irritable has a considerable situational nature and is not a psychological problem that occurs in any situation. Ironically, irritability often manifests itself when we are faced with familiar friends or family, while it can be controlled in unfamiliar environments.

Why is this happening?

Here we temporarily set aside the genetic elements of innate personality traits and only analyze the reasons from postnatal psychological growth:

Firstly, from a subconscious psychological level, we know that our family and friends can tolerate us, even extremely tolerant, just like being hurt many times by Nini and spoiling her as always. Then her subconscious will know that even if she is so irritable, she will forgive her well.

On the other hand, in relatively unfamiliar environments such as the office, in order to maintain her temperament and self-esteem, Nini will try her best to endure even if she is subjected to stimuli that are not conducive to her.

And people with this type of irritable disorder, regardless of gender, actually inflict the deepest unconscious harm on the people closest to them, and the true love and tolerance of family and friends are also the "breeding ground" for "irritable disorder".

Secondly, it is the inconsistency of the cognitive concepts we accept during our growth process. For example, by Nini's side, if she has been hurt by her irritability and feels guilty, and wants to improve, but at the same time accepts the "advice" of others around her:

Who can have no temper at all? When a rabbit gets angry, it bites someone. Besides, in this matter, from the beginning, it was just a matter of right and wrong, which made you angry, didn't it

If a tiger doesn't show its strength, does it think you're a sick cat? You can't just let it go, it'll slap its nose and face another day

These repeated sounds frequently appear, intertwined with Nini's guilt, which does not help her clarify her consciousness and instead increases her stronger sense of frustration. Especially when some people's personality traits are highly suggestive of their surroundings, it is more likely to lead to irritability and irritability.

Thirdly, people with irritability usually have a very strict "mentor" image in their original family. When we are still underage, if we make a slight mistake, fail to follow the requirements, or fail to do it well, we will face severe reprimands and even corporal punishment from the 'teacher'.

This approach can have two negative consequences: firstly, it makes us feel dissatisfied and suppressed during childhood, and this dissatisfaction and suppression will erupt in situations that evoke this emotion in the future; Secondly, the actions of the teacher unconsciously provide us with a suggestion to emulate during our childhood. That's why once such an environment arises, irritability and aggressive behavior will erupt.

The last reason for irritable behavior is that certain diseases or physiological factors (often staying up late) trigger psychological restlessness and easily angered behavior.

Psychological Gate: Guarding Happiness 4- Love's 'Furious Madness'

There is no one in this world who is not sick, as long as the right medicine is given, there will definitely be improvement. Just as we encounter various setbacks and pains, they are inevitable, but as long as we hold onto the desire for happiness and grow with joy and sorrow, we can dispel the fog and see the sunshine. Find the pure white lotus flower in everyone's heart.

5 I won't be a "hot tempered maniac"

I will speak out in the anguish of my spirit,I will complain in the bitterness of my soul.So how to correct irritability?

——Psalm 42:4 of the Bible

Firstly, people who share the same psychological problems as Nini need to understand the above causes of irritability, and understand that this negative personality trait can gradually form positive behavior patterns through long-term self-awareness and psychological therapy or constant reminders from family and friends, in order to achieve the goal of correction.

Secondly, in psychotherapy, there is a form of "introspection therapy" that guides visitors to learn how to gaze at the child in their heart, watching him or her make a scene on the side when communication is difficult, and then watching that crying child. What thoughts do you have?

This is a positive way of self-awareness.

No matter what age group you are in, it is not difficult to notice that the irritable and bad tempered child is still very young and needs your care and reminder so much. You should try to be his ideal parents or ideal partner, always accompanying him and constantly reminding him.

Of course, everyone has a temper, but sometimes getting angry can indeed have a good effect on making things progress, and the targets of our temper tantrums are different.

For some people, getting angry can have a good effect, but for others, getting angry won't have any good effect. In addition to easily occupying your rationality and problem-solving mind at that moment, he can also hurt others badly, and those who are willing to tolerate your temper tantrums are usually the closest people around you. How can we be tolerant if we don't love? Are you still letting your mischievous child act recklessly and playfully inside you?

They are people who are willing to embrace you with silent love. If you are not aware of this, you will inevitably treat them as habitual trash cans every time you lose your temper, and think that you can vent your bad emotions without hesitation? Speak all the malicious words you can find and gather in the world to release your bad emotions.

What are the consequences?

Afterwards, when you watch them suffer immensely from the negative energy and negative emotions you released, you feel sad, upset, and self blame, thinking that this should not be the case... Having such self-awareness is good, so we need to learn to control our temper and emotions, learn to soothe that inner self, that child, and do our best to calm him down instead of letting him control you, right?

Zhang Guangzu of the Yuan Dynasty also mentioned in his book "The Turtle Mirror of Words and Actions": "When a gentleman is raised, he should prevent his irritable and evil temperament from being confined to his body." From this, it can be seen that in addition to learning to be tolerant and tolerant, even if it is for us to have a healthy body, we need to regulate our emotions reasonably and scientifically.

(It is a flower like a dragon but like a dragon turtle.)

After self-awareness, you should pay close attention to the mischievous child in your heart. He needs love and attention so much, his sadness, grief, pain, and discomfort... Be his good parents, patiently accompany him, and remind him when he is about to lose his temper and be mischievous again.

For example, using logical thinking to intervene in emotional states in a timely and urgent manner can quickly count, but it can be a bit difficult, such as "1+3=4", "3+5=8", "5+7=12" ... and so on, adding odd or even classes, urgently calling on logical thinking ability to control or selectively forget negative emotional moments. After completely calming down, what should I, as a rational person, do next?

This is similar to some people reciting the "Clear Heart Mantra" when feeling restless. Firstly, it is for thinking, and secondly, it is to increase firm confidence in being able to calm good and bad emotions.

Secondly, take a deep breath and feel the pure breath coming in from the outside through the nasal cavity, along the respiratory tract, all the way to the lungs, and then feel it downwards, all the way to the position of the navel. In meditation, this position is called the "navel wheel", and after another breath, the turbid qi in the body is expelled. This self positive suggestion method of deep breathing can calm general anger after 5-8 such breaths.

Thirdly, reading. As the saying goes, there is beauty in books, and a golden house in books. Reading books with positive energy can help calm one's troubled emotions and find peace in positive books.

Fourthly, immerse yourself in the beautiful natural scenery outdoors. Nature has a magical purifying effect on all negative energy, just like a polluted river. After years of no further contact and pollution, it can gradually become clean again. This is just like our hearts, no matter how dark they may have been before, as long as we maintain a safe distance from environments that are prone to negative energy or emotional influences, and have a strong desire to improve ourselves, we can persevere and regain the warmth of our hearts, complete self-healing and spiritual growth.

Fifth, go to bed early and wake up early, and develop a reasonable, scientific, and healthy lifestyle habit.

Only when we truly have strong warmth and a mature and perfect personality in our hearts, can we have the ability to feel happiness and obtain happiness. With sunshine in our hearts, we can pass on this light and warmth to our friends around us, making them warm and happy because of you.

Finally, when we have conflicts with people in close relationships, if we do not have the ability to communicate and solve problems rationally, and have to wait for the other person to solve everything, then we will always be passive in problem-solving. How to transform oneself from passive acceptance to a proactive problem-solving expert is also a compulsory course in psychology and social relations.

Psychological Gate: Guarding Happiness 5- I Don't Be a 'Crazed Frenzy'

In this issue of 'Psychology Gate', the explanation is: Every improvement is not easy, even painful. However, for the joy of the loved one, the relieved smile of the friends around us, and for the better self in the future, we all need to work hard. Slowly... you will realize that all the efforts you make are so meaningful.

6 Are you safe in a long-distance relationship?

For the ear tests words as the tongue tastes food.

——Old Uncle 34:3

Introduction:

Do you love me

Love

really

really

Really, really, really

Really, really, really, really

Um... can you say it again

Why do you always not believe me

The psychological development of each of us in infancy requires building a sense of trust and overcoming skepticism in order to possess hopeful and positive personality traits.

During this period, whether we have established a good mother infant attachment relationship directly affects our inner sense of security. And a sense of security is also an important psychological code for whether you can smoothly reach the end of a heart wrenching long-distance relationship and harvest happiness.

In the famous American psychologist Stenberg's love triangle theory, it is pointed out that love includes three elements: passion, intimacy, and commitment.

To achieve perfect love, all three are indispensable.

Intimacy refers to the desire between lovers to care for, nurture, take care of each other, and be together all day long.

But when lovers encounter long-distance relationships, the element of intimacy has to be greatly discounted, so a sense of security becomes one of the important keys to interpreting the perfect love in long-distance relationships.

Why didn't you say goodnight today? "With Nini's questioning, her good sleep was completely awakened.

Well, I forgot

What are you doing now

Sleep well... "There's still a meeting tomorrow morning, and the whole day's work has made him extremely tired.

With whom

What are you talking about? "You're a little angry.

Unexpectedly, Nini on the other end of the phone burst into tears with a 'wow...'.

Do you no longer love me

What's wrong with you? "I was completely awakened by Nini's crying, feeling a little flustered and blaming myself for my heavy tone earlier. It took him a long time to coax Nini to stop crying. Upon closer examination, Nini's abnormality was actually due to:

You... you didn't even say goodnight

Nini and Haohao fell in love a year ago, but the only downside was their long-distance relationship. Nini demands to make a phone call every day after work and say goodnight before going to bed at night. Sometimes, Nini would call over, but every day with the same topic, time, and greetings, both of them felt a bit tired.

For Nini's suspicion, he would have tried to explain it at first, but as time passed, he actually felt mentally tired now.

But his avoidance quickly lowered Nini's sense of security, leading to increasing suspicion and questioning. Repeatedly and repeatedly, at first, Haohao would appear by Nini's side as soon as she cried. But once Haohao left, Nini began to separate and "resist" similar situations, either crying, anxious, decreased appetite, or even insomnia. And being tossed around by Nini is getting more and more exhausting.

He clearly hoped that Nini could be more independent. But this cold expression only resulted in Nini's growing suspicion. In the end, both of them no longer wanted to endure this relationship and just wanted to escape quickly. This long-distance relationship ended in failure.

Although the final indifference and fatigue put an end to this relationship, it cannot be denied that it was Nini's severe lack of security and constant suspicion in this intimate relationship that led to what happened later.

People who lack a sense of security will always do something to destroy their true trust in an intimate relationship.

There are usually two situations: either desperately monitoring the other party, checking posts, checking chat records, or even running to print the communication records of the other party's phone. It is not difficult to find that this is a desire for control derived from a lack of security.

And in the above case, Nini, just because she didn't say goodnight properly, once her sense of security decreased, she began to doubt constantly, to the point where she hated herself for being like this.

Although to some extent, Nini's lack of security is due to her long-distance relationship, the root cause is still her lack of security, which leads to a certain degree of separation anxiety.

If our intimate relationship with partners is about finding a replica template of "ideal parents" and presenting childhood attachment styles through "real parents", in psychology, there is a type of attachment called "rebellious attachment".

People with this type of attachment relationship will be constantly vigilant about their mother's departure due to a lack of security, and will strongly resist her departure, causing great distress. When the mother returns, she seeks contact with her mother while also being vigilant about the next separation. Therefore, in intimate relationships, she shows a desire to have intimacy while often resisting, just like the example of Nini in the above case.

This is a form of rebellious attachment relationship caused by a lack of security.

In this issue of 'Psychology Gate', we often want to control each other due to our inner needs, but in fact, control is a two-way process. When you control someone, you may feel that everything is under control and you are safe, but in reality, you are also being controlled by this gaze. What controls you is not others, but your own way of choosing. This is especially true in romantic relationships, where there is no purely secure attachment relationship, and this sense of security requires internal giving rather than external. If there is an increase in inner determination, then naturally there is a decrease in suspicion and pain. If a happy attachment relationship that makes people feel at ease doesn't need to be controlled, let's think about it, right?

7 Be a Secure Attachment Holder

He is like a tree planted by streams of water, which yields its fruit in season and whose leaf does not wither.

——Old Poetry 1:3

The second form of insecurity is lack of love.

Now let's take a look at the second scenario:

Nini and Haohao fell in love at first sight at a blind date, but unfortunately it was a long-distance relationship. Nini always makes it seem like it doesn't matter whether he's here or not, she still plays her own game. This makes Hao feel very frustrated.

I will come over on Friday, let's have a meal together, "suggested Haojin actively over the phone. He thought Nini would show a very happy expression.

Konini only received a casual, neither cold nor indifferent 'hmm' in return.

He thought it was his arranged program that made Nini uninterested, so he suggested going to the movies together.

I heard that the movie "Monster Hunt" starring Bai Baihe has been released. I remember you said you like watching this kind of movie. After dinner, let's go watch it

Still a 'hmm'.

Thinking hard, I can't figure it out. Is it because my charm is not enough? Why does Nini still look indifferent even though she is already my girlfriend? Xiaobie is better than newlyweds.

On Friday, the company gave a last-minute notice to hold a meeting. With apologies, they called and said they couldn't come. Nini also looked indifferent and didn't feel the loss she had imagined.

On the day when the two had no choice but to break up, ask Nini carefully, "Have you ever loved me?" Nini does not deny loving her well, but what is the reason behind Nini's attitude and way of loving?

It's better not to love than to fear separation. This is Nini's lack of love, she no longer has the ability to love.

In intimate attachment relationships, there is a psychological term called "avoidant attachment". This situation is quite rare. In infancy and early childhood, it is referred to as an attachment free baby. It doesn't matter whether the intimate caregiver is present or not, but fundamentally, it is still caused by a lack of security. Like the first case, it belongs to negative attachment.

It's still the story of Nini and her good long-distance relationship, the third case.

Unlike the previous two cases, Nini and Haohao are lovers who have been in a long-distance relationship for 5 years, but their relationship is as beautiful as the first encounter in life.

What did you have for dinner tonight? "I asked earnestly on WeChat. Nini took a bowl of white porridge and attached a self portrait of a pale face.

What's wrong? Are you sick? "Haojin hurriedly called to greet anxiously.

Hmm. I have a slight cold. I caught a cold by kicking the blanket last night

It's all my fault for not taking care of you by your side. I'll take a leave of absence and come back to see you right away. Please ask the HR department for leave immediately.

Hey, there's no need to take a leave, why bother with work? I'm not a child anymore

It's great that he came back in time. His care and careful nurturing didn't just stop at sweet words, which made Nini understand and affirm that she was the only one in her heart.

Nini herself does not lack a sense of security, and taking good care of her truly deepens her inner sense of security.

Sometimes, Nini would send the movie clips she went to watch to Haohao, and Haohao would watch them again in another city. When they met on weekends, the two would chat about interesting topics.

It has been five years, but the two of them are still like first love, always having endless topics to talk about, creating endless freshness and romance.

Five years was the agreed upon deadline for their long-distance relationship, and they eventually achieved success. In these five years, two lovers full of security have been working hard and striving for true reunion. Five years is enough to achieve one of our dreams, and when we get together, we can work together to advance towards the next dream.

The two people in the third case are both secure attachments, seeing each other as safe bases. When their lover is present, they feel secure enough to actively explore and operate in unfamiliar situations, such as achieving their dreams more actively. There will be no strong sense of insecurity when it comes to the departure of a lover or encountering unfamiliar people and things in a strange city.

When it comes to a sense of security, where does it come from?

To be precise, the establishment of a sense of security occurs before the age of three. If there is not enough attention received during infancy and secure attachment is not well established, then in the later stages of growth, if one can complete the replication of intimate relationships in an environment of unconditional love, have a certain degree of self-awareness in spiritual growth, and have a strong desire to repair, then perhaps under positive guidance, new growth can be achieved in the soul.

This sense of "self-healing" security is equivalent to "secure attachment". It is necessary for someone in an intimate relationship to consistently provide unconditional positive attention to complete the task, or for experienced psychologists to use counseling techniques positively to guide improvement. At this point, if the visitor projects too much of the emotions of past important figures onto the analyst, then "empathy" occurs.

A truly secure person's sense of security comes from deep within, not from someone else's spiritual support. Only by establishing a strong sense of security within oneself can the soul achieve greater growth. People with a strong sense of security are more capable of achieving self actualization, and are more likely to achieve great success and happiness in their life plans.

Couples in long-distance relationships can express their feelings through advanced communication media, such as small gatherings on weekends, where their thoughts and souls fall in love with you more than their bodies. This may be the biggest advantage of long-distance relationships. But it's best to develop a reasonable plan for this relationship, including how to work hard to truly be together and the duration of a long-distance relationship.

If there were no such deadline, long-distance relationships would be like an abyss with no visible horizon, making the words "together" so distant and unrealistic like fireworks in the night sky. Although brilliant, it is just a flash in the pan on your life's love path. What is the meaning of it?

Just like how we achieve our goals, if we exceed the deadline but show no improvement, we really have to consider how to adjust our future path.

Wishing all Nini and their loved ones in the world to be well together, to believe in what they should believe in, to stick to what they should stick to, and to harvest their own true love.

Explanation of this issue's "Psychology Gate": If someone wants to forever curl up in a "shell" due to fear, is it equivalent to choosing to keep themselves in the "incubation period" forever and refusing to grow up. You should know that although it may be hurt to step out and gaze at the diversity of this world, if we turn the scars of each year into some kind of "medal" of experience, we may gain the strength to walk more steadily and smoothly in the future.

8 Choice in Love

like silver refined in a furnace of clay, purified seven times.

—— **"Old Poetry" 12:6**

Introduction: You don't understand why someone decided to stop without you shouting 'stop'? Don't you understand that even though you have your heart set on the bright moon, Xiang Wang has intentions and the goddess is ruthless?

George Bernard Shaw, an outstanding British modern realist playwright and Nobel laureate in literature, once said, "There are two tragedies in life. One is despair; the other is complacency

In love and marriage, whether it's tragedy or comedy, and regardless of who it is, everyone has the right to choose. When love sheds the glamorous cloak of magic, only the cruelty of reality remains to be faced. Making rational choices may also be a true maturity.

A friend recently sent me a private message asking: A long time ago, he wanted to break up with his girlfriend. He knew very well that they had no outcome, but for some reason, every time he made a choice, it was extremely difficult for him. It seemed that he couldn't make a normal satisfactory choice, and in severe cases, he would panic, panic, and even sweat profusely, leading to the inability to make a choice in the end. And such situations only occur in emotional decision-making. Speaking of this, even he himself felt both amused and amused.

George Bernard Shaw, an outstanding British modern realist playwright and Nobel laureate in literature, once said, "There are two tragedies in life. One is despair; the other is complacency

In psychology, there is a term called 'choice phobia', also known as choice difficulty disorder. Choosing fear is clearly a lack of confidence and avoidance of responsibility, a lack of self-reliance, and a fear of failure. People who suffer from this disease will face extremely difficult choices, and they may even be caught up in the daily dilemma of whether to choose to have dinner and take a shower or to have dinner after taking a shower. Fortunately, the above cases only occurred in emotional choices.

In situations where it is difficult to make a decision, aside from the complex and intricate nature of emotions themselves, the main reasons for this are: firstly, the inability to determine one's most important inner needs and achieve psychological balance; 2、 Afraid of bearing the consequences of a decision; 3、 To project dissatisfaction onto oneself as a disguised reaction and avoid oneself.

Let's call this phenomenon love choice disorder for now. On the opposite side of this phenomenon: there is a type of person who has had many experiences, or although they have not had much experience in this area, they have a high level of understanding. When choosing a partner for marriage, once chosen, they are often quite loyal. That is to say, in his inner world, it is already very clear what kind of relationship men and women should develop into, what he should gain from this intimate relationship, and what kind of commitment and responsibility he can give to the other party. Such people have a more appropriate pursuit of marriage and are more rational in their choices. For example, not only should we get along well, but we should also be able to survive, promote progress, or grow mutually beneficial. Marriage should provide both parties with greater space and opportunities for success, or better meet our psychological needs for career, social relationships, and self-development. That is to say, in more mature romantic relationships, such pairing choices are one plus one greater than two. Compared to relying solely on emotional intimacy for a living, it is more secure and solid.

That is to say, choosing someone who has both emotions and is suitable for oneself in multiple aspects can bring a strong sense of security to an intimate relationship.

In addition, I have found that friends with selective anxiety disorder tend to have a tendency towards pursuing so-called perfection.

How to overcome it?

Here, we will only analyze this case:

First of all, let's ask ourselves how well I understand this kind of self, what kind of life I really want in this intimate relationship, what kind of growth I can achieve, and then what I can give. We can temporarily ignore the returns, but we must be clear about where our bottom line lies.

If what the other party wants far exceeds the bottom line you can give, then you can only rely on compromising and distorting your self-awareness in exchange for a brief aggregation, and such a relationship is fragile.

In a mature romantic relationship, if the above is already clear, it is not difficult to manage oneself and firmly accept a choice. When faced with difficulties in making choices, we can try to choose only one option without considering more, focusing only on the word "suitable" and firmly completing the choice. When the choice is made, there is no need to regret, no comparison, just believe that your choice is actually the most suitable positive psychological suggestion for yourself.

Through such positive psychological suggestion, one can completely overcome the shadow of emotional choice disorder.

If you are too conflicted and want to figure out how to take the road under your feet, you can also adopt the method of "comparing advantages and disadvantages" to help yourself make clearer choices. For example, in the above case, when the friend feels difficult and doesn't know how to make a decision, they can take out a pen and paper beside them, list the ten advantages of making this choice on one hand, and list the ten disadvantages of not making this choice on the other hand. By comparing the two, they can definitely help themselves, see the results of their choice more clearly, and make a decision accordingly.

At the same time, we should all learn to appreciate ourselves in intimate relationships.

Only through genuine self appreciation can one truly appreciate others on this basis. Encourage and appreciate the growth gained from intimate relationships, thereby strengthening and promoting the healthy development of intimate relationships.

This also applies to intimate friendships, parental relationships, and the creation of a harmonious cultural environment around us.

As long as the above points are achieved, the inner sense of security is strengthened from the inside out, and one can better understand where to go.

In love and marriage, whether it's tragedy or comedy, and regardless of who it is, everyone has the right to choose. When love sheds the glamorous cloak of magic, only the cruelty of reality remains to be faced. Making rational choices may also be a true maturity.

A truly mature person's way of life is stable, and many choices tend towards this direction, thus possessing the ability to obtain happiness from a smile on their heart. In a calm and peaceful relationship with the surroundings, one can read everything with just one glance and understand everything with ease. So... be grateful for what we have, fill our hearts with love full of positive energy, be safe and secure, and our souls will be rich and satisfied. With such the ability for happiness, what beauty in this world is there that we cannot create or possess?

Psychological Gate: Guarding Happiness 8- The Right to Choose in Love

In love, each of us has the right to choose. Less pain brings more joy and happiness, and we are grateful. May a pure white lotus blossom bloom in all the darkness, like a fleeting moment, knowing how to cherish and love, silently closing my eyes, my heart empty, only wishing for peace.

————The End————

9 Loving kindness and honesty, righteousness and peace, meeting and matchmaking

> Love and faithfulness meet together;righteousness and peace kiss each other.
>
> - "Old Poetry" 85:10

Recently, the topic of "whether cheating men deserve forgiveness" seems to have been heated up again. It's like a home cooking recipe such as Fried Rice with eggs. It doesn't feel bored after repeated frying.

The woman who came to me for consultation last night and cried uncontrollably in a video has been troubled, anxious, and insomnia due to the aforementioned issues.

What are you planning to do? "I listened for nearly 50 minutes before asking her at the end of the consultation.

I don't plan on doing anything, I plan on breaking through with that man. He wants to divorce me and be with the little fairies outside. Then I must make him peel off his skin and make him afraid of women in the future! "The woman gritted her teeth and hated him until her teeth itched.

I didn't say anything, I just showed her the small mirror lying on the table.

She was suddenly taken aback, paused, and said, 'Teacher, how did you...' It was a twisted and grotesque face, and she suddenly realized it herself.

Actually, the way you don't lose your temper, your facial features are very delicate and almost perfect, "I said lightly." It's a pity that even the most beautiful woman may experience aesthetic fatigue one day. If your affection is only based on appearance and lacks the depth of your soul, it won't last long. If you do this, he may be afraid and come back to you because of fear, but he's not afraid of all women, but afraid of turning yourself into a woman with such a face

I don't care, anyway I'm not doing well, and he can't think of doing well either. "The woman fell into hysteria, completely forgetting the beauty of their first encounter, and even though this beauty was fleeting, must it be completely denied?

If he chooses to come back, do you still want him

This question stopped the woman, "Don't... you should, but he still needs to peel off a layer of skin to make it possible

The woman has already come up with a revenge plan, and no matter how the man chooses, she will definitely repay ten times the damage he caused her.

She did this just to let him know how painful the dagger he once plunged into her heart was!

Does it have to be like this

She was caught in a contradiction.

Regarding the issue of "infidelity" in marriage, love, and relationships, many women have a psychological attachment similar to "sexual cleanliness obsession". Women care about sexual relationships deep in their hearts, just like men care about money in their minds, but there are also special cases, and this is just a general situation.

Perhaps two people who were once deeply loved, deeply hurt and betrayed each other, and then forced to be together, squeezed under the same roof, for both sides, perhaps their love has long disappeared. So what is the reason for women's current dilemma?

Firstly, the exclusivity of sexual relationships. That's why that woman wants that man back, but in her heart, she can't accept him anymore. This kind of emotional response is usually related to personality traits. Paranoid people are prone to it, and dependent personalities are also prone to it, that is, "You belong to me, you used to belong to me, so even if I no longer need you, you cannot have the right to choose a new love

Secondly, there is a fear of living independently and facing the future alone, as one has not yet formed an independent and complete personality. The occurrence of such phenomena is usually closely related to one's own economic ability, independence, and self-confidence. Many people like to describe being together as a habit, but in fact, it is the underlying reason behind it. When two semicircles meet and merge into a circle, even if they no longer love or betray each other, no one can live without each other unless they find someone suitable to take care of them. This is true for both men and women. Unless one's personality has grown into a complete circle, then at this point, one can "come and go, leave it to oneself, and do as one pleases

Thirdly, the wounds deep within the soul have not healed. Not only does it need to be repaired, but it is also in the stage of mutual counterattack damage, persisting in the entanglement of mutual damage. You won't be happy, and neither will he, but the precious second half of their lives will be spent on such things, meaningless and without a future.

Until when did this situation persist? When each other's energy is depleted and exhausted, there will be a desire to stop, and only then can we think about healing in solitude. Then there will be more calls for help from family and friends, but preferably a psychological counselor.

Fourthly, the current societal values of marriage and love. Is the cheating party worthy of forgiveness? This article is tentatively defined as the perspective of male infidelity, because due to the established recognition of social values, many times similar issues do not have the ability to be treated equally. For example, when a woman cheats, there is usually only one option - divorce. And the man's infidelity, such as the "article" in the first half of the year, was met with a flood of "scumbag" insults on the internet during that period. However, six months later, with Mrs. Ma Yili's magnanimous forgiveness, the couple appeared together in the same film and made a comeback, becoming another "hero" without waiting for eighteen years. From the overall existing social perspective, regarding infidelity, men are still mostly tolerant.

The reason why my visitor is conflicted is also due to the fourth point mentioned above, because of the tendency of social values. It seems that nowadays, if you don't recognize it, you are a "weirdo".

But is that so? Everyone is born unique, don't forget yourself because of the conformity effect.

The reality is, if you have been hurt by someone and have seriously betrayed your emotions, because a part of the public recognizes and accepts it, do you not have the right to choose?

Both men and women have the right to choose their new love, so you also have the right to choose your future life. The key is, what kind of life do you want? Do you wish for a new future? Or, do you give yourself the right to make such a choice?

For everyone, individual feelings are the most important key. Men can choose what they love and stay away from their original family, and women can also choose to live in a way that makes them happy. The saying 'One parting, two widening, each brings joy' conveys a profound meaning: what you need to pay attention to and respect the most is your own inner needs and feelings, rather than caring about who thinks, who says, and how the public judges comment. Everyone has their own life, and no matter what, besides the topics of conversation after meals, it cannot determine their true life.

You may choose a cheating partner to continue adapting to life, or you can pack up all your old bags and take big steps forward. Sometimes, we hesitate because of habit, and also because we are afraid of changing old framework patterns to embrace new innovations and the reconstruction of new cognitive structures. But on a deeper level of self exploration, there is still a small self deprecating and abused little person in your heart, perhaps hidden in your subconscious level, that needs you to listen carefully - the voice deep in your heart: What do I really want?

Oscar Wilde once said, 'Narcissism is the beginning of a person's romance.' Those intimate lovers who hesitate and don't know whether to forgive their cheating partners make the biggest mistake of not being narcissistic enough. You don't believe that you deserve to be treated with devotion, you don't believe that you will meet a better partner in the future, you don't believe that leaving a cheating partner, life will eventually be colorful and colorful.

As long as there is one partner in this world who does not cheat, he will bump into your arms, perhaps a handsome or beautiful man... at least someone who is suitable for each other. If you have such confidence, then forgiving your cheating partner is not a difficult problem at all.

Of course, the confidence mentioned here is not the indiscriminate abuse of self hypnosis and positive reinforcement methods. As someone often says: Wang Po sells melons and boasts about herself, then you also need to have melons that are worth buying, preferably sweet and delicious.

So, by leveraging your existing strengths and building confidence on this foundation, you can maintain your qualities in a harmonious relationship with each other, have love and honesty, encounter and date, and even have a rich inner peace in understanding and cherishing your own excellence.

So how should we rebuild our own value, or rediscover our own value?

Psychological Gate: Guarding Happiness 9- Love, Honesty, Justice, Peace, Meeting and Matchmaking

Explanation of this issue's "Psychology Gate": If we have been repeating self deception, deception, and being deceived all our lives, then "treating each other sincerely" is already the most basic life practice. The first thing we can do is to be sincere with our little one, and both happiness and hardship are our own changes and choices. Just like whether to change or not, it all depends on the voice of your soul. Believe in beauty, believe in yourself, and you will eventually be safe.

10 We are in the same world, indifferent, tolerant, and cherished

Love can use wisdom, kindness, courage to forgive love of self deception, finally embrace each other.

——The Old Proverbs 10:12

Psychological knowledge and grief management: Perhaps someone is far away from you in physical space, and some people may interpret such experiences as completely or permanently losing that person, which may lead to falling into grief. If one cannot experience the beautiful emotions they once enjoyed between each other, it may also lead to a sense of loss or emptiness. Separation anxiety, imagination that is not equivalent to 'reality', or when desires or dreams are seriously not equivalent to reality, can all lead to a sense of loss or emptiness. This is the experience of sadness.

Here, we will introduce two types of grief experiences and coping strategies for 'Passing Through Your World'. I Belonged to You "is an adaptation of the novel of the same name by Zhang Jiajia. Directed by Zhang Yibai and starring

Deng Chao, Bai Baihe, Yang Yang, and others, it is a romantic, literary, and micro comedy film that was released in China on September 29, 2016.

What the hell are you going to lose

Roll the sheets

Hello, Teacher Chen Mo. I am Yaoji

Hello, Yaoji. I'm Whiteboard. Ha, hey, whoa~

This is Chen Mo.

A man who seems indifferent to everything, a man who seems to speak without restraint and doesn't even bother to be serious about the new intern girl in Taiwan, but has always hidden a sentence in his heart, a seemingly ambiguous past, a warm vacancy that needs to be filled.

If I don't live in your heart, I'll die in a foreign land

Every day, Chen Mo confronts the ace DJ Xiao Rong (played by Du Juan) because he has been on equal footing with the high minded Du Juan since his college days, from being reckless in his youth to being stubborn in his mouth. He once said, "Whoever marries you will have eight hundred lifetimes of blood mold. How about this, I'll be at a disadvantage, I'll marry you

The film showcases three love stories, which, if combined with psychological perspectives and reality, can be accurately described as two ambiguous and seemingly ambiguous stories, one genuine love story, and three missed stories.

Although there are many scenes in the film that tell the story of two brothers other than Chen Mo, as well as the love patterns they portray, or the ways people view love from different perspectives.

In this film, due to the kind matchmaking of Yaoji, Xiaorong played by Dujuan once said to Chen Mo: For you, love is enough. For me, suitability is what matters.

Here, please forgive me for only wanting to analyze Chen Mo's emotional patterns based on the psychological approach to grief management.

At first, Chen Mo thought he admired Dujuan, but after Dujuan said "not suitable", he became decadent and looked like a "waste material".

Previously, with just a casual remark, he could warm the hearts of many people through the radio waves. I hope to have someone like you, like the refreshing breeze in the mountains... as long as it's you in the end

Perhaps many people don't understand, but after encountering Yaoji, they are hit hard by one sentence from Yaoji: "You have warmed the hearts of so many people before, why can't you be here anymore ?

You know you can

That's because those who give warmth are also in a period of lack of warmth or self adjustment, so there may be self deprecation of self-worth, slackness, and speaking without restraint that Chen Mo appears in the film

Why do men always keep desserts in their refrigerators

Not Speaking "is a song written by Huang Weiwen and composed and performed by Li Ronghao. It is the theme song of the" Passing Through Version "of the movie" Passing Through Your World ". I only excerpted this line from the entire song because Chen Mo is a big boy who needs to" keep desserts in the fridge ".

When it comes to emotional experiences, if you don't know how to handle them in moderation, just like this ice cold, you will lose your direction of progress. The only thing that can evoke warmth is warmth. So after losing the warmth of his inner love experience, Chen Mo will only behave like a person with warmth when other warmth naturally arises, such as brotherhood.

In our life journey, everyone may experience important losses. So, it is necessary to flexibly respond to different types of emotional grief by using a quick way to handle grief.

If we look at it from the most basic level, it seems that most people are more concerned about Chen Mo's emotional loss, so he obtained the image of a pure water like girl like Yao Ji to save him. This kind of companionship and comfort is also an urgent grief treatment for Chen Mo's emotional loss.

And at the end of the film, he gained a revelation that he kept the souvenir of the pure girl Yao Ji, a mask of a hairy monkey, chose to let go of that inappropriate and seemingly ambiguous emotion, and chose to continue moving forward.

Although he seemed to have missed the Rooster, he still requested all listeners in Chongqing to flash their lights and search for the Rooster who had saved him under the same starry sky on the show.

When the whole Chongqing was praying for his beautiful wishes, Chen Mo had unknowingly achieved a new peak in his career recovery. The flashing lights of those listeners were the best proof, and it was also his special thoughts on the beautiful imprint of a pure water girl like Yaoji.

Moreover, even without a chicken, he can still choose to move forward.

Some people associate the warm experience of love with their sense of self-worth in their career. Such people usually do not express the warmth of losing their love experience, but instead seize another experience to temporarily replace it when one experience is lost. This may help repair some of the sadness, but it cannot completely repair it.

This belongs to the self healing approach in grief management, and it is also a form of silent and indifferent grief self healing.

The setting of the characters in the film is quite misplaced, as Chen Mo is not silent and hides his grief in a careless way, which is an alternative form of silence. Only pure water like Yaoji can be used as a "medicine guide" to open up his self grief and self healing methods, while Xiaorong is the ultimate silent self grief processor. What she needs is to be understood correctly by the right people.

I wish there was someone like you, but dusk and youth cannot recognize each other... You love to silently listen to the world, please move forward, don't look back. "This film insert song sung by Lin Youjia is a self detoxification and self healing process of Xiao Rong's self grief treatment, and it is also Xiao Rong's choice - please move forward, don't look back.

Perhaps many viewers are on the side of sympathizing more with Chen Mo, and instead overlook the seemingly resilient Xiao Rong. In terms of learning and work, she always stands in a higher position than Chen Mo, from the competitive friendship between classmates to the "best partner" in work.

However, the love experience she desires is not only a pleasurable emotional experience, but also a high-quality simultaneous advancement in her career and work. So, when she has a clear understanding of what kind of future she truly wants, she will hide her psychological sadness and emotional loss well, and self heal to look forward to a high-quality life in the future, demanding herself with specialized work.

Chen Mo almost lost her way for a seemingly ambiguous love experience, while Xiaorong is well aware of the blueprint for her future lover, family, and career. Therefore, she may have a hollow and sad experience in the temporary emotional experience, but she cleverly compensates for this emptiness and loneliness with specialized work experience, and exchanges this waiting for the perfect and happy future she wants.

If there is any sadness that Xiao Rong needs to deal with, it is that the collaborator she originally thought had suddenly fled with the money, leaving her to bear it alone.

In such sadness, there is not only a sense of loneliness caused by the lack of emotional experience, but also a temporary lack of self-worth in terms of career and the future she aspires to. This kind of dual psychological grief belongs to serious grief. And perhaps this is more focused on emotional experience, followed by Chen Mo's clear sense of self-worth. By the end of the film, he can also gain true understanding with time.

Perhaps Xiaorong's side, which the vast majority of the audience may not understand, but I think Chen Mo will give her the most silent and special understanding and fulfillment.

Is Xiaorong a woman who is greedy for vanity, or a career oriented woman who is completely ignorant of emotions?

Is Xiaorong really such a woman?

Passing through your entire world, if it's just passing by, I'll be waiting for you at the finish line, as long as it's you in the end!

Bai, what are the words of hydrangea flowers? I forgot... but I still want to say:remember hope

The last thing she wants, only those who truly understand her can understand, whether it is from the perspective of emotional experience or professional expertise, to give and be given. In the depths of her delicate soul, although there is self repair, there is sadness that needs to be completely healed in the long wait for her "ideal" that is completely different from reality. For an extraordinary woman like Xiaorong, unless reality and ideal are equated, her psychological sadness can be fully processed and healed.

Go to the other person's heart and take a look, understand what each other needs the most, and stop embracing each other in loneliness

This radio love song (promotional song for the movie radio version of "Passing by Your World", produced by Mars Radio)

So, from the initial lack of understanding, it was destined that Chen Mo and Xiao Rong would be the most familiar, unfamiliar, intimate, and distant during their initial time. Chen Mo appeared because of the "medicinal introduction" of Yao Ji, because Yao Ji deeply understood him, allowing Chen Mo to learn to understand and grow in silence, as well as the special mark of longing for a woman like Yao Ji who once held an umbrella for him.

Just as he may ask at the end of the film's ending theme song, 'What do you want, little chicken?'

But Yaoji wouldn't answer, just like a serene smile that disappeared in the wind, which also relieved Chen Mo's heart knot that he might not have been able to let go of.

The ending theme song of "You Wait for Me at the End" was composed by Yao Ruolong. When read lightly, it feels somewhat unique:

I have been following the footsteps of your emotions

Misunderstanded by everyone, we must understand you

Get ready to shine like a floating cloud in your sky

But you're waiting for me at the finish line, with raindrops in your laughter

I am willing to fulfill your cherished past

I just want you to regain the passion that makes you like you

Then he dragged himself to the mountain city to live in seclusion

But you waited for me to live in your heart at the finish line

……

Xiao Rong and Chen Mo both followed Yao Ji's smile that naturally disappeared into the golden sunshine, and they let go of everything, understood the past that should be let go, and the future that should be welcomed and picked up. Without looking back, just move forward.

Psychological Gate: Protecting Happiness "10. We are in the same world, indifferent, tolerant, and cherished

In the moment when psychological grief is properly handled and cured, the truly right person will be pulled into the most beautiful private collection of memories, just like the most beautiful imprint of time. Hold up your chest, lift your head, and welcome the realization, perfection, present, and future of your dreams.

Psychological Gate · **Psychological Film and Television Password**

Main introduction: From popular or classic movies and TV shows, besides seeing fun, humor, humor, suspense, tension, and fantasy creativity, what other differences can we see? What unique insights do psychologists have from their perspective? Let's see how psychologists perceive these novel and unique wonders of film and television dramas? I believe this psychological film code will give you a different feeling.

1 'Despicable Me': How to Rebirth (Part 1)

Blessed is the man who does not walk in the counsel of the wicked or stand in the way of sinners or sit in the seat of mockers.

——Old Poetry 1:1

Release information: "Despicable Me" is a 2010 comedy 3D animated film produced by Universal Pictures and Illumination Entertainment, directed by Chris Reynolds and Pierre Coffin.

I have a strong preference for movies with growth themes, regardless of whether they are science fiction, fantasy, suspense, or animated. As long as the content is appropriate and full of cherished warmth.

Despicable Me, also known as Despicable Me, is a 3D animation produced by Universal Pictures. The plot is roughly as follows: Gru, a big villain who takes becoming the "world's number one villain" as his career and dream, is unwilling to fall behind an arrogant newcomer thief - Vector's unfair competition behavior. So he decided to be more despicable and shameless, and decided to adopt three orphans who had sold him cookies but were rejected by him - Margo, Edith, and Agnes. He took advantage of their opportunity to enter the vector castle and sell cookies to commit theft, intending to secretly dispose of them after the plan was successful. However, in ordinary daily interactions, Gru developed feelings for these three little girls. In order not to affect the meticulous moon stealing plan, Gru had to send the three children back to the orphanage. But when his plan succeeded, the vector kidnapped the children. The ending is that Gru rescued three little devils and the moon returned to space.

At the end of the story, a despicable and shameless villain becomes a true "thief daddy", completing his growth and being able to feel loved and give love.

So, how does a person with a cold heart form and how does they repair themselves and achieve rebirth?

Childhood empathy failure can directly lead to narcissistic fragility. In childhood, we need parents to give us a feeling of being cared for, praised, and protected. If during this period, children can achieve successful long-term empathy, then their inner needs can be met, the energy for their growth is not fixed, and they can also smoothly grow physically and mentally.

Empathy, proposed by the founder of humanism, Rogers, refers to the ability to experience the inner world of others, that is, to open one's mind and see the world, similar to seeing the world with your own eyes. In empathetic relationships, communication is barrier free, and both the receiver and the recipient will experience empathy, emotions, and thoughts. This point was also mentioned in my urban novel 'Manman Unparalleled'.

However, Gru in the film did not receive such treatment since childhood. His mother seemed to be his only guardian during his childhood, but she seemed to have been burying her head in doing her own things. For children, even if they sit aside, it's a pity that they are more focused on themselves. No matter how much Gru tried to attract his mother's attention during his childhood, he received a dismissive response.

One day, he discovered that there was another way to catch his mother's attention, which was to get her attention when he misbehaved. Although the duration of their gaze is still brief, for a child who desperately desires parental attention, this is undoubtedly equivalent to discovering the 'treasure of Alibaba'.

Such brief attention may not be enough for a child, but it does not affect a child like Gru, who lacked empathy during childhood, from drinking poison to quench their thirst.

So he learned to hide his disappointment, not being understood, not being cared for, and even not feeling loved. His heart gradually became cold, learning to isolate the pain of his body and mind, and entrusting himself to be a big villain. This doesn't seem to feel hurt, instead he has become someone who hurts others everywhere. He ignored his understanding of himself and was fixed on the fear point where he couldn't feel love.

So in the movie, we can see him walking down the street and seeing a child crying over ice cream falling to the ground. He pursed his lips and smiled, then magically made a balloon in the shape of a small dog for the child from behind. Just as he noticed the child's face turning from tears to laughter, he used a needle to puncture the balloon and walked away indifferently.

In fact, he is not a villain. He is just using this way to tell every child he meets that the world is cruel, cold, and indifferent. Only by becoming a despicable villain can you avoid being hurt, even if we no longer feel love. This is also the "interpretation" of the love that Gru's mother passed on to him during his childhood.

And when encountering the children from those three orphanages, their innocent and cheerful smiles, is it a turning point for him to regain his life, feel loved and be loved, and improve his own growth?

The spell to break this curse is: to obtain true love and care, until the moment he understands the importance of giving.

I can't help but think of many parents who "accompany" their children nowadays, playing with their phones, following stocks, WeChat, and doing various things of their own, thinking that this is companionship. The body is there, but the mind cannot better connect with each other. At least, every time the child around us calls out our specific title - "parents" - many times before they can refocus their attention on the child.

If love is true, it is the long-term protection and companionship of the body and mind. After all, like the 'despicable me' - Gru, who grew up to meet people who helped him complete his growth, such opportunities are not many, are they?

Explanation for this issue (Psychology): Extreme goodness and extreme evil often lie within a single thought. Where you want to stay depends on whether you are willing to let negative emotions control your behavior.

2 "Despicable Me": How to Rebirth (Part 2)

The price of wisdom is beyond rubies.

——Old Uncle 28:18

The film 'Despicable Me' was filmed in two installments. In the first part, Gru, who is cold and indifferent, meets three sweet little cuties. Perhaps it was fate's arrangement that allowed him to learn something.

He is so indifferent, so impatient, and keeps saying that he is a 'big villain'. In order to use three cute children to enter a competitor's castle and steal a miniature gun, he had to temporarily stay with them. He told himself that it was only for a while. He doesn't want to be attached, he's just a big villain. He may realize that he is' incapable of love '.

Love incompetence, also known as emotional incompetence. They show indifference to others and use various forms of avoidance to avoid entering into deep attachment relationships. If broadly understood, the term 'love incapable' here refers not only to love, but also to the sense of powerlessness in all deeply attached intimate relationships.

Upon investigation, it is likely that there is a frozen place deep within the heart that has yet to be healed. So, once encountering deep attachment emotions, one instinctively avoids and curls up.

So he ignored the obvious attachment and friendliness of the three cute children towards him. He doesn't understand respect, nor does he need respect. He didn't know these things at first. So, when he used dog food boxes as their lunch boxes and used defective missiles as their beds. When the youngest Agnes pitifully and sincerely asked him to tell a story, he chose to habitually escape, leaving her with a cold back

The love of the powerless is just a compulsive repetition in such a way, telling others, 'I have been treated so coldly and cruelly before.' That is the voice of his soul, but he himself is not aware of it.

Everything is so understandable. You can't force someone who hasn't learned how to walk to run immediately. But the key is how to make such people understand and learn one day, and complete this initial growth, which is the key to healing.

In fact, perhaps in the film, Gru has a desire for happy attachment in his heart. Why do you think so? Looking at the group of silly and silly Minions around him, it's clear at a glance.

No matter how bad the situation is, I will always be silly and happy, worship the boss infinitely, have no doubts, and be absolutely attached and loyal. This is the biggest trait of Minions. However, only robots can meet such requirements. Gru set them up as obedient and silly based on his inner needs. In his world, he had already received enough cold treatment during childhood, so he was tired of all opposing voices, only admiration, joyful cheers, and absolute loyalty. But such a setting also limits one's own growth.

Until he met three children.

Why were these three children the ones who initiated his inner transformation and self-healing function?

Firstly, all three children are orphans who are very eager to be loved and cared for, and can achieve strong attachment (so that those who are unable to love can feel it), even if it is an adopter who was not very good to them at the beginning.

Secondly, no matter how the incapable of love resist, the close distance in space will gradually shorten the psychological distance through daily interaction, thus completing everyone's psychological return. Being up close is already a natural psychological reward. That's why many long-distance relationships end in vain.

Thirdly, when Gru tricked the three children into an amusement park and wanted to abandon them, he saw disappointment, frustration, sadness, and a sense of powerlessness from the eyes, faces, and expressions of the three young children due to the attack of unscrupulous merchants

This psychological phenomenon of empathy inadvertently activated Gru's self-healing function. Because he seemed to see his childhood self from an orphan who had no place to rely on, the person who had been neglected and treated coldly by his mother for a long time.

The film ends with the joyful voices of children and Minions. Gru completes self-healing, opens up his heart, and establishes a deep attachment relationship with the three children, thus learning and understanding the need to respect each other and a sense of responsibility throughout history.

Because at the end of the film, he used a self-made yarn finger drawing book to tell the children the story of three little cats, so loving

If he cannot fulfill these requirements for self growth in the first part, he will not have the ability to feel love after meeting Lucy in the second part. Of course, that's another topic.

Explanation for this issue (Psychology): On the path of spiritual growth, only by constantly exploring and analyzing the hidden subconscious can we understand our true needs and gain the inner drive to improve ourselves.

3 "Despicable Me": How to Rebirth (3)

For evil men will be cut off.

—— "Old Poetry" 37:9

S. in Love V. R theory: acquaintance, similarity, complementarity

After a passionate outcry, the second installment of 'Despicable Me' was grandly released. Gru, who originally aspired to become an international villain, washed his hands and began to take on the responsibility of becoming three cute and good fathers. He gave up his original connection with the villainous alliance and began to establish his own legitimate business kingdom. But as a virus called PX-41 was stolen, special agent Lucy appeared in his life. At the same time, the strongest association of the original Evil Alliance also refused to easily forget Gru. His former criminal partner, Mondiago, appeared and tried every means to force Gru to agree to cooperate again in the crime.

In the face of these, Gru's final decision is best portrayed in the family portrait photo at the end of the film.

If analyzed from psychological research, when the old association of evil knocks on the door of the heart again and infinite temptations swarm in, the best self-control and mind are effective weapons to eliminate temptation.

How did Keguru do it?

Firstly, as mentioned in the previous article, he has three cute little ones and has established a deep emotional attachment with them, understanding the meaning of responsibility. Everyone should be responsible for their own actions, their interpersonal relationships, their career blueprint, and self-management.

Secondly, after understanding the responsibilities that a man should fulfill, he also encountered love - Lucy.

If the three children gave him a sense of responsibility, then Lucy's appearance taught him to become stronger, reshape his complete self-worth system, thereby enhancing his mental strength and restraining his addiction.

We have to talk about S. in love here V. According to the R theory, love must go through three stages from acquaintance to marriage: acquaintance, similarity, and complementarity.

The first stage: Regardless of gender, it cannot be denied that both men and women are easily attracted to the attractive appearance of the opposite sex. Beautiful things can easily bring sensory stimulation to people, which is the stage of acquaintance. Gru and Lucy in this film do not have this experience, as Lucy is not of the type that is particularly beautiful and cunning. So, their acquaintance, from "frozen light" to "electric shock lipstick", was just a competition between agents and criminals. Putting aside the attractiveness of appearance and entering into the relationship of understanding may be the dream like pursuit of perfect love for many women. As the female protagonist Wushuang once exclaimed in my novel, "Is there such a person who still loves me when I am old and ugly

I have reservations about the requirement for such a dreamy and ideal perfect love, as the opinions of one family cannot represent everything. But it cannot be denied that such people may really exist.

Phase 2: Mutual recognition of values. But at this stage, the other party's thoughts, attitudes, values, etc. will gradually emerge. The true integration at this stage is an important factor in determining whether the two get along well. Similarity will be valued at this stage, including unconscious imitation. People are all advanced animals that learn from each other. When Gru finally defeated his former criminal partner Mondiago in Lucy's usual way, Lucy, who was tied to a missile, showed a recognized smirk on her face and said, "Roar... he's learning from me

Phase Three: Entering into marriage, placing greater emphasis on complementarity. A mature and stable marriage relationship should be one where men cultivate and women weave, each fulfilling their respective duties. The two have different identities and roles, and the responsibilities assigned to them in the marriage are different, but their status is equal. Such a balanced relationship is the 'code' that sustains a long-lasting marriage that can grow together.

Just like in the film, Gru and Lucy, aside from their perilous love experiences, Gru's youngest daughter Agnes is unable to recite hymns of praise for her mother due to her lack of concept of "mother". And Lucy's appearance made this big family complete, filling the gap in the hearts of the three children's love for their mother, and unintentionally healing Gru's erroneous perception of "love" since childhood. More importantly, Lucy, who possesses independent wisdom and insights, is also a good partner for Gru's career achievements. In the above points, Lucy's role and function are not random.

In fact, whether it is love or marriage, from the perspective of interpersonal relationships, it is a mutual healing and growth between our body and mind. A good marriage and love relationship should be mutually nourishing. Any one party's bias can cause energy blockage or depletion, and cannot sustain each other for a long time.

4 Minions: How to enjoy attachment in intimate relationships? (1)

Turn from evil and do good;then you will dwell in the land forever.

——Old Poetry 37:27

Release information: "Minions with Big Eyes" is a 2015 American comedy animated film directed by Kyle Balda and Piel Coffin, voiced by Sandra Bullock, Piel Coffin, and Steve Carell, and co produced by Illumination Entertainment and Universal Pictures.

The film tells the history of Minions and their quest to find a powerful new owner and assist them in completing their evil deeds. Set in several major cities such as London and New York, the film was released in 3D and IMAX 3D formats in China on September 13, 2015.

When Nini appeared at the door of my consultation room with a tired look on her face, I was watching the recently released "Minions with Big Eyes" on September 15, 2015. This is a spin off of the successful movie 'Despicable Me'. As Minions with an independent language system and distinct personalities, it is not an exaggeration to call them 'professional screen snatchers'.

Perhaps Nini was tired. During her visit this time, she didn't show any impatience at all. Instead, she accompanied me through the final ending before saying, "If only I had someone as likable as a Minion, how great would it be

Aren't you still likable now? "I closed my computer and asked her with a smile. Nini's problem, like most people who have intimate relationships, is that at the beginning of every relationship, she can attract the attention of the opposite sex, but as the relationship progresses, the intimate connection becomes weaker and weaker.

Any intimate relationship will gradually enter the stage of mutual understanding and knowledge from the initial state of mutual attraction. And as independent individuals, no one can be a highly similar body that perfectly overlaps. To promote a close and friendly relationship in a positive way, of course, adaptation is inevitable.

Konini's problem lies in her inability to correctly face the contradictions between the two parties and adopt effective methods of reconciliation. She is just like the Minions in the movie, who initially wanted to be attached to their intimate partners, but lacked the attachment advantage traits like Minions.

Once faced with a conflict, even if it's just a small matter, when her partner tells her that both parties need some space to calm down, Nini will adopt an extreme approach to pursue and not let go, commonly using "attacking to gain attention". I am angry, I am angry, I attack, and even I pull out a knife at each other. In fact, I just want you to pay attention to me, love me, and make me feel that you love me

This type of 'crazy lover' cannot successfully detach themselves from the peak of negative emotions when encountering conflicts. Instead, they ignore and almost lose their rationality in pursuing all the attention of the 'intimate link body', even resorting to removing all the 'obstacles' that prevent them from obtaining intimate links.

The most typical example is the well-known character Li Mochou in Jin Yong's "The Return of the Condor Heroes".

Asking what love is in the world, and teaching people to commit to life and death, "said Li Mochou, the fairy of Chilian. She is a failed character in her emotional relationship with Lulang, not because she lacks beauty, lacks sufficient attraction to the opposite sex, nor because she lacks good external conditions, including a thriving career, family background, education, etc., but because she cannot regulate the conflicts that arise in her marriage and love relationship.

Lulang hopes that she will have a harmonious and gentle temperament, not easily get angry and hurt innocent people, and kill indiscriminately. She doesn't care, she says, 'I love you,' and then kills someone, or hits someone she thinks may be close to her with just one palm. Lulang already sees these as 'attackers' against her in her cognition, and there is no need to put 'morality' on a rational level anymore.

This should be placed in Nini's relationship, where she and Haohao enter the stage of deep understanding of the relationship through suspicion and doubt, and constantly check Haohao's phone communication records, text messages, QQ, Momo and other chat communication tools to gain an inner sense of security. And such groundless doubts and suspicions are one of the most serious psychological elements that harm this intimate relationship.

Here we need to talk about a concept in psychology about PU, which is Paternity Uncertainty (PU), originally referring to the male's uncertainty about their offspring. Of course, women can always determine who the father of the child in their belly is, but men are inevitably troubled by such relationship uncertainty in this regard.

Someone said, can't we do a paternity test?

Data facts are one thing, but human cognition is deeply rooted in the mind, triggered by specific events that result in neural transmission reactions, followed by inappropriate handling of relationships during emotional peaks.

Just like how Little A hated eating eggs since she was young, but one day someone or a fact told her that eating eggs could help her become smarter. Ask her if something she disliked from childhood to adulthood could cause her to completely change and say, "Oh, I love it so much

In terms of an individual's inherent cognition, this is like a fairy tale, isn't it?

Unless there is a cognitive change, it is difficult to accept and impossible to change habitual processing behavior patterns.

That's why Nini always harbors suspicion and suspicion no matter what kind of intimate relationship she encounters, which is not related to the event itself, but only to her cognition. When we mention that women have high PU, it means that they appear to make men feel uneasy. When we mention that men have high PU, it means that they are not very comfortable with all women. Anyway, this is ultimately related to the development of intimate relationships, where one party's emotional investment in the other even involves investment in future generations.

The way these 'crazy lovers' handle emotional conflicts and express their needs in romantic relationships is actually counterproductive.

You cannot make a wounded and sick person, whose arms and legs have been repeatedly blown off by your 'gunpowder bag', turn back and repeatedly attack you several times.

Even if it's your pet dog, when you beat it hard, whip it, or even cut it with a knife, when it chooses to escape or hide under the bed or in a crevice, you still tirelessly bend down and lie on the bed, calling out to it trembling inside, "Come on, I love you, I need you, come out quickly

May I ask, will that little dog covered in injuries come out?

Even dogs are like this, let alone humans?

So in an intimate relationship, it is not advisable to use constant "attacks" without considering the other person's feelings to gain attention in order to achieve a positive development of the relationship.

Just like a married housewife who has been penetrated by countless mistresses, going crazy, angry, hurt, entangled, and attacking everyone, including your lover, and beating them up together with mistresses and mistresses, that kind of way does not make your lover understand that you actually need his love, but drives him away, faster causing your marriage castle to collapse and disappear.

If you need love and need your loved one to turn back, first learn to love yourself, express your needs well, and communicate in a positive way, which is the best policy.

There is a saying that has been said a hundred or a thousand times: "If you love me, please speak well." However, Minions have always been successful in expressing intimate attachment relationships.

5 Minions: How to enjoy attachment in intimate relationships? (II)

No king is saved by the size of his army;no warrior escapes by his great strength.

——Old Poetry "33:16

Whether in the first and second parts of "Despicable Me" or "Minions with Big Eyes", it is not difficult to find that Minions always have fresh and bright elements of happiness shining on their bodies, deeply attracting people's lips to rise.

From the moment a person is born, regardless of their status, it is difficult to guarantee that they will not encounter any setbacks in life, because there is no "pure emotional vacuum zone" in this world.

Living completely on one's own, disregarding the feelings of those around them, can be called selfishness; However, excessive attention to the words and actions of those around us, constant self suggestion towards oneself, and acceptance of what is happening, from the inherent cognitive reactions in the inner self consciousness, can lead to a lot of troubles. This way of processing information can make people physically and mentally exhausted, and it is no better than the former.

Where is the root of our pain and troubles?

Some people think it's because of what they've encountered and feel regretful about their bad luck throughout their lives. However, when we think about it calmly, the root of our troubles and pain lies not in what we've encountered, but in our inherent cognition in our minds. This is related to the education we've received since childhood and the life experiences we've encountered. But it's precisely the existence of these cognitions that leads us to have certain thoughts or ideas when we encounter certain specific events or symbols, which in turn breeds our troubles.

In short, cognition leads to afflictions, and the key transition point between happiness and afflictions is not what we encounter, but what we want to decide.

Just like the Minions in the movie, whether they are kidnapped to the Big Bad Alliance or injected with PX-41 virus to alter their biological genes, they can always find a genuine smile from self mockery and mutual ridicule among their partners. Because their brains, as single celled organisms, do not feel that they are experiencing unfortunate cognition. Without such cognition, there are naturally no worries.

So, to truly be happy, we need to change our inherent cognition, which is the way we used to view similar issues. This job is a long road that can be taken by professional psychologists to help people with this problem with behavioral cognitive therapy, improve irrational cognition, and even reshape missing personalities.

Cognition refers to a person's understanding and perception of an event or object, their own views, thoughts about others, their understanding of the environment, and their insights into things.

Cognitive behavioral therapy believes that human emotions come from their beliefs, evaluations, interpretations, or philosophical views of the things they encounter, rather than from the things themselves. As A.T. Beck, a leading figure in cognitive therapy, said, "maladaptive behaviors and emotions stem from maladaptive cognition

For example, a person always "thinks" that they haven't performed well enough, even their parents don't like them, so they have no confidence in doing anything, feel insecure, and have a bad mood. The strategy of treatment is to help him rebuild his cognitive structure, re evaluate himself, rebuild confidence in himself, and change the perception that he is "not good".

Cognitive behavioral therapy believes that the goal of treatment is not only to address external manifestations such as behavior and emotions, but also to analyze the patient's thinking activities and strategies for coping with reality, identify erroneous cognition and correct it.

It must be mentioned here - the cognitive "ABC" theory: A refers to activating events that are related to emotions; B refers to beliefs or ideas, including rational or irrational beliefs; C refers to the emotional consequences and behavioral responses related to the event. The relationship between events and reactions: It is generally believed that event A directly triggers reaction C. In fact, there is a mediating factor of B between A and C. The significance or response of A to an individual is influenced by B, that is, it is determined by people's cognitive attitudes and beliefs.

Just like the most common example in marriage and love counseling cases, Nini began to suspect that her long-term travel partner had betrayed her due to the lack of normal communication and interaction at home for a long time. As a result, her partner's parents also had a different attitude towards her, seeming neither cold nor hot towards her. She became an dispensable person at home, not only depressed and anxious, but also unable to feel a sense of presence at home.

When she visited, she almost cried for an hour. Later, I asked her, if your partner is on a long-term business trip but is actually preparing a unique gift for your birthday this year, and their parents are also responsible for concealing this surprise, would you still cry?

She stared at me blankly, her eyes suddenly widening: 'Of course not.'

I told her that your unhappy emotions are all caused by your pessimistic thoughts and beliefs, not the behaviors you have experienced, isn't that correct?

That's why the ancient saying goes, "There is nothing in the world, mediocre people disturb themselves

What you mean is that it was actually my idea, and my thinking conclusion led to all the unhappiness. "She seemed to understand something.

When she left, she turned her head and gave me an apologetic smile, "I'm not feeling that bad anymore. Thank you

Watching her departing figure, I lifted the hollowed out white veil of the countryside, and a ray of sunlight shone into the room, playfully jumping onto the personality test I had just taken for myself as a Minion.

Our lives are short. Since happiness is a day and pain is also a day, why don't we choose to live happily for ourselves?

In life, some people are obsessed with right and wrong, while others are obsessed with gains and losses. However, there is no absolute truth in the world. From some perspectives, perhaps someone has won at a certain point, but they are only obsessed with the biased cognitive concept of "must win". But from another perspective, they may have lost the moderate warmth of laughter and joy that should have been cherished around them.

This is not to say that we cannot cling to our own desires and feelings, but if that attachment carries the power to destroy our body and mind, making us unhappy and unable to feel the breath of happiness, becoming more like a soul crying in the dark night, then perhaps at this time you need a professional psychological counselor.

He can help you distinguish between reasonable ideas and unreasonable ones at the cognitive level, which need to be improved and discarded.

If it is a good cognition or obsession that will not harm the people you care about or innocent people around you, then try to be good at it. At this time, the more you aspire, the more you must go through the wind and rain.

But if this obsession leads to the evil cause and effect, can we still persist in our gains and harm those around us?

A true man (whether male or female), anyone with rational qualities of high intelligence and emotional intelligence, should be able to do what they can afford and let go of.

With good intentions in mind, one's heart becomes pure.

Because happiness and joy can only be given to oneself, if your mind does not have such a function, then you must find a way to learn it.

From a psychological perspective, in addition to "dispersing attention, relaxing training, and fully accepting the hardships encountered", there are also a series of activities that allow oneself to turn to happiness. Don't wait until your emotions are very depressed to engage in these activities. Learn to schedule these lovely activities regularly, because similar to exercise activities, they can make the body secrete pain relieving endorphins, making you immediately feel happy (just list a part of the "Minions Happy Attachment Method" below):

——Chatting with friends on the phone;

——Eating chocolate (which is useful for you) or other favorite foods;

——Going out to visit friends;

——Entertaining friends at home;

——Eat your favorite ice cream;

——Do beauty treatments;

——Exercise is a killer of depression;

——Organize a meaningful party;

——Go to the library;

——Go to the bookstore to read a book or a new disc;

——Doing yoga, practicing Tai Chi, or enrolling in a class to learn new life skills is beneficial for both body and mind;

——Go to the park or take a quiet walk;

——Prayer or contemplation;

——Riding a bicycle;

——Travel and save up enough money;

——Swimming;

——Learning a foreign language that one usually dares not challenge;

——Do something exciting (surfing, rock climbing, skiing, skydiving, riding a motorcycle, kayaking, screaming at the roaring train);

——Ball sports (basketball, bowling, handball, golf, table tennis, squash);

——Recall the lines or lyrics of your favorite movies or plays;

——Join a public discussion organization and write a speech;

——Adequate sleep, going to bed early and getting up early, and having a regular body routine are beneficial for endocrine stability;

——Do puzzle games or on-site CS;

——Attend a cooking class or learn a new dish;

——Draw flowers, trees, people, and beautiful houses with a brush or fingers;

——Read various positive books

May everyone find the cute little yellow person in their heart and find their own happiness. I am optimistic, intelligent, and steady Dave. Who are you?

6 "Lost in Hong Kong": What other troubles do you have in your heart that make you feel uneasy?

All is riddle, and the key to a riddle...is another riddle.

——Emerson (American poet, essayist, philosopher)

Release information: "Lost in Hong Kong" is a romantic comedy film jointly produced by Beijing Zhenledao Cultural Communication Co., Ltd., Beijing Enlight Film Co., Ltd., and others. The film was released nationwide on September 25, 2015.

Xu Zheng plays Xu Lai, a young man full of countless hidden troubles. Perhaps in his youth, he initially wanted to pursue a literary and artistic path, but fate played a trick on him, and he had to be polished by reality and time into a small businessman who designs women's underwear - a middle-aged bald man.

His brother-in-law Cai Lala is a literary 2B youth who loves movies.

May I ask what your dream is? Who did you give it to for the first time? Did you experience premature ejaculation

I found that you have many little secrets in your heart

You actually took a set behind my back

No, that was sent to me by someone else

I found that you have many little secrets in your heart

The film basically starts with these conversations that can almost make a mature man's heart collapse. What kind of unsettling story does it unfold for us?

This is a story of a man and two women, but it was only uncovered by Cai Lala, a second rate person.

During his college years, Xu Lai gave a speech with the dream of becoming an artist. He returned to his seat amidst a confident round of applause. At this moment, Yang Yi, a beautiful oil painting artist in the front row, turned her head and said to him, "Very artistic." This is undoubtedly a fitting praise and encouragement for Xu Lai, who also has the dream of oil painting art.

However, at this moment, Cai Bo, a second-generation wealthy girl from the management department in the back seat, reminded him that the zipper on his pants was not pulled properly.

Uh... Although such a reminder is well intentioned, it is also a true fact that brings Xu Lai, who is currently immersed in infinite imagination, back to reality and implies that there is still a huge gap between his dreams and reality.

From a psychological perspective, the phenomenon of attitudes gradually becoming negative as rewards decrease and positive as rewards increase is known as the "Aronson effect" in social psychology.

The Aronson effect also refers to the fact that people like people or things whose likes, rewards, and praises for themselves increase the most, and dislike people or things that appear to decrease the most.

At the first meeting, in Xu Lai's heart, Yang Yi was undoubtedly far superior to the carefree Cai Bo. Of course, when two people walk together, develop feelings, experience first love, and share a common artistic dream, there will naturally be endless topics to talk about.

But setting aside the similarities and common topics in marriage and love, let's just analyze Xu Lai's inner thoughts in detail from the perspective of the Aronson effect. Why did he choose Yang Yi instead of Cai Bo in the beginning of the film?

The main reason is actually the inner frustration at work.

The Aronson effect experiment involves dividing participants into four groups and giving different evaluations to one person in order to observe which group they have the most favorable impression of. The first group always praises it highly, the second group always belittles and denies it, the third group praises it first and then belittles it, and the fourth group praises it first and then belittles it.

After conducting this experiment on dozens of people, it was found that the vast majority of them had the most favorable impression of the fourth group and the most unfavorable impression of the third group.

The key point of the Aronson effect is the diminishing reward. Although the most obvious scene in the film is the encounter between Cai Bo and Xu Lai, it also implies their future rules of getting along.

The Aronson effect reminds people that in daily work and life, they should try their best to avoid the reversal of negative impressions caused by their own improper performance. Similarly, it also reminds us to avoid being influenced by it and forming incorrect attitudes when forming impressions of others.

What Cai Bo made Xu understand was the laws of reality in life, which were naturally vastly different from an idealized life. For example, a talented oil painting graduate who designed underwear and even "switched" to his wife's family business not only to become a son-in-law, but also to strive for his wife's entire family business instead of pursuing his own dreams.

The inner unwillingness and frustration, the escalating sense of frustration, and the fact that the two had no offspring, all led to a hidden emotional crisis between them. In the end, the old relationship with their first love became difficult, and naturally sprouted in Xu Lai's restless heart.

Long term suppression and imbalance can lead characters to resist the status quo.

So, under the guise of accompanying his wife and family on a trip to Hong Kong, it was inevitable for Xu Lai to embark on the path of his first love in a private university.

I hope to open a small studio in a small place in Italy, where I can realize my dream as an artist. This was Xu Lai's idealized dream when he was young.

But the response from her first love, Yang Yi, was that she chose to give up this relationship and accept the opportunity to become a foreign exchange student, leaving far away.

In the previous text, the "Aronson Effect" was mentioned. Although when Xu Lai first met Cai Bo and Yang Yi, two women who would have a significant impact on his future life, Cai Bo's words "You didn't zip up your pants properly" made Yang Yi, a lively and sweet woman, quickly gain recognition in Xu Lai's eyes, as the plot developed, Yang Yi left Xu Lai with an unfinished dream figure engraved with traces of youth. In addition to regret, there is also the diminishing effect of the "Allen effect".

Since Cai Bo met Xu Lai, he has been silently waiting for him. When he was in love with Yang Yi, she secretly stayed aside and dared not approach. When Yang Yi left and Xu Lai felt lost and lonely, she handed him a steaming hot boxed meal; When he failed to submit his self recommendation letter after graduating from college, she took him to their family business and made him a lingerie designer, fulfilling his role as the breadwinner in a family; She carried their only regret - never having a child, but still remembered Xu Lai's dream of a small Italian studio when he was young. Taking advantage of a family trip to Hong Kong, she secretly met with a foreign seller, mysterious and just to surprise him. This was her little secret when she came to Hong Kong, even though she didn't know that Xu Lai also had a little secret hidden; And she had already made sacrifices and choices for him during her college years, secretly giving up the opportunity to be an exchange student without telling him anything. Xu Lai only learned about it after meeting her first love Yang Yi later and listening to Yang Yi talk about it

It is not difficult to see that Yang Yi and Cai Bo represent two distinct characteristics of women in society. The former emphasizes dreams and freedom, preferring to spread their wings and fly freely like a free bird, constantly exploring the magical melody of self exploration in life; The latter, Cai Bo, is undoubtedly a model of a virtuous wife and mother in the family. Even reminding Xu Lai to take medicine should be recorded and carefully placed in his pocket, caring for him step by step.

These are two completely different individuals, and the two women in the film have no intersection in their respective growth pursuits. In today's society, there are also many examples of such individuals, and there are very few women who can perfectly overlap the two human roles.

Anyway, it can be seen from the above that as a wife, Cai Bo's role in Xu Lai's "Aronson Effect" is increasing.

She is not only the bond that maintains Xu Lai's awkward status as a son-in-law, but also the "lubricant" for the harmonious coexistence of the entire family.

In the family, such a woman balances relationships with love and silent dedication. Her role is so important that it is like salt, which must be included in every meal, but it is easy for people to overlook her importance in the daily, steady flow of life.

Especially Xu Lai, who is experiencing a midlife crisis, was filled with excitement, unwillingness, and unfinished kisses and sexual fantasies when he heard the news of his first love again... The bombardment of this information completely made Xu Lai forget the existence of his wife - the role he played, and it was a silent sacrifice.

So he must go see his first love, this is the unbearable palpitation and dream in his heart.

In a sense, 'Lost in Hong Kong' actually tells the story of a man like Xu Lai's attitude towards the midlife crisis and personal growth gained from it during the passing of his youth. We have to talk about another psychological effect here - the Chekoni effect.

The Chekoni effect refers to the tendency of the general public to easily forget things that have already been completed and achieved, while always remembering things that have been interrupted, unfinished, or not yet achieved.

For example, if you write a paragraph and are interrupted midway before finishing it, you will always remember it in your mind while doing anything else; Alternatively, we are often captivated by a puzzle novel, whether to read it in one go or put it down and read it again tomorrow. Perhaps most people choose to read it unconsciously, even until 3am; Similar phenomena will appear on a TV series disc, and we will also watch it with relish.

The reason for this phenomenon is that people have a natural drive to do things from beginning to end.

Don't believe me? Please try drawing a circle, but don't finish it. After a while, take another look at it and see if you really want to draw it completely in your mind.

Yes, complete, cloze, and do not want to have any shortcomings. This is the positive and positive application of the Chekoni effect by most people, but there are still some people who may go to extremes:

Either it can never be completed, or it must be completed, and not completing it will definitely be uncomfortable.

Both of these people need to adjust their completion drive, and they are likely to be psychologically stuck at the level of infancy or childhood (usually due to insufficient secure attachment during infancy). Moreover, this group of people also possess the terrifying traits of macrosomia: paranoia, black-and-white, perfectionism, equating imagination with reality and fantasy, even delusions, and so on. The most terrifying feature among them is omnipotent narcissism - that is, imagining oneself as an omnipotent person who can only say and do what is right. Such people are afraid of failure.

A person who gives up halfway, the reason for giving up halfway is because they are worried that they will be criticized or criticized by others after completing something. Therefore, they simply choose not to finish it, so that no one will criticize their unfinished work. And another type of person who must complete it also has the psychological characteristic of fearing failure, because in their dictionary, there is no failure, and they cannot accept the occurrence of failures in their "omnipotent self", which naturally blocks the opportunity to summarize, think and gain experience from failures.

And in our current society, there are still a considerable number of people with a "giant baby" mentality. In the movie "Lost in Hong Kong", there are actually two "giant babies".

The first obvious giant baby is of course "Cai Lala" (played by Bao Beier), whose Chekoni effect is reflected in the VD that filmed the documentary. Even when the young couple kiss and their brother-in-law Xu comes to the bathroom, he takes pictures without any regard for the feelings of others. For the sake of a VD, he would jump off a pedestrian bridge without caring, even neglecting his own safety. This is a typical giant baby.

And another less obvious' giant baby 'is Xu Lai.

Although he appears mature on the surface and has entered middle age, when he encounters a mundane life with no passion day after day and a virtuous wife who exists like salt, he finally bursts out in anger when he encounters the dilemma of "tearing apart" the entire Cai Bo family from the succession of his family. He unleashes all his accumulated grievances and unwillingness, including giving up his dreams, becoming a son-in-law, and serving as a cow and horse for a family business, etc

He may be able and worth venting, but he magnified these experiences infinitely in an angry way, ignoring his wife Cai Bo who has always been by his side and silently striving for harmony in the entire family.

And the unfinished circle in his heart is to meet his first love again and continue their relationship. This behavior, in a sense, is just a psychological comfort for him as his youth is about to pass away and he mourns his dreams, lacking rational thinking.

However, people who encounter a midlife crisis may forget their responsibilities in reality, including the responsibilities that a role in the family should shoulder. Cai Lala forgot that she was already an adult who could take responsibility for her actions, while Xu Lai forgot that there was still a wife who silently dedicated herself to him like salt and loved him at home.

So how can we avoid being negatively affected by the Chekoni effect?

Firstly, before carrying out a task, weigh its value. If in the long run, your efforts and rewards will be severely imbalanced and not in line with normal values, then give up boldly. It is your rationality that requires you to give up on it, not your failure. Learn to invest your limited energy and time in more meaningful and valuable things in life.

Again, if there are no issues with the first step, then develop a reasonable short-term, medium-term, and long-term plan, write down the steps to achieve it on paper, and plan the process from method A to goal B based on reality. If you can clearly feel progress or gains within the specified time period, then the current method or goal is suitable for you to spend valuable time pursuing. Otherwise, you should change the method or replace the goal.

Finally, it is necessary to train the ability of self-control, telling oneself that even if it is not completed, one can stop and think about whether their current state is really suitable for themselves. If not, then bravely correct it.

In fact, at the end of the film, Xu Lai truly understood that the person who is truly suitable for him is not the first love who freely pursues his dreams, but the virtuous wife who has silently made many sacrifices for him.

This little understanding is so rare and difficult, because it means that the protagonist has bravely completed another deep self exploration and thinking, and has truly grown from the state of a middle-aged crisis baby. This is more important than anything else.

Explanation for this issue (Psychology): When you have the ability to face life and difficult environments, or the ability to deeply reflect on your past gains and losses with hope, inner strength, and courage, and finally make changes, you have already gained the opportunity to bravely step out of the first step of growth from a giant baby.

7 Understanding the Transcendent Power of Mindfulness Therapy DBT from "The Dragon Quest Technique"

Release information: The film started filming in August 2014 and was released on December 18, 2015, in multiple versions including 3D, IMAX 3D, ScreenX, etc.

When you have eliminated the impossible whatever remains, however improbable, must be the truth.

——**Sherlock Holmes is a famous detective in the works of Sherlock Holmes and Conan Doyle.**

Searching for dragons, dividing gold, and observing winding mountains,

If there is an eight fold insurance when closing the door,

One entanglement is one hurdle,

There is no Yin Yang Eight Trigrams.

The mnemonic of 'The Search for the Dragon' comes from the brave commander Hu Bayi, who is proficient in the Feng Shui Eight Trigrams of the 'Sixteen Character Yin Yang Feng Shui Secret Technique', and is also known as the 'Touching Gold Colonel'.

This fantasy thriller suspense film, which has grossed over 950 million yuan in just one week of release, mainly tells the story of the three person duo Hu Bayi, Shirley Yang, and their friend Wang Kaixuan, who are about to wash their hands of their golden pot. Suddenly, they accidentally learn about the "other shore flower" from a deal with a heavy buyer, thus opening up the dusty memories of their first love "Ding Sitian" twenty years ago.

The mnemonic for touching gold at the beginning of this article has come from Hu Bayi's mouth more than once in the play, and is used to divide gold and break acupoints. The original passage is actually adapted from the representative work of Tang Dynasty feng shui master Yang Yunsong, "The Dragon Shaking Sutra". But here, as an original psychological counselor, I don't want to discuss Feng Shui Bagua or the art of escaping armor with readers. Instead, from a psychological perspective, I want to take a look at a certain psychological science knowledge point presented in this film - the transcendent power of mindfulness therapy DBT.

Firstly, find and recognize the transcendent power of oneself, so that one's inner strength will be stronger.

Perhaps each of us has experienced despair or helplessness at some point in our lives. At that time, the parties involved may experience significant changes or misfortunes, sudden breakdown of intimate relationships or loss of health, and the business they have been painstakingly managing for many years may be on the brink of bankruptcy, or even be violated... At that time, the parties involved are prone to symptoms such as fatigue, anxiety, loneliness, and even sleep disorders, decreased appetite, narrow consciousness, mania, depression, post-traumatic stress disorder (PTSD), etc.

If, at these critical moments, having faith in extraordinary power can actually help you rediscover the source of your own strength in the midst of adversity, and regain your beliefs or goals in life.

In the mindfulness therapy we are discussing, recognizing your self transcendence power does not necessarily require us to believe in God or religion. It can be an object, a sentence, or even the power of goodness in an important relationship. The prerequisite for finding such transcendent power is that we must have unwavering faith. The psychological explanation for this belief in positive energy is the belief in the power of goodness, beauty, divinity, nobility, and extraordinary things that can help us overcome certain extremely difficult times. The combination of introspection therapy or Morita therapy can achieve the soothing function of enduring pain and self-healing.

And this way of finding our own faith and belief, that is, finding our transcendent power, is the psychological code that helps us overcome difficulties and hardships.

Secondly, taking introspection therapy as an example, find the source of one's own strength and fully experience it.

NaiKan Therapy was proposed by Japanese scholar Yoshimoto Yoshinobu in 1953. Yoshimoto believed, "To know if you have confidence, you can look up the days you spent in the past

Its core essence is based on introspection meditation, focusing on, facing, and perceiving, mainly revolving around three themes, constantly reflecting on the important relationship that is most deeply connected to oneself: what has he done for me? What have I repaid him for? What troubles have I caused him, and what are they?

Pay attention to breathing, self-awareness, and current feelings, until you discover the wisdom and love inherent in each person's heart (referring to oneself), thus gaining insight and achieving the goal of spiritual growth, stability, and peace.

The specific operation method can be assisted by a psychological counselor with experience in this operation. Introspection therapy is not only a quick and effective way for visitors to treat physical and mental illnesses such as marital discord, non social behavior, addiction, obsessive-compulsive disorder, and neurosis, but also a good medicine that many psychological counselors should master for a long time to relieve work pressure and negative emotions.

Here, we have to go back to the golden mnemonic mentioned at the beginning of 'The Legend of the Dragon', showcasing the power of faith of each person in the film and understanding the transcendent power in 'The Legend of the Dragon'.

Due to his frequent exposure to elements such as ancient tombs and corpses that can easily cause negative illusions, Hu Bayi's faith clearly leans towards seeking help from the Taoist Xuanzong Qimen Dunjia technique. This is his inner transcendent power, and he always manages to remain calm in times of danger, activate mechanisms, and find a way out.

The pioneering explorer Wang Kaixuan, played by Huang Bo, is Hu Bayi's most loyal friend. In the 1960s, when he switched teams in Inner Mongolia, he "competed" with Old Hu to pursue Ding Sitian. Later, he reunited with Hu Bayi and began his career as a junior officer in the imperial examination. By nature, he is rough and generous, seeming to have nothing that can ignite his inner universe, but the "other shore flower" symbolizing his first love Ding Sitian is the life and death code of his transcendent power.

Even if it's in the underworld, I'll bring it back for you. "This was the promise he made to Ding Sitian twenty years ago, and Xiao Ding's death not only became a psychological trauma for Hu Bayi, but also a knot in Wang Kaixuan's heart.

Both of them seemed to have never let go of Ding Sitian, who had been in their hearts for twenty years, but in fact, it was the guilt and helplessness of her death that left a mark on their hearts.

Shirley Yang, played by Shu Qi, is a Chinese American who graduated from the United States Naval Academy and worked as a photojournalist for National Geographic magazine. Having a passion for archaeology, I met Hu Bayi and Wang Kaixuan upon returning to my home country and formed a stable team to embark on an adventure. During the process, I developed feelings for Hu Bayi. The typical personality of 'fierce on the surface but weak on the inside' may appear indifferent on the surface, but in fact, the love for Hu Bayi who accompanies her through life and death is the transcendent power within her.

It is worth mentioning Ding Sitian, who stars Yang Ying. She and Shirley Yang actually have many similarities, both of which are beauty and intelligence, and the ability to make rational decisions in critical moments. Ding Sitian said, 'Without cutting that wood, none of us three can leave...' Her self sacrifice perfectly demonstrates her rational and calm understanding of the overall situation.

So, what was her transcendent power at that time? Can a fragile little woman sacrifice her life for righteousness and protect two big men without hesitation?

She did that back then to make you live well, "Shirley Yang revealed in a sentence from the grave.

Survival "is Ding Sitian's transcendent power, but it doesn't matter whether she lives or not. The key is for the two of them to live well.

This reminds me of the plot where there is a contrasting character whose transcendent power is also about "survival". However, whether others live or not is not important, the key is for her to survive on her own. This character is the Himalayan Supreme Master Ying Caihong, who is seriously ill.

In order to survive, she is willing to play tricks and drag others into dangerous situations. She regards others' lives as worthless and not worth mentioning.

When the tomb was just opened, she said, "To live, one always needs a little spirit

Yes, when we use self-awareness, introspection therapy, and self perception to find our own transcendent power, we become calm and feel unprecedented stability and strength. Some people may go to the library to read a large book of positive energy; Some people may hike up mountains to admire the vast ice and snow world of the snow capped peaks; Some people may recite scriptures; Some people also choose to go to church and pray and repent in front of the statue of God; Some people, through astronomical telescopes, carefully observe the stars in the sky and think about the faint self in the universe; Some people go to the vast grassland to lie quietly and feel the freedom; Or it could be meditation, using introspection therapy to reflect on the important relationship between people and things in life that can provide a source of self strength. What kind of person or thing does it look like, what special qualities does it have that can bring soothing and calming power to one's soul

When encountering changes and difficulties again, deep in my imagination, I am the source of that power. It can be faith, a place that will always bring you peace, or someone else; At this point, let's take a look and immerse ourselves in our imagination. How would he handle the current problems and difficulties?

Thirdly, the theme of "The Search for Dragons" is to explore the mysteries of life.

In a discussion between Shirley Yang and Hu Bayi, it was mentioned that what you see is not determined by your eyes, but by your brain, that is, empathy and countertransference.

When the flowers bloomed on the other side of the ancient tomb, the crowd experienced negative hallucinations due to the influence of a meteorite.

Hu Bayi saw the dead Ding Sitian again, as if he had returned to that day twenty years ago. However, the two people who escaped from the cave were no longer Hu and Wang, but Hu Bayi and Ding Sitian.

This illusion, analyzed from a dynamic perspective, actually reveals the trauma of Hu Bayi's subconscious and expresses his true wishes.

We sometimes reminisce about past events and dig into unforgettable memories, which is true but not always. It cannot be ruled out that some people may often trace back their past memories, especially those that trigger negative emotions, leading to obsessive-compulsive disorder (OCD) - an anxiety disorder that often originates from themselves, and the more they resist, the more difficult it is to control themselves, such as "forced thinking", "forced doubt", "repeated examination", and "fear of dirt and poor washing".

This group of people may spend a long time thinking about past events that have been turned over, mistakes made, or unfinished events, leading to negative emotions such as guilt, regret, anxiety, and self conflict. So, there may be two situations, either indulging in the past or fantasizing about the future, so that the part of paying attention to current feelings is obviously less.

But the plot in "The Legend of the Dragon" that unties Hu Bayi's knot of heart gives us the profound meaning of exploring life:

Originally, in this illusion, there was a beautiful and wise first love, a vast and beautiful grassland, and an intimate embrace. This was Hu Bayi's subconscious self soothing of the past trauma, like a dream, just a certain wish of his subconscious. Nothing was missing from the illusion. But when Hu realized that the badge on Ding Sitian's chest was reversed, his self-awareness suddenly woke up and realized that this was just an illusion, and living better in the present with the current interpersonal relationships was the meaning of life.

It's not difficult to have such a high level of self-awareness as the Gold Commander. Starting from the first deep breath, feel our breath. What is the feeling of that breath entering your body through your respiratory tract? Is it deep or shallow? Is my current psychological feeling anxiety or calmness? Are you excited or indifferent? Is it happiness or depression?

Looking at the surrounding environment again, seeing what your eyes can see, what feelings do they bring to yourself? What are the feelings of the self, and what are the true attributes of those things, rather than projections of the self.

When you feel all of this, this is the present, this is reality.

If you feel that your current psychological emotions are painful or uncomfortable negative emotions, then use rational and scientific psychological processing methods, such as using the techniques of mindfulness therapy for pain tolerance mentioned above, to quickly eliminate your current negative emotions. Wait until the negative emotions disappear before thinking about what caused such feelings.

The meaning of life lies in living in the present, trying to live as authentically as possible. After being able to correctly understand oneself, whether beautiful or ugly, one can gradually learn to fully accept that self, manage oneself well, and naturally treat others well.

8 "Mi Yue Zhuan" • Women's Chapter: An Analysis of the Influence of Personality Traits on Social Relationships

Release information: The drama premiered on Dragon TV and Beijing TV on November 30, 2015.

Faith is not just a mind dominated thought, it is a mind that can control the mind.

——Robert Oxton Bolton

The Legend of Mi Yue "is not an ordinary palace intrigue drama, so compared with the former" Empress in the Palace ", it is more majestic and grand. The focus of this drama is not on the story of several women fighting and scheming for imperial favor, but on the rise of Mi Bazi's power path, where power and sadomasochism blend together, palace intrigue is just a" child's child ".

The reason why Mi Bazi's life was exciting, including her harem, previous court, and abusive love, is closely related to her personality traits. From a psychological perspective, this article analyzes the typical women in "The Legend of Mi Yue" and discusses the two types of typical personality traits in the novel.

Personality, Latin for "persona", originally refers to the mask worn by actors in ancient Rome when performing plays. It wasn't until the 19th and 20th centuries that it gradually evolved from a person's appearance type to a subjective concept, leaning towards psychology and evolving into the current meaning of "personality".

Personality refers to the characteristic patterns of a person's thinking, emotions, and behavior, as well as the hidden or explicit psychological mechanisms behind them. It reflects the consistent behavioral patterns exhibited by individuals in social and living environments, namely the stable and predictable psychological characteristics exhibited by individuals in general.

Simply put, a person's survival behavior pattern has stable manifestations, which also determine the development direction and impact on individual social relationships caused by their behavior.

Here, let's take Mi Yue as an example to analyze the inner personalities of those beautiful women?

Mi Yue: Loyal to oneself, unyielding, neither humble nor arrogant. To put it simply from a psychological perspective, low neuroticism, high agreeableness, high rigor, and high openness (creativity).

Back then, due to Mi Yin's frequent framing and baseless slander, Mi Yue was placed under house arrest and poisoned by Empress Wei, and her life was in imminent danger. Even if you get beaten, you still have to insist on telling the truth; Later, due to the death of King Huiwen of Qin, Mi Yue and her son Ying Ji became hostages in the state of Yan, falling into a difficult and miserable situation from their former place of honor. Additionally, Mi Yin colluded with the government to frame her for theft, resulting in the death of people around Mi Yue who were considered family and friends, and putting her in danger.

Although she understood that there was no excuse for wanting to add guilt, she still insisted on stating that she had never done it before! She also brilliantly swung a whip at the bullying dog official, and in her bones, she had a strong and unyielding character that was no less than that of a heroic man.

In terms of romance, Mi Yue has had three relationships.

Although the endings of the childhood sweetheart Chun Shen Jun Huang Xie, the gentle and steady Qin Wang, and the domineering and persistent Yi Qu Wang are all different, each paragraph represents the most genuine emotions:

When she was young, she stole a Mantou from the kitchen and gave it to the cute little boy. Then she taught "little fool" Chun Shenjun to swing a whip, jokingly called him by her master and apprentice. Then she went to the hall. The graceful and graceful dance of the Sacrificial Dance of Shao Siming showed her feelings with Huang Xie. Her feelings with Huang Xie were pure, pure, sweet and meaningful.

Afterwards, Mi Yin forced her to marry Huang Xie but failed, and instead used her power to vent her anger on her. As a concubine, she married Princess Mi Shu to the state of Qin, with a poor status. At the age of fifteen, she was far from the thirty year old Qin King Ying Si. However, her intelligence and wit still made the Qin King look down upon her, naturally recognizing that she was different from ordinary women. He cared for and accompanied her, and although he was a noble ruler of a country, he was also her husband. After Huang Xie and Huang Gongzi had "passed away" for several years, the patient listening and care of the Qin king made this "old man" so heartwarming that he once again opened Mi Bazi's heart.

Two emotions are incomparable. If we were not to compare the feelings between Huang Xie and the King of Qin, in the episode when Ying Si was about to pass away, this once stubborn and not easily shedding tears Mi Bazi cried like a "tearful child", praising the saying "Old man treats me like a father and a brother".

From this sentence alone, it can also be seen that Mi Yue is a person who insists on being her true self. Even when Ying Si was dying, she did not want to deceive him in the slightest about their marital relationship. They always prioritized their family over their child's love. In this regard, they cannot be compared to Huang Xie's innocent and innocent relationship, nor can they be compared to the passionate love between men and women between the later Prince Yiqu. So Ying Si said, 'In the end, I will still be like a father and a brother,' and shed a tear of the emperor's tears.

What he loves most is the sincerity of the little girl in front of him, but this is also a bit regretful in the evaluation of the ending of his relationship.

After the death of King Huiwen of Qin, Mi Yue's fate once again encountered setbacks and twists and turns. She met Yiqu Jun again and formed a relationship with him when his life was on the brink of death. In order to encourage him to have the courage to live on, she said, "Don't you want me to be your woman? If you survive, as long as you get through this hurdle, I will agree to you." Yiqu Jun, who loved her to the point of infatuation, risked his life for her and blocked Huiqu Jun's hidden arrows for her. Just because she called him "black horse and foal", he laughed foolishly like a child. For him, she may have been moved, passionate, sympathetic, and had no choice but to seek benefits.

Until around the age of thirty, Mi Yue, with the help of King Yiqu and her younger brothers, overcame all obstacles and gradually ascended to the supreme throne, achieving the historical Empress Dowager Xuan of Qin.

Is it fate's arrangement? Or is it 'personality determines destiny'?

The answer is personality.

This is precisely the conclusion drawn by psychologists after years of research: personality traits affect an individual's social relationships, including the development of romantic and professional relationships.

The characteristics of personality are related to genetic, physiological, and environmental factors. This article temporarily avoids the influence of neurotransmitters such as serotonin, dopamine, norepinephrine, or congenital genetic factors on personality, and only analyzes the interrelationships between personality in friends, family, love, and career——

Taking Mi Yue as an example, low neuroticism, high agreeableness, high rigor, and high openness (creativity) have a positive effect on individuals' successful social relationships and personal achievement development.

Firstly, the level of neuroticism determines an individual's attitude and ability to recover from challenges and setbacks.

1. Individuals with low neuroticism have stronger resistance to pressure to some extent compared to the general population, commonly known as the "neural big strip" or "small strong family". Psychologists have conducted experiments and found that for individuals with high neuroticism personality traits, the internal reactions and effects of the same external stimuli are several

times higher than those of low neuroticism individuals, and the magnification level varies depending on individual differences.

Firstly, regarding Mi Yue's experience and her reactions, she is not a petty and narrow-minded person, which is determined by her low neuroticism personality traits.

Faced with numerous hardships, yet living a thriving life like a 'little strong', and seeing each experience as a tempering of time to advance to higher heights.

Of course, from a cognitive perspective, this is also significantly related to a person's fundamental way of thinking, and whether the thinking generated by the brain is positive or negative during each setback directly determines what kind of emotional response an individual will have.

For example, when Mi Yue was placed under house arrest by Empress Wei, she indulged herself in hardship and thought to herself, "Okay, I'll stay here for a few days and see what you can do to me." If it were Lin Meimei from Dream of the Red Chamber, she would have dug a pit and buried herself before anyone else could do it, singing a self pitying song called "Burial Flower Song" while digging.

The opposite of low neuroticism is high neuroticism, so what are the characteristics of high neuroticism?

2. People with high neuroticism are usually more sensitive to external stimuli and may even exhibit pathological reactions. Of course, it is not entirely believed that this personality trait is bad. It depends on how individuals make good use of these "talents" to believe that any trait has two sides.

Looking at the two princesses Mi Yin and Mi Shu in the drama, and then at Lin Meimei in Dream of the Red Chamber, it is clear that they belong to the "Long Eared Rabbit" series.

For example, in the scene of Mi Yin stealing the Night Pearl, if it weren't for her highly neurotic personality traits, she wouldn't have discovered Wei in advance and would have thoroughly investigated the matter, nor would she have taken immediate action. Just self-protection is not wrong, but harming others' interests for self-protection will inevitably bury a big pit for one's future path, whether it is social relationships, romantic relationships, or career development relationships, the disadvantages outweigh the advantages.

Due to the fact that individuals with high neuroticism may often experience emotional fluctuations, be at risk, or be caught off guard, their thinking and emotions can be more complex and chaotic than those of ordinary people, and they are also prone to excessive mental stress, which is not conducive to their physical and mental health development.

As a subject of vitality and energy, human beings have limited energy. If too much of their physical and mental energy is consumed in overly complex thinking and agitated emotions, then the energy that can be used for positive individual development will naturally be much less.

This is detrimental to the long-term development of individuals.

Secondly, the harmony of an individual's social relationships depends to some extent on the level of suitability for human nature.

Balanced agreeableness tests an individual's attitude towards others, which includes being close, empathetic, trusting, tolerant, and soft hearted, as well as hostile, cynical, manipulative, vengeful, and emotionless. What is referred to here is the broad range of interpersonal orientation. Yiren represents "love" and whether cooperation and interpersonal harmony are valued.

People with high agreeableness are empathetic, friendly, generous, and helpful (with strong altruism), willing to sacrifice their own interests for others, holding an optimistic attitude towards human nature, and believing that human nature is inherently good.

From a psychological perspective, individuals with high agreeableness are more likely to benefit from harmonious interpersonal relationships and a virtuous cycle of teamwork.

And what is the pleasantness of Mi Bazi?

From beginning to end, she remained loyal to herself and never forgot to cherish her friends, family, and loved ones around her. She makes friends not because of one's social status, but more because of her high and helpful nature.

If that's the case, she won't rescue Zhang Zi, who is struggling and destitute in the bustling city; She wouldn't just bandage the wound of Nanhou Zheng Xiu and casually befriend Wei Meiren in times of hardship, saying, 'Meeting by chance, make friends.'.

At first sight, she treated everyone she met as equal and balanced, without being snobbish or wearing colored glasses to look at others. Only with frequent persecution and accusations like Mi Yin, Mi Shu, and Lady Wei, would she be able to distinguish between the two.

Having a high sense of humanity, this has complemented Mi Yue's social relationships, and on her path to becoming Empress Dowager Xuan, she has achieved great success, becoming an important support for her upward mobility.

High human nature refers to getting along well with the surrounding social relationships, understanding and empathizing with others, understanding and experiencing the difficulties of other individuals, and being able to consider others properly. To gain a detailed understanding of the personality traits that are highly compatible with human nature, simply search for the top ten words in the vocabulary of "most popular personality traits" and it will be clear at a glance.

And low suitability for human nature is obviously the opposite of the above traits.

People with low agreeableness prioritize their own interests over those of others. Essentially, they do not care about the interests of others, and therefore are unwilling to help others. Sometimes, they are very suspicious of others and doubt their motives.

So after Mi Yue encountered the Killer Bee incident, she took the initiative to approach Mi Shu and requested to take her son Ying Ji to the fiefdom of Bashu. Mi Shu would squint her eyes, furrow her brow, and ask, "Do you really think that way?" Mi Yue calmly replied, "Nothing is more true than this moment. At that time, Mi Bazi, who was vying for favor in the imperial harem, was so worthless to her. She just wanted to live quietly with her child and had no other desires. When it comes to why she eventually became Empress Dowager Xuan, it's not so much a matter of fate, but rather the hard work of Mi Yin, Mi Shu, Lady Wei, and others.

If Mi Yue wants to treat Mi Shu, Mi Yin, Lady Wei and others as good as ever, regardless of old and evil, even if Mi Bazi can do it generously, the difficulty level of these "nobles" who are high in neuroticism and low in humanity is too high.

If you treat others with sincerity, they may not believe as firmly as you do. Mi Shu had already had a murderous heart towards Mi Yue since the partition of Bashu, how could she believe it?

Thirdly, high rigor determines an individual's personality traits of prudence, meticulousness, and keen insight, as well as their level of responsibility and diligence.

High rigor, which is different from high neuroticism. High rigor means being meticulous and sharp, doing things carefully, having a sense of responsibility, having a clear beginning and end, and being able to work hard and take responsibility for the chosen plan. The latter is only the "long eared rabbit" series, "wave" series, and "non conservative emotion" series mentioned earlier.

The former focuses on the focus and exquisite quality of handling affairs, while the latter focuses more on the individual's excessive emotional reactions and external attack defense mechanisms.

Fourthly, high openness refers to a person's high creativity and the ability to solve problems with breakthroughs.

Individuals with high openness can choose careers related to research or art. In jobs that require creativity, high openness often adds points to the progress of the work and promotes it.

From the plot of Mi Yue unraveling the mystery of the authenticity of the He Shi Bi, it can be seen that she is able to unravel the mechanism of embedding the He Shi Bi with "Northern Xuanwu, Southern Vermilion Bird, Left Green Dragon, Right White Tiger", and with "Bian He's blood and tears" that are difficult for ordinary people to detect like hair, she has integrated into the He Shi Bi to distinguish between real and fake He Shi Bi. This intelligence and wit are related to innate inheritance, but also closely related to her love for reading various classics since childhood.

The third and fourth personality traits have laid a significant foundation for Mi Yue to successfully turn danger into safety in every disaster she encounters.

So how can we avoid negative personality traits that we cannot easily change, and how can we establish and cultivate positive personality traits that have a positive impact on our social relationships?

Firstly, we all know that personality has stability and is not easily changed. To a certain extent, it is determined and influenced by genetic, physiological, and environmental factors. But at the same time, due to changes in the environment, the acceptance of individual value frameworks has a constantly evolving nature.

1. Read more high-quality books, absorb knowledge, and integrate it.

In terms of personality traits, if the level of neuroticism is closely related to innate inheritance and may be difficult to change, then the level of agreeableness, rigor, and openness can largely be learned through continuous cultivation and absorption of knowledge. Just like Mi Yue needs to first read the Eight Trigrams of the Book of Changes and the technique of Qimen Dunjia to form a relevant knowledge system, in order to be able to apply it in solving the problem of the He Shi Bi.

2. Participate in social practice activities that benefit both others and oneself.

Everyone's knowledge framework system will continue to develop with their observations. By participating in outdoor activities and social practices, as well as with the help of professional psychological counselors, and through systematic training, individuals can gradually change and improve their tolerance, broaden their horizons, enhance their value, and naturally undergo cognitive changes.

Just like 10 years ago, when someone dropped 100 yuan, they would have been in a state of fluctuating anger for several days, but 10 years later, when the same person dropped 1000 yuan, they may not have as many negative emotional reactions anymore. The reason is highly likely that this person has successfully acquired the ability to create self-worth. Imagine a person whose daily income is many times higher than their expenses, would that tiny mistake affect their individual emotions for several days?

3. Cultivate self-control, improve the level of superego (moral level), and constantly explore oneself.

Freud divided humans into three levels: id, ego, and superego. The id represents the desire self - basic needs, the ego is the regulating self - responsible for regulating the individual's needs and self-control, and the superego is the moral self - the level of an individual's moral outlook also determines their altruistic behavior and self-control in the face of temptation.

Why did Huang Xie say to Mi Yin in "The Legend of Mi Yue", "Even without Yue Er, I wouldn't like you

This is not about identity, status, wealth, or appearance, but about values, personality traits, and charm.

Imagine if Mi Yue and Mi Yin exchanged bodies, and the body with Mi Yue's appearance showed Mi Yin's words and actions, I believe Huang Xie would not like Mi Yin's version of "Mi Yue".

The appearance remains unchanged, but the personality charm is different. Naturally, the attitude towards external social relationships will also change accordingly.

To enhance an individual's personality charm, the first step is to learn self-control. While improving self-control, cultivate a virtuous cycle of superego (i.e. moral self).

Here, it does not necessarily mean that the higher the superego, the higher and more desirable it is. However, it cannot be denied that people who have reached a certain level of moral excellence are more likely to be recognized by society. Everyone has their own choices and ways of survival, but regardless of an individual's superego or self-control, there must be a path that makes them feel most comfortable developing. However, no matter how it develops, if the goal of self satisfaction and happiness is achieved through frequent sacrifice and harm to others in society, then the development of individual social relationships will inevitably show a parabolic downward trend, and even cause negative adverse reactions to individual social life, romantic relationships, workplace relationships, etc.

American psychologist Ernest Fromm once wrote a book on the goodness and badness of human nature - humans have two abilities: the ability to do good and the ability to do evil, and they must choose between good and evil, blessing and cursing, life and death.

Good people are willing to sacrifice their own interests in order to help others; And for the sake of one's own happiness, one is willing to frequently harm others and sacrifice others' interests by any means necessary to achieve one's own happiness. This is evil.

What is good and what is evil? Different value frameworks will have different interpretations, but the key is whether you truly know and understand yourself? Does the pain of social relationships closely related to you really not have a negative impact on oneself?

No matter what choice you make, it is the right of individual freedom, but can you fully take responsibility for every firm choice from beginning to end?

This is a process that requires continuous self exploration and self-improvement of one's body, mind, and spirit.

Perhaps we may encounter difficulties and confusion on the path of self discovery, but seeking professional psychological counseling is a wise path that is increasingly accepted by the general public.

At the end of life, isn't everyone's life scale still measured and grasped by themselves? Only by truly finding oneself can we discover the true meaning of the word 'I', return to the inner self, and explore in a simple and calm way. Eventually, we will understand the true meaning that life's circumstances require us to understand, perhaps - a faint smile can also captivate us.

9 Heart of the Mermaid: I am narcissistic but not arrogant

Release information: "Mermaid" is directed by Stephen Chow and was released in China on February 8, 2016.

> **Pride makes people can't love me, prejudice makes me can't love others.**
> **——Jane Austen's Pride and Prejudice**

Legend has it that there is a group of humans living under the sea, who have beautiful fish tails, soft long hair, beautiful dance moves, and captivating singing voices. The Little Mermaid is the seventh daughter of the sea, with a graceful fish tail and thick golden hair like seaweed

This beautiful fairy tale of the same name by Hans Christian Andersen was adapted into the New Year's film "The Mermaid" and was released to the audience on the first day of the Lunar New Year.

The film mainly tells the story of humans and mermaids, as the real estate plan of young wealthy man Liu Xuan involves land reclamation projects and the placement of high-power sonar in the deep sea area of Clear Water Bay, forcing the mermaids in the area to curl up in a broken ship and struggle to survive. Mermaid Shanshan disguises herself and enters human society, hoping to use love to influence Xuan Shao and save the mermaid tribe

The film only retains Xingye's unique humorous style. Compared with previous works, "The Mermaid" relatively weakens the comedic elements and focuses more on sadness and speculation, making people reflect more clearly on the theme of the film and making a loud declaration on how development and environmental protection can coexist harmoniously.

Just for positive energy themes like environmental declarations, we need to label this film with high-quality labels.

But if we analyze this film from a psychological perspective, what kind of film and television voice is it interpreting?

Narcissism "is one of Freud's most important and effective discoveries.

Freud pointed out, "Once born, we take a step from an absolute self satisfied narcissism towards perceiving a changing external world and begin to discover various objects

From a psychoanalytic perspective, zero narcissism is the most desirable ideal state. However, in the world of humans and nature, individuals without narcissism will lose the motivation to work hard for survival, because the meaning of survival for individuals who do not even care about their own survival is dangerous.

So, narcissism is not only a necessity for survival, but at the same time, excessive narcissism is also a threat to individual survival—— That is to say, pathological and malignant narcissism.

We can find many narcissistic psychological language in the film 'The Mermaid'.

Deng Chao played Xuan Shao in the film and once sang a song called "Invincible" with the mermaid Shan Shan. The lyrics are as follows:

Invincibility is so lonely

Invincibility is so empty

Alone at the peak, the cold wind keeps blowing through

Who can understand my loneliness

……

When thoughts like "I am invincible," "I am omnipotent," and "I am God" appear in our minds, we may need to explore ourselves. Do we have an excessive tendency towards narcissism?

Because omnipotence and invincibility can serve as signals of excessive narcissism, narcissists often feel lonely, which is why words such as "loneliness", "emptiness", and "who can understand me" appear in the lyrics.

It is not difficult to analyze that Xuan Shao, played by Deng Chao, is a "narcissistic madman" at the beginning of the film. Excessive narcissism breaks his sense of balance and makes him feel prickly all over. His words and actions of "stay away from strangers" interpret the loneliness of a billionaire:

Having experienced hardships since childhood, starting from the slums and working hard from scratch, I have become the Xuan Shao of today. I firmly believe that as long as I have money, I will definitely be respected, and I expect others to envy me, thinking that I deserve the best things. I may even appear arrogant and short-sighted, willing to do anything to achieve my own development goals, such as placing underwater sonar for the reclamation project in Clear Water Bay.

And these 'narcissistic maniacs' often have a sense of privilege, can compete with each other for benefits, and the friends they gain are mostly from the perspective of benefits, rather than being companions protected by their hearts.

So, in the film, Zhang Yuqi played the domineering queen Ruolan, who was once his girlfriend, because Xuan Shao was originally the same type of narcissist who would do anything for profit as her.

So, what harm can excessive narcissism (i.e. malignant narcissism) bring to individuals?

Firstly, the most terrifying consequence of malignant narcissism is the distortion of reasonable inferences, resulting in a lack of objectivity and rationality in the conclusions drawn.

Narcissism - Individuals do not view their entire individual characteristics as objects of narcissism, but can also focus on certain aspects they have invested in, such as achievement, honor, wisdom, physical strength, beautiful appearance, etc. It can be divided into benign narcissism and malignant narcissism. The key word for benign narcissism is "creation", and moderate narcissism has a promoting effect on an individual's survival in society; And malignant narcissism, the key word is not "creation", but "possession".

The object of malignant narcissism is often regarded by narcissists as the most valuable (good, beautiful, the best), and is usually labeled as "perfect". Narcissists idealize it, but the label of "perfect" is not inferred and judged based on objective value, but rather derived from narcissists' self love, that is, "because you are a part of me, or because you are me, this is mine", which leads to the conclusion that "you are perfect no matter what".

This is a clear bias that comes at the cost of distorting objective facts. This is also why malignant narcissists often cannot see or understand the subtle emotions of others, lack empathy, and often encounter "Waterloo" in interpersonal relationships.

Secondly, malignant narcissism is one of the sources of insane jealousy, violence, and aggression.

Ruolan, played by Zhang Yuqi in "The Mermaid," once spoke arrogantly to Xuan, saying, "... my pursuers lined up from here to Paris, France, and I came out with 30 billion to play with you, but you just

Exactly what? Unfortunately, I didn't choose her.

In fact, in a certain relationship, everyone has the right to choose whom. It's not that if you like me, I have to choose you. Mature and independent individuals understand this principle. Why doesn't Ruolan in "The Mermaid" understand?

Because she is a narcissistic maniac.

When a person with a normal level of narcissism is criticized by others, and this criticism is truthful and has no malicious intent to attack, we will not get angry.

But once malignant narcissism encounters criticism, it will regard any criticism that focuses on the narcissistic object as a malicious attack, resulting in the individual being unable to tolerate all criticism and emotionally reflecting an imbalance. Narcissists have two choices, either to overthrow the critic or to overthrow themselves. But usually we can see that 'narcissistic maniacs' use actions to overthrow those rationalized explanations and existences.

In the film, Ruolan expresses her anger at not being chosen by "exterminating" the mermaid tribe. However, from a deeper perspective, that anger actually stems from her deep-seated fear of her self absorbed image on the brink of collapse. She takes her idealized state as evidence of her own existence and is overly narcissistic. Therefore, she cannot accept Xuan Shao's rejection, nor can she accept the fact that her "perfect" image has been shattered.

So, how can we moderate narcissism and prevent overgrowth?

In the movie, Xuan Shao is very lucky. After meeting the pure mermaid Shan Shan in his heart, everything quietly changes, including his malignant narcissism.

It's precisely because you don't understand that I'm appearing in front of you, "she said to him with a calm and sorrowful gaze.

Firstly, maintain a benign narcissism that is balanced with the level of social acceptance. As mentioned earlier, malignant narcissists cannot understand the subtle emotions of others and lack empathy.

In the story of the chapter before (Psychology Gate), the Old Testament of the Bible was quoted: "Love your neighbor as yourself." Here, when it comes to loving your neighbor, from a psychological perspective, it means that we should try our best to overcome individual excessive narcissism. Trying to widely accept people, things, and objects other than 'me', to integrate and experience them, in order to better understand the true meaning of the four words' empathize ', that is,' I accept you not because you like me, nor because you are a part of me or you are me, but only because you are you, I am me, but I can accept you, perceive you, go to the places you have been, see the world with your heart, perceive the world. '' I 'accept different parts of' you ', not just the same parts.

In the film, Xuan Shao gradually integrated into the world of mermaids, seeing the world through the eyes of mermaids Shan Shan, and went to the research laboratory to personally try sonar. Only by "empathizing with others" can he "feel pain that is not mine, love that is not mine". Perhaps from the moment he stepped into the research laboratory, it was the happy beginning of his successful bid farewell to his old malignant narcissism.

Secondly, harness your creativity and cultivate scientific thinking, rather than relying on delusions to create the real world.

By constantly creating and finding objective and reasonable evidence in reality to prove your self-image, reality is to some extent transformed by your creativity, thus conforming to your narcissistic image.

For example, if someone claims to be a scientist, then they need to make creative achievements in the scientific community in real life in order to be reasonably and objectively inferred as a "scientist", rather than exaggerating and excessively acknowledging themselves. After all, "empty talk, talk on paper" lacks objective evidence in reality and has no scientific empirical power.

Thirdly, change the narcissistic object and direction of excessive narcissism.

All malignant and pathological narcissism is caused by the excessive infusion of energy at the level of narcissism, leading to explosive destructive power that disrupts the balance.

If we can reduce the narcissistic energy of individuals and redirect a portion of their narcissism towards their families, careers, achievements, and social contributions, that is, to form benign narcissism, the personal growth they achieve should be quite precious.

The concept of "enlightenment" has been mentioned in the classics of Confucianism, Buddhism, and Taoism. What is ' true enlightenment '? In fact, the 'true enlightened' is someone who has overcome narcissism. Although as individuals living in society, we cannot completely 'zero narcissism' in order to survive better, we can gradually distinguish from reality what belongs to 'self illusion' and 'delusion', and whether their ultimate direction is negative or positive. From this, we can gradually cultivate the awareness to change the object and direction of narcissism.

When every sip of water or every breath of air in this world is toxic, what's the use of making so much money

At the end of the film "Mermaid", Xuan Shao has freed himself from the vicious narcissism of being arrogant and self deprecating in the past, and successfully transformed into an environmental spokesperson who connects with the world. He accepts and loves this world, not because it is the same as him, but because it coexists with him in similarities and differences.

Explanation for this issue (Psychology): What is heaven and what is ultimate

happiness. In fact, heaven and paradise are two seeds in our hearts. Today, when you decide to coexist with this world warmly, the world will also treat you warmly in the future.

10 Journey to the West: White Bone Lady: The Freedom of Good Power

Release information: "Journey to the West: Sun Wukong Beats the White Bone Demon Three Times" is a 3D action fantasy film produced by Xinghao Film Co., Ltd. The film was released in Chinese Mainland on February 8, 2016.

When you look long into an abyss,the abyss looks into you.

——**Nietzsche**

Before watching this brand new film, I once thought that the story of "Journey to the West"'s three battles against the White Bone Demon had already become a classic, and the understanding and grasp of those classic character images and roles could not be surpassed.

After watching it, I realized that there are still stunning aspects to this movie 'Journey to the West: Sun Wukong Beats the White Bone Demon Three Times'.

The story of the Three Beats of the White Bone Spirit goes without saying, but the adapted story of Lady White Bone is still worth exploring together the wonderful language of the soul.

I married into a village, but soon someone died there. The villagers blamed me for bringing bad luck into the village, calling me a demon and leaving me alone on the mountain

The White Bone Lady who told this story to Tang Sanzang was then transforming into a human form, trying her best to seduce Tang Sanzang into falling for it. She ate Tang Sanzang's flesh, which could make her forever a demon, and told so many lies. Deceiving people can go deep into their bones and emotions, but unfortunately, this story is a true past.

That was when Lady White Bone was still human.

She said, "You mortals are heartless

In the eyes of a Buddha, all sentient beings are Buddhas, in the eyes of a bodhisattva, all are bodhisattvas, and in the eyes of ordinary people, all are ordinary people. Pessimists see the world as bleak and failing; Enterprising people see the world, and the world is beautiful and bright. Whether your world is bright or dim depends on your mentality and wisdom.

Similarly, a heartless person only sees ruthlessness.

So what kind of psychological code has forged the ruthless and frosty face of the White Bone Lady today?

Firstly, the experiences of childhood or significant life stages leave a deep and lasting impression on one's heart.

The flower season girl, filled with the joy of being ready to marry, married into a village that was still unfamiliar to her as a woman. However, due to the superstitions and exclusiveness of the villagers, regardless of right or wrong, her flower like life ended. There is no right or wrong, it's just that she is not accepted by the villagers. At that time, her experiences and inner feelings were very heart wrenching and pitiable.

I can imagine the pain and despair of falling into hell after thinking my heart was in heaven.

It's like a child being raised by an invisible boundary from a young age, and someone playing the role of a mentor telling the child that as long as you're in the boundary circle and behave well, they'll give you candy to eat.

At first, the child must have crazily wanted to cross that line, seeking warmth and hugs, because those educators were there, and the child's soul needed to establish an intimate connection with them, both physically and mentally needing the comfort of love (i.e. the spiritual encouragement system). But the fact is exactly the opposite. Every time she crosses the line, she will encounter serious conflicts. Gradually, the child will realize that the educators she wants to connect with intimately do not need her so much, and she cannot integrate into that group of educators. From a caregiver to an independent individual recognized by the taught, during the important stages of her life, the only thing that accompanies her is the invisible boundary and the beautiful "candy" (material encouragement system) in that boundary circle.

So, once the trauma of the soul is planted in the young heart, if such wounds are not seen, discovered, and corrected, the injured soul will no longer heal. So, children have both deep love and deep disgust and hatred towards such educators.

In the above small case, the child wants to integrate into a group that is closely connected to their own soul, which is similar to the psychological needs of Mrs. White Bone when she first became a woman.

In Mrs. White Bone's important experience, when she was treated as a demon and betrayed by the group she thought she could be intimately connected to, amidst the many voices of "you are a demon", she needed to repair or identify with those external perceptions of herself through continuous self betrayal, even though she had always known from the beginning that the distorted external perceptions were not true.

When a person cannot gain external recognition and cannot be certain of who they are, they either overthrow themselves or overthrow the outside world. This is also why many visitors do not want to hear any questioning or opposing voices, because their past experiences can distort a cognitive pattern for them.

And the candy in the above case is like the fatal temptation that Madame White Bone wants for the demon.

In this way, after such individuals grow up, they will either pretend to be strong, with cold-blooded and ruthless eyes; Either it's a person who finds it difficult to control their beliefs at the slightest temptation of "candy".

Psychologically, this phenomenon is known as identification and anti identification. A person consciously and purposefully uses methods of self-identity or self-identity, and its process is to integrate the fragmented and uncoordinated parts of a person's power (unity) center into a whole, coordinated, and complete organism.

For a person who identifies with themselves based on their role or dominant function, it also has an equal effect, which can prevent a person from experiencing the necessary "continuity" in the development or process of life. In the film, when Lady Baigu is identified as a demon by the village community, she needs to experience self betrayal, which goes against her self-identity of "I am alone".

So much so that in the end she had already become a deadly white bone demon, and she still said to Tang Sanzang, "I hate others calling me a demon the most

The body and mind are the ability to resist external temptations, and as this ability diminishes, the individual's inner self becomes increasingly weak.

Being a person is painful, it's better to be a demon. "This is the approach chosen by Lady Bai Gu. But the intentional close-up portrayal of her blood sucking spirit in the film, silent yet fully absorbed into her body, may be her subconscious desire and voice: I am a person or I want to be a person.

In this painful and intense conflict, Madame White Bone finally chose to betray herself and accept temptation, becoming a demon, but she still couldn't let go of my desire to be a person, or my idea of being a person. When inner desires and behavioral expressions are inconsistent, an individual's external behavioral image is opposite to their self-identity, thus creating a more intense breeding ground for inner conflict.

When an individual is in a long-term intense and difficult psychological conflict, and lacks the ability to self regulate and guide, it is necessary to seek psychological counseling.

Secondly, vanity and excessive narcissism result in the loss of the ability and freedom to choose goodness.

In my article 'The Mermaid', I mentioned that narcissism is divided into benign narcissism and malignant narcissism. Benign narcissism can create something from scratch, which is a recognition of a creative reality matching from the inside out; Malignant narcissism is not the case.

Individuals who cannot create or do not realize that they have equal creative abilities can lead to vicious narcissism, and the keyword "possession" emerges.

This is one of the causes of collecting and fetishism.

For example, some people who never use pencils to write inexplicably like to collect pencils and erasers. Such collection is harmless, as long as it does not harm others or oneself, it may not necessarily affect social function and interpersonal relationships. From this perspective, we can also discover some celebrity collectors who enjoy collecting antique and jade artifacts, willing to invest heavily, but not for value-added investment, just because of their hobbies. The White Bone Lady in the film, after absorbing human blood and soul, built her cave into a fortress of human bones.

In fact, sometimes we encounter situations where when you hear about a magnificent treasure, you really want to own it, but in fact, you haven't fully understood its specific function, whether it suits you or not, whether it harms others or yourself

I just want to buy it back and put it on the shelf, even if it's of no use to me in the future, and it doesn't matter if I don't get questioned. At this moment, have you ever thought about whether the personality traits of excessive narcissism and vanity are being coated behind the desire to possess so much?

So, why are we doing this?

Thirdly, the response to all actions only stems from the fear of the recurrence of pain.

Madame Baigu once said, "What does it mean to be in hell

I am hell

When a person encounters significant psychological fear, they either eliminate the fear and become stronger, or simply become afraid and let others fear them.

The former choice requires strong willpower, spiritual cultivation, and gradual growth and strength through setbacks and hardships.

The latter, on the other hand, is quick and easy, without the need to overcome or face fear on my own. I am the spokesperson for fear myself.

Madame Baigu also has a deep fear in her heart, which conflicts strongly with her inner self needs and breeds even greater fear.

Madame Baigu no longer wants to be human, even if Tang Sanzang keeps saying that he wants to tame her, she would rather die than become a demon, because she has evolved that fear that is not recognized by humans into her own image or spiritual symbol, producing the spirit symbol of "making everyone fear me, that is me".

It is said that a person can only truly love one person in their lifetime, and other successors are just substitutes or similar products of that spiritual person. That is actually a mode of seeking psychological recognition from the outside world, but after all, newcomers may just happen to conform to the individual identity pattern, that is, the imagined appearance, and once the gap is discovered in reality, it will lead to such individuals falling into a bad mood. Because she couldn't accept another collapse of this identity model.

So, in the film, the White Bone Lady couldn't let go of her obsession and was determined to eat "Tang Monk's flesh". As a demon, she also hoped to be recognized by the crowd. Such conflicts were hidden in her subconscious, tearing apart her spiritual consciousness bit by bit. Over time, no matter how much blood and spirit she absorbed, she couldn't fill the "black hole" of her psychological trauma.

When the White Bone Lady in the film is captivating, she only sees her own needs and never sees the emotions of others, such as pain, helplessness, fear, and pain

When an individual chooses to live by sucking on the happiness of others and watching their pain, they have already lost the freedom to choose goodness.

Do you think that Lady White Bone is actually a pitiful person after reading my words so far?

So, how can we use psychological codes to break the fate of Madame White Bone?

The degree of freedom in body, mind, and spirit determines the degree of freedom in choosing between good and evil.

A. The decisive factor in choosing better rather than worse lies in cognition: every individual has a self constructed cognitive system of good and evil since birth. If the system is distorted during the growth process, then a person who focuses on this field is needed to work together. Everyone should work conscientiously and responsibly with the goal of discovering the underlying causes of individual pain, and increase the percentage of normal cognitive balance, in order to possibly improve the situation.

B. When it comes to making decisions in certain situations, one can think carefully, but try to avoid indecision: a person will only experience serious psychological problems in the midst of self contradiction and conflict between becoming a human or a demon, just like Madame White Bone wants to be a demon to eliminate her fear of being a human, but also wants to be recognized by others, emphasizing that she dislikes others calling her a demon the most. If you want to be a good person, then speak and act with dignity and righteousness; If you want to be a demon, you can openly declare yourself a demon. So, if you want to be yourself to the extreme and become yourself, as long as you can bear the domino effect of your words and actions, why not? In fact, among the five cultivators in Journey to the West, only Tang Monk is a human, while the others are all demons. However, they all abide by their duties, protect Tang Monk from the West to obtain scriptures, and become the ultimate demon. By practicing brightly in this way, they can avoid pain and distortion that could tear apart their souls and personalities.

C. Being able to perceive the subconscious needs behind one's own actions, finding and discovering them: for example, an individual's true needs are the satisfaction of narcissism and vanity, rather than necessarily possessing a pile of "bones" and "souls" that are not of much use to oneself. Interpreting such needs, we can try to rephrase them and satisfy them in other ways, such as leveraging one's strengths in a certain field to gain extraordinary fame and fortune, which can greatly satisfy narcissistic and vain needs. As long as one does not harm others or frame their own needs on the pain of others, it is the beginning of regaining good power, and the freedom of choice is also expanded.

Rejecting irrational emotions is the key to finding the direction of one's emotions.

People who are influenced by irrational emotions often force themselves to do things that go against their true self-development patterns. When "candy" appears, it is important to firmly establish the voice of the subconscious (of course, the prerequisite is to first learn to explore and discover it). With the extension of time and changes in the environment, it is often easy to gradually change a person's original true beliefs, lose the "consciousness" of cultivation, and gradually lose oneself in various vivid experiences, becoming numb, cold, and even ruthless.

So, loudly say to yourself three times: 'I'm not eating candy now because it goes against my development plan and life pattern. Don't eat candy! Don't eat candy! Don't eat candy!' Gradually, you will find that there are many people around you who, like you, focus more on individual planning, development, and growth. And fortunately, you are also one of them who is subtle but resilient, willing to pay for your dreams and actions.

3. Fully understand the possible consequences of behavior and enhance willpower.

As we saw before, the child who was raised by candy is prone to compromise when he sees temptations such as "candy" as he grows up, and easily give up the "original intention" that almost deceived him before. Once the true essence is lost, one will inevitably indulge in the temptation of short-term gratification and ignore the consequences of words and actions. This' neglect 'is a natural occurrence that has almost become a conditioned reflex event from childhood or past experiences.

This is one of the reasons why we do not advocate material rewards over spiritual rewards to encourage children's learning in the education of the next generation.

When faced with temptation, the spiritual platform should have a clear consciousness, rational logic, high-quality and comprehensive cognitive system. In the long run, when the gorgeous sugar coating on that candy falls off, it is the beginning of the opposite of pain and the pursuit of a happy life plan. So, returning to the present moment, there may be a sudden burst of inspiration and a realization of enlightenment - no matter how delicious the candy is, it's not worth it.

Explanation for this issue (Psychology): Goodness may be an ability, the ability to water, help germinate, grow, bloom, and bear fruit for the seeds of inner happiness. Happiness lies deep in everyone's heart, and our attitude towards being treated by others depends to some extent on the individual's attitude. When you treat others kindly and view the world objectively, then at least the majority of people in this world will also treat you kindly; If you are grateful for your experiences and hardships, then those experiences and hardships will help you grow. It depends on whether you can discover it, or whether you can take care of and be responsible for it. A single thought of obsession is sentient beings, and a single thought of enlightenment is Buddha. Perhaps everyone still has a white bone lady living in their heart, but whether to turn her into a Buddha or a demon depends entirely on the power of consciousness and time in their heart.

11 Discussing Dream Systems with Bert Hellinger from Inception

Release information: Inception is a film directed by Christopher Nolan and starring Leonardo DiCaprio, Marion Cotillard, and others. It was produced by Legendary Pictures in 2010. The shooting date is July 13th, 2009.

When you dream, what do you feel?

——S Jing Goldtouch

I watched Inception again because I recently read Bert Hellinger's book 'Who's in My Hellinger Family System Arrangement'.

Bert Heilinger is a German psychotherapist and the founder of the Family Constellations method.

In the modern era where materialism is the mainstream of scientific debate, this is a rare work. This book discusses a large number of insights into the arrangement of family systems, all of which touch on topics such as gods, souls in family systems, and other mythological stories, which may be related to his 16 year missionary experience with the Zulu people in South Africa.

He attempted to integrate Zulu music and rituals into his missionary Mass, believing that he could do better without any constraints.

The belief that divinity is everywhere allows him to obtain the information he wants to collect without being confined to a single point, and flexibly integrate these valuable healing experiences and information through collective dynamics, psychoanalysis, Gestalt therapy, primal therapy, and interactional analysis therapy.

Among them, he mentioned a brief account of dreams, which is about a visitor's dream therapy record and has some similarities with the interpretation of dreams in the 2010 film Inception. This is also one of the reasons why I want to revisit this classic movie.

This new film starring Leonardo DiCaprio and Christopher Nolan, in the words of the male lead, Dom Cobb, is: "I am engaged in a very special security job, protecting people's subconscious

Dom Cobb (Leonardo DiCaprio) and his colleagues Arthur and Nash fail in a dream stealing operation against Japanese energy tycoon Saito, and are instead exploited by Saito. Kobu, who was wanted and exiled overseas due to Saito's coercion, helped him break up his competitor's company and took extreme measures to plant the idea of abandoning the family company and starting his own business in the deep subconscious of his only heir, Robert Fischer.

In order to return to the United States, Cobb was forced to take on this job and secretly sought help from his father-in-law Miles, recruiting young dream designer Ariadne, dream actor Ames, and pharmacist Joseph to join the action.

However, after entering a series of progressive dreams, Cobb encountered Fisher's subconscious instinctive resistance and had to face the constant destruction of his deceased wife Mel

For old fans who have watched this film, there is no need for me to say much about the plot, but here, I believe it is necessary to briefly explain my views on dream therapy by combining the viewpoints mentioned in Hailinger's Dream Memoirs.

In the film Inception, there is a character that Cobb finds difficult to face but must confront, which is the destruction of his deceased wife Mel in the dream world.

In Cobb's real world, Mel may be a nightmare that Cobb hardly wants to mention in his real life, but in his dreams, his wife is his perfect companion. Regarding Mel's destruction, Mel's explanation is that Cobb has transitioned from actively entering the final layer of LMBO (Lost Domain) during dream missions to unconsciously entering LMBO (Lost Domain). People who enter this public dream space unconsciously, even dream thieves, cannot return to the real world without being killed or committing suicide, unless someone comes to the Lost Domain through their dreams in the real world and tells them. So at the end of the film, Cobb's wife Mel attempts to inform Cobb through death that this is the Lost Domain, hoping that he will wake up and return to the real world.

But there is a node in the dream cycle here, which is in Cobb's real world. Mel is a dead person, and whether Cobb consciously or unconsciously enters the Lost Domain, he remembers this very clearly and distinctly. So, according to this logic, Mel is just a misguidance in the lost domain of a dream.

So, in terms of the plot setting of the film, it is a self contradictory inner loop, and Cobb may serve as a balance point for the dream.

The viewpoint of Bert Hellinger's Dream Brief:

A visitor has a continuous dream or often thinks of it, always worrying about someone in the dream.

Hailing Ge will ask that person if anyone with such an image has died in your big family system.

According to Hailing Ge's viewpoint, he would connect a person's often troubled dreams with the entire family system.

Just like in the movie Inception, Cobb had to face his wife Mel in layers of dreams because in Cobb's family system, his wife Mel was a deceased person who was very important to him, in other words, also Cobb's inner demon.

After carefully analyzing and reading this work by Hellinger, and eliminating the cognitive attitude of taking things out of context, I adopt Gestalt therapy, Primitive therapy, and Interaction Analysis therapy in psychology. With a cognitive attitude of mutual respect and communication among psychologists, I would like to talk about Hellinger's views on dream classification and family system arrangement.

According to Bert Helinger's classification of dreams, in the usual sense, derivative dreams are defined as people's dreams that are created to escape from real events. They are dreams in which people instinctively avoid certain things without being responsible or showing respect, and are considered derivative dreams.

Secondly, it has memory encoding and there are not too many dramatic and exaggerated dreams, called native dreams.

There is also System Dream, which is the main psychological analysis method used by Bert Hailinger throughout the entire work: family system arrangement.

Under normal circumstances, categorizing a dream character that always influences visitors into a family system arrangement to find answers does not pose significant problems. After all, where there is a cause, there is a result. The loss of one person in the family system will lead to the gain of another person later on. This is the method used in the Hailing family system to heal certain visitors who are unhappy by using almost mythical stories.

Just like in dream movies, Cobb often sees his deceased wife in his dreams because she has already passed away in his real world family system. But because she was once an important person to Cobb, that's why she dreamed about it.

According to this viewpoint, there is no problem analyzing it up to this point, but Bert Helinger overlooked a detail, which is Cobb's inner demon, also mentioned in Bert's dream perspective as a shadow dream.

Bert Hellinger mentioned that these dreams allow us to see the side of ourselves that we don't want to see, and we are even unwilling to talk about it.

That's equivalent to Cobb's real-life deceased Mel in the film, who is his inner demon and created his shadow dream.

Shadow dreams can potentially mislead visitors' system dreams. In other words, if a dream therapist interprets a dream based on the system dream and simply searches for answers in the family arrangement, they may have already been misled and confused by shadow dreams.

Therefore, in Bert Hailinger's family system arrangement and the analysis and treatment methods of system dreams, the misleading shadow dreams created by each different person and members of his family system cannot be ignored.

That is, what we commonly refer to as the inner demon, it may mislead us to ignore, exclude, or even miss moments of treasures or treasures that are quite important to ourselves.

Just like Cobb in the movie, perhaps Mel could be his heartthrob or his treasure. So, the entire film ends with a somewhat contradictory inner loop.

So, taking this film as an example, how can we face and overcome the impact of shadow dreams on the correct treatment of system dreams in the arrangement of family systems?

1. Believe in yourself: No matter what the shadow dreams may mislead us about, as long as we firmly trust ourselves and clearly understand who we are and what has positive development value for our future, both in dreams and in the real world, we also need to have a clear and intuitive understanding.

2. Patience and waiting: This is a small technique that I have learned from reading Bert Hellinger's work, which can be applied in both psychotherapy and daily life. That is to say, no matter what kind of confusing or misleading situation we encounter, we should not be controlled by our inner confusion and anxious emotions. Instead, we should patiently and calmly wait, and face what we encounter with a mindset that is close to nature. So I believe that at some

important moment in the future, the self who firmly believes in clarity will definitely have a chance for redemption.

This is also exemplified in the film Inception, where Cobb's wife, or Cobb, who was once eager to return to the real world, or his companions, may have missed the opportunity for redemption and become lost by forcibly revealing the answer too early without fully understanding the situation. Just like those people who are forced into the realm of lost dreams without knowing themselves, isn't this the best interpretation of the meaning in the film?

3. Cherish the special value of life: Bert Hailinger once mentioned a circular therapy in his healing notes. The original intention of his setting up this is to prevent every member of the motivational psychotherapy group from being attacked by collective defense on the basis of an individual personality that is not very strong and solid.

So, his beautiful therapeutic intention is to achieve perfect healing in an atmosphere where no one will be attacked, blamed or praised.

However, he overlooked a seemingly subtle factor that could potentially destroy the entire power therapy with even a slight mistake, similar to the variables mentioned in Inception films. Under the surface peaceful tranquility, there are either variables that are prone to causing great waves of difficulties and setbacks, or variables that are extremely lucky to bring peace back, such as Saito, who Cobb encountered when he failed to steal his dreams at the beginning, or his wife Mel, who hinted at Cobb's lost domain.

Combining Bert Hellinger's peculiar work with the wonderful movie Inception, the circular therapy proposed by this Hellinger family system arrangement psychotherapist is not bad for those visitors who are not physically strong in their personalities. However, in such a peaceful and peaceful healing group, every serious therapist engaged in healing the soul must consider preparing a relatively strong emergency defense attack ruler. If circular therapy is compared to harmony, then a rigid ruler can also serve as an effective measure to defend the orderly, long-term, and stable treatment of the entire family arrangement system.

Under the close connection of rigidity and flexibility, it is possible to discover different special values of life when facing treatment from different visitors, while also cherishing the original driving force of equal life.

Explanation for this issue (Psychology): Only in such systematic therapy can visitors appreciate themselves more clearly. Even in situations of misleading or confusing situations, they will focus more on a clear understanding of their own actions, rather than the destructive power that may be triggered by negative emotions such as fear, anxiety, anger, blame, or avoidance. After all, cherishing oneself and the value of life is the topic that should be paid more attention to - life is full of practice!

12 Identifying Kind Wisdom from 'Magic Teacher'

Release information: 'Magic Teacher' is a science fiction comedy film directed by Terry Jones, starring Simon Pegg and Kate Beckinsale. It was released in Chinese Mainland on August 14, 2015 (UK) and September 9, 2016 (China).

Control his anger and forsake his wrath.Don't be unfair,So that they do evil.

————Old Poetry 37:8

According to the powers granted by the Galactic Council, the unknown single high school teacher Neil (played by Simon Pegg) is unintentionally selected and becomes a routine test subject in alien random selection, endowed with strong super energy. During this process, a series of comical stories happened, and aliens hoped to see in this little person their ability to recognize good and evil, and use their super energy to do things that punish evil and promote good.

Neil woke up from a night's sleep and suddenly discovered that he possessed a wonderful superpower that could make all his dreams come true with just saying his wishes and waving one hand, including things he had never dared to imagine before, such as dating and having dinner with his dream lover Catherine

From ignorance to the subsequent forced use of machinery, Neil, this ordinary person, began to greatly admire such superpowers and increasingly regarded himself as an omnipotent being, like a god. He needed this feeling so much, and by helping his friend Lei and making the girl he was pursuing crazily admire him, he could uncover some basic psychological codes that the film wanted to convey.

It is obvious that a small person, in the sudden stroke of luck, did not truly utilize such abilities properly. Firstly, he did not initially have a clear ability to distinguish between good and evil, but instead abused most of his abilities to satisfy personal desires. From a teacher's perspective, his initial wish, which came out of nowhere, was to destroy his own class. Psychological analysis techniques show that he does not truly love his job, and as a teacher, he did not initially realize the responsibility of the word 'teacher'. There seems to be a conflicting conflict deep in his soul. So, after a series of losses, he will try his best to make up for them and feel extremely guilty.

This reminds me of a real-life case where there was a girl who liked to dream. She often dreamed of being a teenager, but in reality, she was actually a very dependent person. She has had too many dreams and even likes to be inseparable friends with the boy in her dreams, even fantasizing about being partners. Over time, she began to have difficulty remembering what happened in her dreams and gradually developed some problems, which is that she tends to mistake some of the unpleasant things that happened in her dreams for events that happened in the real world.

The feelings in those dreams made her feel difficult to express, even ashamed. That deep sense of shame kept devouring her mind and had already had some impact on her normal life. Until I discovered her like this, given the phenomena that had occurred with her, I rationally suggested necessary psychological treatment and counseling for her.

Just like the second half of the movie 'The Magic Teacher', the magic teacher's abuse of abilities has led to a series of negative consequences. For example, his friend Lei no longer likes him because he thought he was humorous but turned his only friend from an ordinary faculty member into an extraordinary "saint" in the eyes of a good girl, and finally became disgusting. That made Lei go from ecstatic and flattered at the beginning, to panic and running wildly due to fear, and finally, like hearing a dry thunder explode and being knocked down from the clouds, as if he had had had an extremely absurd dream. Looking at reality, but even more cruel, love seemed suddenly dull to him, leaving only a face full of sadness.

For example, Catherine, whom Neil most expected, also left angrily because he chose to temporarily abandon his rumored love on his last wish in order to break free from the control of his rival. But afterwards, he felt extremely guilty. The personality trait of evading responsibility is once again reflected in Neil, as evidenced by his explosion of his class at the beginning of the film. And this time, surprisingly, he wanted to choose to escape everything from being born lightly, rather than using his superpowers to properly repair his mistakes.

Neil's personality traits in the film are like that of the girl who often treats her dream experiences as real. Neil's situation is like a dream, something that doesn't exist in real life. Unfortunately, many ordinary people are too eager to satisfy their aspirations of becoming big shots, and thus choose to use various behavioral patterns to escape the responsibilities they should bear in reality. Just like how Neil, filled with guilt for friendship and despair for love, would rather choose to jump off a bridge than try to make up for his mistakes. Based on the above personality traits, combined with interactive analysis therapy, I also observed an extremely subtle personality trait of Neil and that girl, which is perfectionism tendency.

Only individuals with a perfectionist personality can't tolerate making mistakes. They usually show humility and politeness, and often make people feel very good in all aspects. Unfortunately, these appearances are only meant to maintain the perfection they cannot achieve. They hope for perfection, but reality tells them that they cannot achieve it. So, they cannot accept the painful spiritual feelings that should have been triggered by self-awareness and self reflection in this step, and only then will they become negative, and even have temporary suicidal thoughts.

Taking the realization generated by Neil's mistake in the film as an example, it can precisely solve the problems and doubts of my young girl:

Firstly, having kindness requires sufficient wisdom in order to have the ability to distinguish between the truth and falsehood of goodness and evil.

Secondly, possessing the appropriate strength and balance to counter evil, which is also reflected in the self-control of behavior, is the key to hitting a beautiful home run. It is neither belated nor self harming, nor is it a violent tactic. It is a mixed fight that harms innocent people. It is too much to do.

Thirdly, respecting the past and grasping the present will lead to a better future. Just like the girl I treated with psychological therapy, she became willing to confront her feelings of shame and guilt and realized that they were just false interpretations in her dreams, just to make her feel uncomfortable.

Now she has completely let go of those shame and guilt. Recalling her brief thoughts of suicide due to the scenes in her dreams, she finally felt willing to let go. Because holding onto the past means not letting go of oneself. So, in my hypnotherapy, she used a particularly wonderful way to say goodbye to the boy in the dream, 'Goodbye, but never see him again.'.

After more than a month of treatment, I accidentally saw her again. She works in a large supermarket, and her facial features have become more beautiful, radiating a spring breeze like radiance. However, she was enthusiastic about her job as a supermarket tallyman at the time and didn't notice me.

In my heart, I am sincerely gratified.

Only by being caught by a greedy enemy in the movie "The Magic Teacher" and fully utilizing it, like going to hell, not daring to face one's past self, feeling ashamed and guilty, jumping over a bridge, but also daring to save one's owner because even a loyal dog who cannot swim dares to do so, can one gain reincarnation from past experiences.

Explanation for this issue (Psychology): Let go of the past and gain new life.

Psychological Gate · **Listening to Children**

A: Educators cultivate children's concentration by allowing them to focus on themselves - who they are at this moment and what they should do, rather than focusing their attention on "where I am right and where I am wrong" - from various external misleading information. Wishing the children happiness.

B: Growing through gradual discovery requires transformation. This process may involve some normal emotional expressions during the growth period, even missing out on some enjoyable learning time, and may also wrongly blame partners who already care about themselves. Until we find precise answers through self reflection and contemplation, and then remember the knowledge that has helped us grow. In the end, it will be discovered that what is truly worth cherishing and paying attention to for children's growth has not been missed at all.

C: In the same environment and circumstances, knowing how to give urgent desires a sense of self tranquility and peaceful waiting, what should be seen can always be seen. But as educators or parents, or in a big family atmosphere, when it comes to children's small slip ups, we need to distinguish whether they need more attention or if there are other deeper reasons. But I always believe that all questions will receive a satisfactory answer.

D: Around September 27th, 2016, I received a great picture book called 'Flowers Know, Wind Has Passed'. I read it carefully last night and told the story of a little fool looking for a dream flower everywhere. No matter what situation he encounters, he can remain calm and his faith cannot be erased by any setbacks, because the flower he is looking for has always been with him.

E: I don't know how many years ago, it seemed like a long, long ago. In my hazy memory, there was a boy with golden hair who once said to me, 'I love the feeling of being with you so much.' To put it simply, 'Who am I when I'm with you?'. But I vaguely remember that I only received his text message again at the end of 2013. The phone case is very cold, and the words and lines of the text message are familiar. The content that can be written is still this sentence, 'Who am I when I'm with you?'. Stranger, familiar, even stranger, there are still scattered remnants of familiarity

I asked, 'Who are you?'

He said, "I am... I am someone you once said such a thing to me, you know ……

Good child, you are still wrong. The key is not who you are with me, but who you should always know who you are and what kind of talent you will become in the future

……

Um... vaguely, I may have said this sentence before, or that feeling, I said it myself, but it's not, is it? Perhaps if that blond kid really talked to me, I have a

92% chance of saying it. Usually in such situations, I would say something like this, and I would calmly and calmly look at the child as usual, but still scare him. I speak fast... maybe I'll rephrase it.

That sister said you're a pig, are you a pig

In the faint and lingering memory, the blond little boy said, "No pig

Perhaps he would also pout his cheeks and reply to me, "You pig."

1 Teaching students according to their aptitude is the most reasonable educational philosophy

I believe everyone still remembers the TV drama "Tiger Mom and Cat

Dad" played by Zhao Wei and Tong Dawei. After watching it, I believe many viewers have resonated with the educational philosophy of the parents in the drama.

Five year old little princess Luo Xiqian was first taken care of by her grandmother and grandfather. As the saying goes, 'babies come from different generations', emphasizing the cultivation of children's temperament in a free environment. The grandmother gave children full respect and the right to choose, but lacked rules, which led to many bad habits such as being unable to endure hardship, hating poverty and loving wealth, and being spoiled.

Tiger Mom "Bi Shengnan realized that if this continued, his child would be ruined by unruly indulgence, so he took the child home and took care of it himself. She, who received the "Victory" education from a young age, inherited her father's compulsory education method. Excessive protective desire leads to a strong desire for control, which is almost irrefutable: she does not allow her children to participate in extracurricular activities, believing that outdoor sketching is just a waste of study time; At night, tired children who have already gone to bed will be pulled up by her just to remind them of the principle of "finishing today's work today"; She even sneaked a peek at the child's diary... This kind of love, with more rules, but with less respect, creates a barrier to genuine communication between the child and the mother.

In fact, the age of three to five is the embryonic stage of children's self-awareness and also the age with the strongest plasticity. The behavior pattern of children at this time is often more interactive with the emotions on their parents' faces, rather than deeply recognizing the values of right and wrong in their consciousness.

A five-year-old child is in the stage of self-evaluation, and he does not yet understand what is right and what is wrong. (Moreover, this world cannot be fully explained solely by black and white.) For example, in the drama, grandparents often play the game of "Little Princess and Servant" with Rosie, and both adults and children are happy. As a result, the child's feedback from the smile on the adult's face is, "Ha, I'm doing this, they're happy, and I'm happy too." Then they assume that there is no right or wrong in continuing this interaction. Later on, as a mother, Bi Shengnan forcefully read and edited Qian Qian's diary, ignoring the fact that five-year-old children also have their own initial values, as well as the right to choose and privacy. However, she plays a crucial role as a mother in family relationships and exerts strong pressure, making the child wonder and explore from their own uncomfortable emotions. "Is it wrong to think that I don't like my mom reading my diary because she gets angry

Continuing to evolve in this way, under high-pressure and dominant education, children will gradually be deprived of their own choices, creativity, self happiness, and the free development of interests will be suppressed. Such children will become indecisive and timid, always wanting to pay attention to the emotions of those around them before doing anything, and increasingly ignoring their own needs and feelings. Or it is also possible to fully grow into a more dominant opposite, surpassing even the elders.

From the perspective of a mother, interpreting this educational philosophy actually comes more from Bi Shengnan's father. Because Tiger Mom grew up in an equally high-pressure educational environment since childhood, although she has always had a shadow over her father's educational methods and instinctively expressed opposition, she naturally replicated the educational model she received from her elders in her own educational behavior and philosophy. Although the high-pressure and forceful education of "winning the game" has been quite effective on Tiger Mom herself, it has overlooked the personality of the educational object.

So far, there is no fixed educational philosophy or model that can be applied to all children with different personalities. This is not like choosing clothes. In education, there are no "versatile styles", only whether they are suitable or not.

In this world, any normal family, without parents who do not love their children, wants to pass on their true love to their children and receive reasonable and equal feedback.

Respect+rules=true love. The feeling of love in true love is fluid, not closed or silent. Because of harmonious communication, understanding, and seeing the world in an equal way with each other, our love can flow. The warmth and acceptance of love are like the warm embrace of a mother. While warming our young self-esteem, it also teaches us how to recognize whether our own shadow is incomplete or perfect in the eyes of others, examine our own way of dealing with things, and slowly grow step by step until... when we can walk independently and face storms and difficulties independently, form clear values of right and wrong deep in our hearts, and gradually improve them through our different experiences and summarization. Only in this way can we integrate true love into acceptance and respect. We can see the world through our own eyes, as well as through the eyes of others. With a new way of truly understanding self love and loving others, we can pass on love and let our blood and life find new ways to adapt and survive.

The "Tiger Mom" Bi Shengnan in the drama went from blindly following education due to lack of experience to groping, and finally formed his own faction, understanding the educational philosophy of "teaching students according to their aptitude". In this process of transformation, parents and children are actually exploring and growing together, adapting to each other, and ultimately finding the most harmonious way to convey true love. If we blindly adhere to any fixed educational philosophy and apply it to children, it is like watering and nurturing a small sapling. There is only one chance to give and nurture it, and once it takes shape, it is impossible to start over. If it weren't for 'teaching students according to their aptitude', we might have sown bitter fruits, which is the most worrying thing for us and our children on the path of growth.

2 Try using differential addition to control your small mouth

Your psychological counseling room is absolutely amazing. "These were the first words Huirong said when she first came to my psychological studio. Although there is a pleasing tone in the tone, there are also dirty words used to curse.

She is a 7-year-old child. But every time I speak, there is a pile of dirty words stored there, and swear words can be used anytime, anywhere.

Your pen is pretty good, it's so damn cool, it's really dazzling

Your sofa is so damn good, comfortable

This glass of juice is so damn delicious, I'm just thirsty

Not bad, Huirong is a child who never leaves TMD greetings in three sentences. For this reason, her parents were at a loss and relied on their friendship to find me and seek help.

Huirong's parents spoil their children very much. They don't want the teacher to overly criticize Huirong at school for this, so that Huirong won't lose face, nor do they want the teacher to punish her for it. So Huirong's problem is getting worse and worse, and she is also developing herself more and more on the road of growth, without any hesitation. It really lives up to the saying that children have "no taboos" when it comes to speaking.

Ke Huirong's parents are both intellectuals. Whenever they take Huirong out as a guest, she uses vulgar language, some of which are unheard of by adults (not repeated here). When asked by others, it made Huirong's parents feel ashamed. They knew that if they didn't care about Guan Huirong anymore, this child might be ruined.

I have a general understanding of the situation and said to Huirong, "Why do you like every sentence to have dirty words

This is not easy, because it makes me mature. "Huirong shrugged her shoulders and sat down on the fabric sofa in my consultation room, crossing her legs." This way, my classmates will be afraid of me and dare not provoke me

Children in this age group may not be mentally mature enough, but they crave adult like attention, which is why Huirong experiences this phenomenon.

We might as well adopt a differentiation enhancement strategy to control her small mouth, "I suggested.

The first thing I did was to provide a week of psychological counseling for Huirong. During this period, let me become Huirong's "big banyan tree". I have a big tree hole where Huirong can freely express her thoughts.

At first, Huirong was very happy about me not restricting her from using dirty words when speaking. My tree hole also played the best role in listening and acceptance. Actually, I am also observing the frequency of Huirong cursing dirty words from the perspective of caring about her.

After a week of evaluation, we learned that Huirong curses with dirty words more than 15 times a day on average. So, I started talking to Huirong and said, "You know what? Actually, cursing dirty words doesn't necessarily indicate your maturity. True maturity is the way we handle things and our ability to handle them. Classmates are not afraid of you, but because you curse, they stay away from you. If this continues, no one will want to play with you. Besides showing your bad behavior, cursing dirty words can also turn you from a good girl to a not so good child. Are you willing to do that too

Huirong was taken aback for a moment and retorted, "I fucking like to say things like that. What should I do? I can't change it

I picked up a stack of "Douluo Continent" dance stickers and waved them at her, saying, "From now on, if you curse less than 6 times a day, I will give you a sticker of this kind. It's the first time you've come and said you like it

She reached out to grab the sticker from my hand, but I stopped her and hid behind her.

She withdrew her hand and rubbed her nose, saying, "Okay, only six times. There's nothing I can't do

On the contrary, if you can't do it, you will be punished for helping your mother take out the garbage

So, we agreed to come to my consultation room at 4 pm every day to conduct evaluations and implement rewards and punishments with her mother.

After a period of implementation, indeed, Huirong went from cursing dirty words 6-8 times a day, to later 5-6 times a day, then 3-4 times a day, and finally agreed to 1-2 times.

One month later, Huirong gradually reduced her daily standard from 15 times to 7 times, 5 times, 3 times, 2 times, 1 time, and finally 0 times, completely breaking her habit of cursing.

My little dance stickers are also just finished: "You look more like the little dance in Douluo, not bad

Analyzing this case, it is not difficult to find that our basic principle for tutoring Huirong, who has become accustomed to cursing dirty words, is not to expect her to improve completely at once, but to adopt a gradual approach. As long as the frequency of bad behavior is reduced, positive reinforcement will be given, and she will be rewarded with small dance stickers. She will use objects she likes to reinforce and gradually improve, and then gradually reduce the frequency standard to finally achieve the goal of improvement.

According to research, aggressive children are prone to losing their temper when faced with setbacks, being argumentative, using verbal abuse and fighting to resolve conflicts, and ignoring the rights and expectations of others. We can use differentiated reinforcement strategies to tutor these children.

3 How to be a parent with high emotional intelligence

Getting angry can destroy a child's spirituality, but not getting angry can make them feel uncomfortable. What should we do?

I believe many of us have raised children before, and in our consciousness, we all want to be excellent parents. However, when it comes to raising children, most people cannot always maintain a calm and composed attitude. Is this a big problem? Will our emotions affect children?

Firstly, from the psychological perspective of children, every time we lose our temper, there is always a sense of fear in their eyes. What we don't know is that what children are truly afraid of is not our anger, but the fear that from then on, we will no longer be friends with them, and they will never be able to receive their parents' love again.

The feeling of no longer being loved is more frightening for children than being scolded and beaten.

Secondly, since you said the child is so afraid of us getting angry, I will hide my anger and try to restrain myself from getting angry with the child again. Is that okay?

No, this is also not advisable. Because we are flesh and blood people, we all have moments of losing our temper and experiencing emotional outbursts. There are almost no people who don't lose their temper. Unless it's a 'walking dead'.

And every time we want to get angry at the bear kids, we actually try to restrain our temper. This bad way of dealing with negative emotions is captured by the sensitive and young minds of children. They can already feel a strong message from the restrained tone, intonation, behavior, demeanor and many other aspects of adults: "Don't provoke me now, otherwise I will get angry. If I get angry, you bear kids don't have good fruit to eat. Get out of here, where it's cool, where you stay

Because children can feel our restrained emotions, they are likely to learn how to handle negative emotions in this way over the long term. The biggest problem is that in the future, they will not tell you what they encounter outside, but instead choose to keep it to themselves. If emotions do not flow positively, it will be extremely detrimental to the psychological growth of children in the long run.

So, you said that children who get angry are afraid of losing love, and not getting angry is not conducive to their psychological growth. So, we are normal flesh and blood people. When we have negative emotions, we have to communicate with our children. So how should we interact?

When we encounter mischievous children, such as smashing your beloved porcelain; Or ruin your work documents; Or scribble on the walls of the house; Or fighting with the neighbor's bear child... and so on, there are countless moments when the bear child ignites a raging anger in the parents' hearts. At this point, as educators, we should choose the approach of "dealing with the situation but not the person", reason well, and explain the reasoning behind what the bear child did. We should guide them to understand what kind of mistake they made and how to handle it next time they encounter the same situation.

2. As parents, we should try our best to give necessary warnings to our children before negative emotions arise. For example, saying to a child, 'I'm not in a good mood, I have to be alone for a while now, and we can talk about your affairs later.' This way, before the emotions come, we can be in a calm state with the child, and after the emotions pass, we can call out to the bear child.

3. After calming down, if we speak ill of our children, the first step is to explain to them why we get angry and how we feel when we do so, so that they can understand your difficulties when you are about to explode.

The key to true love is to rebuild the relationship after getting angry.

Some parents never apologize to their children, they may think that there is no reason in the world for parents to apologize to their children? For a long time, it has been the only way for children to apologize to their parents. In fact, this idea is somewhat biased and not conducive to the positive flow of emotions in the family. After all, no one is perfect in this world, and no one ever makes mistakes. If there is, that would be the biggest joke in the world.

So how to rebuild a good relationship with children?

If we get angry with our child and hurt their self-esteem, we must apologize and say "I'm sorry" to them as soon as our emotions calm down. This occasional low posture parenting style allows us to relax and make our child understand that although we get angry with them, it doesn't mean we don't love them anymore. We still love them very much.

Why do we suddenly get angry when we talk to our children about our worries? For example, "Mom, things didn't go well at work today," or "I accidentally made a mistake and got scolded by someone today. At the same time, we also need to tell our children that when they are in a bad mood, they can also get angry. It does not mean that once a child makes a fuss, it is certain that the child will not behave or listen, so do not stop the child from crying, confiding or venting.

This kind of parenting style of chasing and blocking is a "double standard" and not conducive to children's growth. To have a healthy and stress tolerant mindset, he needs to allow children to have a clear understanding of their emotions and teach them how to handle negative emotions positively.

After chatting with the child, we returned to each other's hearts and asked if we had reconciled? After confirming this, give each other a warm hug.

In a good family, there must be one or a pair of parents with high emotional intelligence. This kind of open and cheerful approach can effectively vent negative emotions and promote positive emotional flow in the family. It should be slow, steady, and not impatient, always guiding children to live freely, strong, confident, and happy and healthy lives.

4 How to give your child a strong inner self?

How to give your child a strong inner self? This is probably the expectation of many parents for their children, but how should we proceed?

In short, please praise him more.

We often say that it's easy to make a child feel inferior. Just keep hitting and denying them, constantly comparing them to other children, not recognizing their unique strengths, and denying their words and actions... As parents, with just this operation, you can easily give your child a strong and powerful blow to their confidence, and over time, become a child with a strong sense of inferiority or fragile glass heart.

On the contrary, it is not easy for us to establish a strong inner self in a child, especially to build the confidence of a child who is very insecure. It is not a simple task at all.

It's like it's easy to do something bad, but difficult to do something good.

So how can we praise a child who has been criticized and self doubting? How can a child still firmly love and believe in themselves when faced with external questioning voices?

What is the reason why you don't praise your child?

Some parents believe that if their children are not educated on setbacks from a young age, they may not be able to withstand criticism from others when they enter the workforce in the future, or they may choose to commit suicide at the slightest setback. Some parents also believe that some children can be praised to heaven, but in the end, they will achieve nothing.

But in reality, deep down in every child's heart, whether or not we are criticized or questioned by the outside world, we all need to receive a lot of praise from our families. Only by receiving these praises can children realize the shining points in themselves when forming an independent personality, and these shining points can gradually light up their humanity, gradually form normal and healthy values, illuminate the weak parts of their personality, and then dispel them. Only in this way can children who grow up in constant affirmation have enough confidence to withstand the baptism of wind and rain.

2. Children who have not been praised by their parents since childhood actually have a lot of inferiority complex in their hearts, and they have been proving that 'I am actually great' all their lives.

Xiao A has never been praised by his parents since he was young, and he grew up under their pressure. In his bones, he believes that he is not good enough and that no one else can do a great job. As an adult, my relationship with my parents became very distant. Later, after establishing a small family, the other half often praised themselves. Even the smallest things, such as peeling a fruit for their lover and placing it on a fruit platter, would be praised by their lover as "artistic and talented." Gradually, Little A could also see these good qualities in his life. He gradually became courageous, recognized his strengths and weaknesses, and began to work hard for the dreams he could achieve. He smiled and said that it was his significant other who gave him a second chance for self growth.

So, praise is so important for a child's growth process. It can help children gradually establish the boundaries of their self-awareness, knowing what to do and why not to do. He can clearly understand where the boundaries of his own abilities lie? I will neither aim too high nor give up easily due to self pity.

What are the thoughts of parents who do not praise their children?

Parents also grew up in the setbacks of criticism and suppression from a young age, and this growth process naturally replicates in their own children. The childhood memory is: 'I also grew up in pain like this, you are my child, and you should also grow up in such pain.'.

This analysis is not meant for us as parents to prevent our children from suffering, but rather to encourage and support them when they encounter difficulties or setbacks. By saying 'I have faith in you', our children can truly walk through the storms of setbacks alone and gradually grow up with sunshine.

2. Parents reflect their inner worries and anxieties on their children through continuous criticism and insults.

Parents themselves do not have the ability to handle negative emotions, so they vent on their children to relieve them. Over time, they actually develop a habit. If you are in a bad mood or acting improperly, use your child as your 'emotional trash can'.

Little do they know, the child's psychological resilience has reached a certain peak. Gradually, children also vent their negative emotions by hitting and scolding other classmates, leading to issues such as "campus bullying". Another type is when children encounter emotional violence and are unable to express themselves to others, they resort to internal attacks such as self harm and self abuse to vent their suppressed dissatisfaction. As a result, we occasionally see two wounds on children's bodies that have been cut by blades.

These types of children are seeking happiness and release in their own pain.

3. Parents' authority is overly maintained.

These types of parents do not know how to be friends with their children, but only know how to use the authority of their parents to suppress them, expressing love and authority through constant urging and critical words. In the end, when their children become adults, their relationship with their parents may become increasingly rigid, and their family ties may become farther and farther apart.

So how can we praise children correctly?

1. Try to recognize the child's true strengths and praise them. Don't be unrealistic and exaggerate your praise, as it will only make the child feel that you are just perfunctory, rather than really thinking that they are good.

2. Timely praise the child's strengths. After discovering a child's strengths, we should give them timely and appropriate praise, so that they can leave a deep impression in their memory and form the perception that 'I can perform well in this area'.

3. Some parents are not good at words and don't know how to praise their

children. After discovering your child's strengths, if you really don't know what to do, give him a warm hug. Hugging can deepen the bond of family.

So, what is a person with a strong inner self?

1. Recognize the value of one's own existence.

2. Have a clear boundary awareness of one's own abilities: what I can do and what I cannot do so far.

3. Able to control oneself: not easily hindered by negative external evaluations, whether to do what should be done or still do what.

4. Able to quickly recover from setbacks: commonly known as having strong resistance to pressure.

5 Step out of the haze of the past and free yourself from the twitching

When Xiao C first came to my consultation room for help, he was alone and he was still underage.

At a young age, life gave him extraordinary pain and experiences. When he saw me, he had an unstoppable frown and a slight shrug as he spoke. He told me that when he had this symptom a year ago, it was even more severe and he kept nodding. At that time, everyone saw him as if facing a monster, and as a result, his old wounds did not heal and he added new ones, which also increased his sense of shame and illness.

The condition of Xiao C is called Tourette Syndrome, also known as Tourette Syndrome in children. This is a type of neurological and psychiatric disorder that occurs during childhood and adolescence. Children with this condition may experience repeated motor and vocal tics in multiple areas, often accompanied by complications such as obsessive-compulsive disorder, attention deficit, and hyperactivity disorder.

Due to the negligence of my assistant, I was informed during my first medical consultation that it was ADHD. Therefore, my consultation was based on providing psychological counseling for ADHD. How should I start consulting with Little C?

When did you first realize you had this illness? "I thought for a moment and asked him the first question. Xiao C appeared very reserved in front of me at first, although he was young, he was very sensible. From his description, I learned that his initial illness was caused by the people closest to him leaving him forever.

I observed his incessant twitching and eye squeezing behavior in his narration, and based on my past consulting experience, I immediately had a completely new consulting plan in mind.

Have you received medication treatment in the past year or so? "I know that generally, this type of neurological and psychiatric disorder requires medication treatment, along with psychological counseling to assist in its progression.

Yes, I used to take an oral medication before. After taking it, I felt dizzy and swollen, and couldn't study or concentrate at all. Later, I switched to another medication that was applied to my back and shoulder blades, "Xiao C tried to recall. I noticed that he tried to control his words and actions in front of me, perhaps because he was worried that his unconscious behavior would scare me.

You can try to relax and release yourself in front of me, without being so deliberate, "I reminded him. A good counselor is like a cradle, providing visitors with a warm and safe harbor.

Considering that the main cause of Xiao C's tic disorder is the strong stimulation caused by the passing of a loved one, and now, after a year, he is still immersed in sadness and unable to extricate himself.

However, the knowledge conveyed in books indicates that the etiology and pathogenesis of Tourette's syndrome in children are not yet fully understood, and may be related to various factors such as genetic, neurophysiological, psychological, and environmental factors.

In light of this situation, I have timely adjusted my consultation plan for Xiao C

Firstly, during the gradual counseling and treatment process, I constantly told him that this condition can be treated and improved, in order to gradually eliminate his sense of shame and enhance his confidence in treatment and recovery.

At the same time, I asked about his interactions with others at school, which can help determine whether his illness has damaged his social functioning, especially in terms of interpersonal relationships.

Fortunately, there were no mocking or mocking classmates among Xiao C's classmates, and the teacher also showed great care for him, which made Xiao C feel very warm.

I like going to school, "he said with a rare and slightly happy expression on his face as soon as he mentioned school.

Well, that's great. If Xiao C can receive a lot of support from the environment and society during his illness, it will help him build confidence in his recovery.

Secondly, I plan to provide supportive guidance and behavioral therapy to Xiao C in subsequent consultations to help him arrange the child's normal life reasonably.

Due to this type of tic disorder, most children can gradually improve in their symptoms as they enter late adolescence. Although some children may continue with these symptoms into old age, it does not affect their intelligence and lifespan.

Thirdly, because Xiao C still cannot let go of the passing of his loved one over a year ago, based on this characteristic and past experience, it is necessary to provide him with grief counseling.

To make visitors who have been immersed in grief for a long time understand that grief is only a part of life and cannot replace everything, what we need to do at this time is to integrate grief.

1. Enhance visitors' sense of reality towards the loss of facts, increase their sense of lost reality, that is, accept this fact.

2. Help visitors deal with emotional and behavioral pain, assist parties in dealing with expressed or potential emotional emotions, and express sadness.

Some inexperienced caregivers may raise doubts at this time, and when the child is grieving, they are more inclined to help the child hide this sad wound, and over time, it becomes very deep. They think that by doing so, the sick child will no longer feel sad and mournful. Some caregivers even stubbornly believe, "As long as you can't see him crying, it's good

In fact, doing so is not conducive to the child's recovery from grief at all. The wound needs to be exposed to sunlight, and once it is exposed to light, it can be looked at directly, which is beneficial for the healing and scab formation of the wound.

However, considering the situation of children with Tourette's syndrome such as Xiao C, when dealing with grief counseling in the counseling room, the principle of not excessive stimulation should be followed.

But this does not mean that it does not help them recognize reality and deal with grief.

3. Encourage the parties involved to bid farewell to the deceased and calmly invest their emotions back into a new relationship in a healthy way. As for Xiao C, I encourage him to socialize more with classmates, make friends with one or two of them, handle family relationships with his current caregiver at home, embrace more, confide more, get closer, and allow for the establishment of new dependency relationships.

4. Introduce and educate visitors about mindfulness therapy, which involves observing oneself and others in the present without criticism, and healing oneself with Buddhist concepts.

The overall principle of grief counseling is: those who leave have a good ending, those who stay have a good parting, and those who are capable have a good life.

Finally, may every wounded soul have something to rely on, be comforted, stand up from sadness, bravely walk through the dark path, and move towards a bright life.

PS: Due to the principle of confidentiality in consulting, the case analysis in this article is fictional and only mentions Tourette's syndrome. We hope it will be helpful to everyone.

Psychological Gate · Our Emotions

1 Create a "transfer plan" for yourself to carry with you

Whoever of you loves life and desires to see many good days, keep your tongue from evil and your lips from speaking lies.

——**Old Poetry 34:12, 13**

He appeared at the door of the consultation room with a tattered plastic bag in his hand, empty and full of anger. He is today's visitor, named Qiaonan.

Do you need help? "I asked softly as I looked at the young visitor.

I don't know! "His answer still contained a lot of anger, and his eyes seemed to be looking at me, as if he was awkwardly looking away when I was staring at him.

I realized that his anger was still there, but it was clear that this anger was not directed towards me, who was sitting in the consultation room waiting for visitors. So I stood up straight from the sofa, put down my book, naturally poured a glass of plain water for him, and handed it to him.

He was stunned and stood there, unsure whether to answer or not. His gaze glanced at my still smiling face, and a hint of embarrassment appeared in a daze. I greeted him to come in and sit down. He took a sip of water and lowered his head somewhat dejectedly, "Why aren't you angry

Do you think I should be angry? "I was pondering his logic. Is someone in his world who hurt him the kind of person who will definitely repay ten times? So where does this anger come from?

You shouldn't be angry? "He looked at me like a monster, but soon said dejectedly," I think I do need help - my problem is, I... I often can't control my temper, and then I often pay for my anger

How did you view yourself at that time? "I asked.

In the past, I used to think that people around me should understand me, so those emotions, once understood, should be endured. But later, as time passed, some experiences gradually made me realize that no one is born to pay for my bad temper. But if I don't vent, I feel like I'm about to explode. Do you understand

But venting recklessly, you feel inappropriate again, don't you

As soon as I finished speaking, he nodded and told me that before coming here, he was carrying a bag of apples in his hand. However, because he answered a call from a friend and the other party did not cooperate with his cooperation plan as he expected, he couldn't help but want to lose his temper. The other party hung up his phone because of this, which made him furious. He suddenly dropped his phone on the ground and cursed at any time and place. He was so angry that he walked recklessly, hooked open the plastic bag, and scattered apples all over the ground. At that moment, he felt like everyone in the world was mocking him

What kind of development did you originally expect

I hope that as soon as my friend calls, I will receive good news that our cooperation plan has been successfully implemented, and I do not want any delay

You don't expect any changes or breaks in your thinking plan, do you

He nodded desperately and chopped the railway, 'Yes, I don't like it very much. I just like everything to go smoothly.'

But in reality, that's just your thinking, not reality. Will there be no change in reality

He thought for a moment and said, 'No. Actually, I know that reality is real and it won't change with my thoughts. I can't control the variability of reality with my thoughts.' Then, the frustration on his face deepened.

Yes, you actually understand this truth, but your main problem is just that you can't control your temper

What do I need to do

I laughed and said, 'You need to establish a transfer plan and carry a urine stick with you.'

Transfer plan urine strips, specifically tailored for those who are prone to losing control of their temper. This requires the parties involved to choose to create a distraction plan for themselves when calm, on which they can write down some things they want to try. This method of transfer and self soothing can effectively pull oneself out of a situation where anger is almost overwhelming. When feeling a little anger stirring in your heart, quickly take it out and choose one to implement.

Here are several commonly used "magic weapons to make bad temper disappear":

——Quickly recall some unforgettable and enjoyable experiences from the past. Think as carefully as possible, such as the beautiful details and moments that caught your attention at that time, what colors, smells, and textures do those "attractive" things have? What kind of feelings did it give you at that time?

——If you are on the street or in a public place, quickly look around or outside the window to see if you can find beautiful people and things in the distance and observe them. If you find it and start focusing on it, then think about what state he is in and perhaps there are some little stories behind it?

——Keep a famous quote from your favorite or most revered person. When you feel angry, take it out and read it. Imagine if one day you could stand at his height and become someone like him. What would he do at this moment? Will it be simple and rough to turn oneself and the surrounding environment into a primitive jungle? Hey, isn't that right? You're not a fool, so close your eyes and imagine that at this moment, a auspicious light appears above your head, starting to shine on you, soothing you, and dissipating all the unpleasant energy around you. You will become more and more intact.

——Has it been a long time since any new interest was developed? haven't you? Just think of one, one is enough, even if it's a small thing like turning over the soil in a flowerpot.

——Doing household chores, such as washing a bunch of family clothes and hanging them on the balcony.

——Take a hot bath and also wash and blow dry your hair.

——Polish your leather shoes to a shiny finish.

——If you are trapped in a small environment, count your breaths, listen to your breathing, be quiet, and then feel the breath around you.

——Activate your sense of smell and taste, smell some calming aromatherapy or simply go to your favorite food restaurant to smell the aroma of the food there, and guess what ingredients and spices are in this dish. Then enjoy it to the fullest, as long as you're not afraid of gaining weight:)

——Activate your hearing and listen to pure music. You can listen to nature friendly music similar to Bandray's, and imagine yourself freely wandering in such a beautiful environment.

——Activate your senses, place a piece of jade in your pocket, gently caress the smooth texture, and sense the natural composition inside the jade. A humble gentleman is like jade. Or do a self soothing massage, massage your palms, arms, shoulders, or even hug yourself.

……

If you have already read my transfer urinal, why not go home and make your own. Then when you still want to get angry in the future, take it out, select one, mark it with a pencil, and immediately implement it. You will find that the bad temper has disappeared without a trace.

When Qiao Nan left, he also borrowed my urine stick. He plans to choose a relaxing drink like a large cup of hot chocolate. After he calms down, he will call his friend at another time to ask if he can modify the cooperation plan.

Can I come and listen to your advanced techniques for enduring pain in the next episode

Of course." I maintained a faint smile and walked out the door with him, facing the sunshine.

Explanation of this issue's "Psychological Gate": Perhaps happiness is around us in our lives. If we complain about the pain that life rewards, it is difficult to feel the joy it bestows calmly. Work diligently, actively adjust one's body and mind, and simply be prosperous and happy.

2 Can you fully accept yourself like this?

Has no slander on his tongue, who does his neighbor no wrong and casts no slur on his fellowman..

——**Old Poetry 15:3**

Thousands of phone calls told me that he wants to hurt himself and even wants to burn down the house he currently lives in with a fire.

I was listening to soothing music at the time, and I didn't immediately ask him why. Instead, I said, "Can you tell me what your favorite music is

He remained furious and said angrily, 'No. Nothing!'

What's your favorite movie to watch? "I asked again.

No, when others watch funny movies, I usually don't laugh or find it funny

What about cartoons? "I continued.

Who watches things that children watch? Can you tell me that you enjoy watching such childish movies? "His tone was no longer as angry as before.

If I were to honestly tell you that sometimes I do watch cartoons and giggle like a child, would you despise a psychologist like me

No. "He answered quickly, like a monkey worried about being stepped on by someone's tail.

The contract we signed earlier stipulated that visitors must provide genuine emotional responses to the psychologist, "I said.

He pondered for a moment and said slowly, 'Hmm, okay, a little bit.'

Now, where are you

Of course, I'm on my way to your clinical consultation center

I put down the phone and estimated that he might arrive in another 15 minutes. Obviously, he had forgotten about setting fire to the house just now.

This kind of crisis intervention is very common for a psychologist. Actually, perhaps my friends have noticed that when dealing with pain, the available strategies are only three: transfer, transformation, relaxation, and coping.

No matter what we encounter at the moment, we may experience emotions or behaviors such as anger, anxiety, irritability, sadness, pain, congestion, depression, timidity, self isolation, verbal aggression, and even insulting language, self harm, or hurting others. At this point, the usual way for ordinary people to deal with it is to confront it.

Because they cannot accept the sudden reality in front of them, especially those who have a tendency towards perfectionism, they may find it even more difficult to accept after their regular control is broken.

Based on the above case, let's talk about the advanced skill of pain tolerance - comprehensive acceptance.

Fully accepting something does not mean you give in and passively accept any bad things happening to you. For example, if you have suffered unfair insults and attacks. But aside from those situations, there are still some situations that are worth considering. When they occur, we should take responsibility for the imbalance in our interpersonal relationships caused by improper handling.

The transmission of negative emotions such as anger, self harm, anxiety, and irritability can harm oneself and others. And comprehensive acceptance is equivalent to opening up our multi-dimensional perspectives to observe this relationship. We have to admit that the current reality is the result of a series of events in the past and the decisions we make with other people we interact with.

Every choice has a certain degree of directionality.

So, we need to take full responsibility for accepting this result.

Based on the above case, we can analyze several aspects in detail:

Firstly, what caused the current situation of thousands?

Because he had conflicts with several classmates who lived in the same dormitory, he felt that he had been excluded all along. Today, he forgot to bring his dormitory key and went back to knock on the door during lunch break, but surprisingly, no classmates opened the door for him.

What responsibility should thousands bear for the current situation? (Don't irrationally conclude that Qian Qian has no responsibility, all the classmates in that room are crazy. The cause of the matter must have twists and turns, right?)

It is obvious that the initial way Qian Qian wanted to deal with the problem was to harm himself and expand the impact of the harm, shifting from attacking inward to attacking outward - the way he dealt with emotions was incorrect.

Again, if you encounter unreasonable treatment from classmates who live with you, and there is indeed injustice, then carefully consider why they can treat you this way? And has the same thing happened to others? In this interpersonal relationship, whether Qian Qian was too confrontational or too humble in balancing harmonious coexistence among classmates, with a bullying attitude, etc., what kind of self-image did he display among his classmates that led them to ignore his feelings in this way? These questions are worth considering. Only by understanding how to explore inward and think about the reasons behind it can one gain the value of thinking.

What responsibility should those classmates take for this matter?

Indeed, in this matter, those classmates have shown a phenomenon of ignoring thousands of needs. If it is only for the reason of 'sleeping soundly and not knowing', then if it is not thousands knocking on the door outside, but teachers or student union disciplinary inspection officials, can they still use such an excuse to evade? Or, if there are really thousands knocking on the door outside, but their request is not "please open the door", but "there is a fire", "an earthquake", "someone across the street is throwing money and dancing a erotic dance" ... and such reasons really happen, then can the tightly closed door really be so silent?

The answer is obvious, no.

What is the current situation that can be grasped by thousands?

The reason why thousands of people are anxious and angry is because they want to go back to the dormitory, which happens to be during their lunch break. And the reason why he wants to go back to the dormitory is not for lunch break, but to find out during self-study in the classroom that he didn't bring the National English Test Band 6 question book, only the vocabulary book. According to the original plan, he needs to memorize 200 words every day and then do a question book. But when he finished reciting, he found that he didn't bring the question book and went back to the dormitory to get it, and encountered this kind of thing.

So, what parts can he master? If you have to enter the dormitory, you can ask the dormitory administrator to bring the key to open the door. If you don't have a key and insist on opening the door, there are many compromise and effective ways, which I won't go into detail here. I suggest I can tell you during psychological counseling.

Alternatively, he could flexibly change his plan for the day by memorizing 400 words, and then go back to the dormitory to get the exercise book after lunch break. There is no need to make a fuss with classmates who have been with me for four years in college for such a small matter, causing me to be in a negative emotional environment for a long time. It is not appropriate for my good physical and mental growth.

What is the current situation that Qian Qian cannot grasp?

If Qian Qian only treats his classmates like this because of his introverted, dull, and repressed emotions, then even after being true to himself, he still cannot grasp the short-term attitudes and opinions of his classmates towards him. This requires a series of stable and well intentioned behaviors and words, such as long-term self-improvement, proactive communication, friendly exchange, mutual respect and mutual help, in order to gradually change. So, based on the current situation, it is impossible to change the students' perception of him in the short term, unless he deeply explores, improves himself, and grows, in order to gradually improve the attitude of others towards him.

How did the initial reaction of thousands of people affect the consequences of this matter based on the current situation?

During his lunch break outside the door, Qian Qian made a scene and cursed loudly, which not only made his classmates dislike his behavior even more, but also worsened their attitude towards him. Thousands of people have unconsciously woven a network of inverted interpersonal relationships for themselves, causing harm to others and themselves, and affecting normal learning function. It is recommended to seek psychological counseling or college counseling.

How should Qian Qian change the current situation and handling methods to reduce the pain of him and his dormitory classmates?

He could have chosen many good methods to deal with and solve his troubles and anger, fully accepting such a situation, considering the problem from multiple perspectives, and re examining the possible direction of the current situation, which could have resulted in different outcomes. The worst option is to change dormitories. Although the growth obtained in this way is not maximized, it can at least protect thousands from being immersed in negative emotional networks for a long time, suffering and affecting their learning.

Assuming that Qian Qian fully accepts the issue of 'not opening the door', what would happen?

If he is keenly aware of the anger of being treated unfairly despite thousands of unopened doors, he may choose to go to the dormitory administrator to open the door, or go back to the classroom, take a dictionary, choose a beautiful and quiet grassy area, and recite 200 words. After taking a nap, he can return to the dormitory and not take this matter to heart. However, he can tactfully express his regret to the dormitory head that he did not open the door despite his efforts. Sometimes we may find it difficult to refuse the way others treat us, but learning to take the first step instead of suppressing emotions is a brave growth. Without repression, learn to express your feelings correctly and tactfully. Pay attention, just express your feelings and give advice, not for you to judge. Adopting such a compromise approach to express oneself is a wise move.

In the future, let's continue discussing statements of self affirmation

Time flies so fast, anyway you're going to finish work, why don't you let me take you home on the way? Can you tell me about it on the way? "Qianqian's face overflowed with happiness and he made a request.

I looked at him, raised an eyebrow, and politely declined, "No, you know everything I do is help visitors book time every day. This is my job, that's all

Okay, I know you're going to talk about the code of conduct for psychologists again, "Qian Qian understood without forcing," See you next week.

Explanation of this issue's "Psychology Gate": As the ancients said, the meaning of the phrase "the benevolence of women and men" is to encourage people's compassion not to take a small path, but to show great compassion and love. That's why "the benevolence of women and men" is used, rather than referring to some startled and screaming "benevolence"——Taken from 'Nan Huaijin'

3 Interpretation of Dreams - A Psychologist's Dream Analysis

It is not only the old who are wise, not only the aged who understand what is right.

——**Old Uncle "32:9**

After consulting for a while, I think I should calm down. "A male psychologist friend named" Rational Rose "suddenly stopped talking to me. The reason is that he saw a painting, which happened to be placed in a Weibo post I showed him.

That is a picture of majestic lions crouching beside a pure white lamb, with a gentle expression on their faces.

What's wrong with you? "I noticed something unusual about him.

Very harmonious, this painting. But... can lions really be vegetarians? "He began to explain to me that his strangeness stemmed from a dream he had.

What kind of dream is that

Repeatability, continuity

He began to speak eloquently: There was a time when I often fell into the same dream. In the dream, there was a black cheetah wandering back and forth in front of the barbed wire fence, walking around anxiously. Its deep gaze was only fixed on a bright sky, a light blue clear sky. And I stood on the other side of the barbed wire, watching it. A voice from the bottom of my heart asked me softly:

Can you make a leopard not eat meat? A black panther.

can you do that?

……

When I woke up from my dream, I felt a heavy burden on my shoulders. It seemed that the mission I carried made me sweat profusely and feel pain when carrying heavy loads, but I couldn't take off the burden and let the breeze clear my sleeves.

Analysis of Dreams:

The material of dreams, to some extent, comes from real-life experiences. Perhaps at a certain moment, a certain time, or a certain period of time, it is easy to form recurring themes in dreams. The repetition and continuity of dreams are due to the fact that the materials hidden deep within have been processed multiple times by the brain. Then, the content of the dream needs to be directly compared with real-life experience, which requires careful consideration.

And my male psychological counselor friend's dream of 'Rational

Rose' repeatedly appeared during a certain period of time, which should be related to his real-life experience. At that time, his work as a psychologist had undergone at least 6 years of refinement, and the psychological industry had evolved from a small-scale development to a better planning direction. However, he may be facing some things that make him physically and mentally exhausted or anxious. He said he almost has to face visitors with different questions every day, although there are appointments, the combination of various psychological work may be due to his fatigue and anxiety. However, as an experienced senior psychological counselor, he still cannot explain the source of his dream material - the black leopard and the bright sky.

The psychoanalytic perspective represented by Freud holds that dreams have significant psychological characteristics and represent our unnoticed memories. It may be forgotten in a fragmented memory space in a conscious state of reality, but it will reappear in different ways in dreams, thus allowing us to recall it in a special form of expression.

There was once a painter in the past who, in a state of wakefulness, had no inspiration, could not paint, or made terrible paintings. However, in his dreams, he was able to gain wonderful inspiration. Under hypnosis or in a dream state, he could pick up his pen and draw beautiful color compositions. Some people jokingly call him a genius in his dreams, but in real life he is worthless.

In fact, from the perspective of psychological psychoanalysis, this statement is a fallacy. Because even dreams come from real-life experiences. This person, perhaps when awake, traveled around and then remembered those wonderful colors in their mind. And at a certain stage, it is strengthened through the theme of dreams.

This person is a painter named Kurdis Watkins from Michigan, USA. He created excellent works in his dreams, and he painted with both hands in his dreams, but when he was awake, his left hand could not paint. The fact we all know is that dreams are easily forgotten, and the reason for their forgetfulness may also be the source of their creation.

Whether the perception is weak or the excitement points accompanying us in our dreams are weak or not is not actually the reason for being remembered. If the material in a dream is often repeated or psychologically reinforced in life experience, and forms appropriate connections and classifications in perception and consciousness, it is easier to remember and remain in the memory of the dream.

Dreams do have unexplainable space, but psychoanalytic perspectives suggest that dreams have emotions and emotional colors. For example, in the dream of 'Rational Rose', negative emotions such as black panther, wandering, and staring may have remained in the consciousness of the visitor on a regular day, manifested in the dream. And 'black' represents seriousness, caution, and silence; And the cheetah's wandering implies a certain level of anxiety in the 'rational Rose', perhaps caused by a slight unease about her grasp of psychological counseling work and some unknown future plans. And some people even have the ability to use the will in their dreams to guide the direction of their dreams, that is, when dreams express strong emotional colors, the desire for sleep is replaced by another preconscious desire.

So, as far as the dream of 'Rational Rose' is concerned, the barbed wire fence and the bright sky he gazes at are also a positive suggestion and hypnosis of himself. Wire mesh, perhaps symbolizing rationality, also represents some kind of boundary. The feeling of iron wire is cold and hard, which is not easily broken by ordinary animals and represents a certain rigidity characteristic. But the safety boundary formed by the bent wire mesh also implies a certain flexibility. The light he gazed upon in his dream also meant that his consciousness could perceive his future direction and development prospects.

At this point in dream analysis, it is not difficult to see that the 'rational Rose' is already observing her own dreams as an observer, and giving it a certain degree of controllability. When a person begins to have the perception of such dreams, then when they wake up, the dream is actually easier to remember clearly.

Dreams represent the desires of the subconscious, combined with the remnants of the day, and with the assistance of the subconscious, they rush towards consciousness through the efforts of the preconscious. It is necessary to mention the condensation and substitution effects of dreams in psychoanalysis. Everyone's consciousness has a system of inspection, which is equivalent to the level that we can perceive in a conscious state, just like the barbed wire in the dream of 'rational Rose', representing rationality.

When the dream encounters the inspection system, it will be distorted and transferred with the help of recent life experiences or materials. Following the program of the dream, it begins to retreat, and in this process, the dream takes on a form of expression, namely condensation.

And a person will have at least 5-6 dreams every night, and the reason why they are not noticed is because our memories in dreams are generally easier to remember in nightmares than in good dreams. And the 'rational Rose' woke up in this dream. Although his will could guide the dream towards a certain degree of controllability, such a dream, as well as the negative emotions contained in the dream, brought his reaction. Obviously, as a psychological counselor with comprehensive analysis and flexible experience, the best way to deal with it is to help the 'rational Rose'. My male psychological counselor friend extracts and focuses on positive, mindfulness, and positive self spirit, and maintains a balance index of internal goodness.

　　Explanation of this issue's "Psychology Gate": Just like every competent psychological counselor, visitors facing various problems may have encountered some hidden fears, wanderings, or doubts about the unknown represented by the black cheetah in their dreams during the early stages of their career. Perhaps in such ups and downs, have we also tried to hold our shoulders tightly and ask ourselves, why can you make a black cheetah not eat meat? This is clearly the anxiety caused by our eagerness to solve the visitor's problem. But over time, most people won't think like this anymore. Instead of rushing to give someone a "That's right" answer to their dream, it's better to give some moderate advice. On the basis of psychological counseling "dream interpretation", the "rational Rose" will explore and comprehend her own survival rules during a certain period of waiting, and move forward with the pain in the problem. Perhaps one day, I will understand——

　　What is the true meaning of the sentence 'When God closes a door for you, he also opens a window for us?'.

　　After all, no matter what we have encountered, we cannot lose the ability to make ourselves stable, happy, and content.

4 ways to recognize one's own value

The healthy man does not torture others. Generally it is the tortured who turn into torturers.

——Carl Jung

When it comes to the word 'value', we may first think of physical concepts such as gold, treasures, stocks, futures, investments, real estate, villas, etc. If we must add an annotation to "value" from the perspective of psychological science popularization, then from a cognitive level, it refers to the effect relationship between the object and the subject that can meet the needs of the subject, which is the mutual connection between the subject and the object.

Teacher, do you think I'm useful? "This visitor named Ben often asks me similar questions during consultations.

'Useful' equals' value '. Such questioning is equivalent to the materialization and functionality of self recognition. And... any visitor who raises such questions is indeed someone who excessively values themselves in the eyes of others, has inferiority complex traits, and emphasizes the function of self external object relations, that is, the value of others.

That depends on which aspect you're referring to. After all, it encompasses categories such as ethics, principles, ideals, standards, or morals. Everyone has different values in life, so what problems have you encountered when asking this

Yes, I've been in a low point in my life lately, "Ben lowered his head." My girlfriend often thinks I'm useless. I don't seem to know anything

What makes you think like this? Did she explicitly say that? "I noticed Ben's wording -" think ".

Ben lowered his head, pondered for a moment, and remained silent. Suddenly he said again, "Even if she doesn't, I know she thinks so

The cognition of everything is based on evidence, which means that your partner did not say so, but you have such a belief, right

Yes, I often feel that way

Ben came to consult with me to find his value.

A person's life values can determine the direction of their choices and coping strategies when facing difficulties. So, exploring one's own value is a very important topic in life.

Here, several popular science methods can be provided to rediscover value, please note that it is "re understanding" rather than "re picking". The former is that you may ignore its existence for a long time, or you may never realize your own value direction, which is one of the reasons for low self-worth. The latter is a mechanism to clarify self-worth, or adjust oneself, pick up again and rebuild after encountering major setbacks or changes.

So how can we rediscover your value?

Firstly, conduct a questionnaire test to clarify life goals and preferences.

In Wilson, 2002; In Wilson&Murray's 2004 Life Value Survey questionnaire, it can be seen that the level of self value exploration in the ten directions of life is clear:

1. Family (excluding romantic relationships and parental relationships)

2. Love (marriage, lifelong partner, dating, etc.)

3. Parental affection

4. Friends and Social Life

5. Work

6. Education and Training

7. Entertainment and leisure

8. Spirit and religion

9. Citizens and Communities

10. Self care (self stabilization and self appreciation through exercise, diet, rest, hobbies, etc.)

The above 10 points are classified by level, with 0-3 points indicating "not important at all", 4-7 points indicating "relatively important", and 8-10 points indicating "extremely important".

Based on the above table, it is not difficult to find out which part you value. For example, if Ben values love and work more, then the next step is to perfect a goal on these two points - that is, to give us a more complete goal in the life direction we value.

Ben's goal in love is to have a harmonious and happy long-term relationship with his partner; In terms of work, new goals and heights are set to achieve a new recognition, such as attending an elite class to master a new technology and gain weight for obtaining a new position.

Secondly, make the accuracy of the goals concrete and actionable, and reject fantasies.

So, what actions do you need to take towards these goals in the end? "I asked Ben.

Ben thought for a moment and decided to concretize and take action on the above life goals. He even immediately filled out a course registration form and assigned it to action.

When our lives are filled with specific goals and actions, our minds will also undergo some noticeable changes.

Do you still think your sense of value is lower now

Ben breathed a sigh of relief when he saw the goals and life directions he had filled in on the questionnaire, "It seems to be a bit useful

We can use this method to address one or more goals by asking ourselves, "What do I think are the valuable parts of my life?" "What actions have I taken to achieve those goals?" "So, how did I do it specifically?" These three questions can be used with the help of Wilson, 2002; Wilson&Murrell, after finalizing the 2004 Life Value Survey questionnaire, repeatedly thinking and putting it into action, it is not difficult to find the meaning of life.

If the purpose of the first step in conducting a questionnaire is to find our preferred life direction and goals, then the second step is to establish our ability to take action. This cannot be done by others, but can only be perceived through our own hands, eyes, body, mind, and spirit. At least in terms of self recognition, you will find that you have direction and goals.

Thirdly, establish a notebook of personal achievements and goals, and determine your internal and external rewards.

Divide the achieved goals or achievements into several levels, based on individual circumstances and the difficulty level of the goals. For example, if a person wants to become a business elite and earn a bucket of gold for themselves, they need to at least establish steps and complete them in a hierarchical manner, rather than achieving success overnight. The greater the effect of the ultimate goal reward mechanism, the more it is necessary to divide the reward levels in detail and gradually. This avoids achieving goals without any conventional methods and scientifically conforms to the role of the Pygmalion effect.

The Pygmalion Effect refers to the expectation or prophecy formed by people based on their perception of a certain situation, which will cause the situation to have an effect of adapting to this expectation or prophecy. Psychologist Rosenthal, the proposer of this theory, believed that you get what you expect. What you get is not what you want, but what you expect. As long as you have confident expectations and truly believe that things will go smoothly, things will definitely go smoothly. On the contrary, if you believe that things are constantly hindered, these obstacles will arise. Successful people will cultivate a confident attitude and believe that good things will definitely happen. This is what psychology calls the Pygmalion effect.

When all three parts are completed, you will find that your confidence gradually increases as your sense of self-worth is established. And the sense of value established in this way is built by yourself, rather than being "liked" or "recognized" by external objects. So, in terms of establishing our own value and maintaining a clear self-image, our complementary links can be well integrated.

So what is the difficulty in finding the value and meaning of life?

In this issue of 'Psychology Gate', to use an old saying, 'Do not admire other teachers, shape yourself'. On the path of life, there will inevitably be people who like us, those who belittle us, those who have nothing to do with us, and so on. Perhaps at some point, our emotions will be affected by being belittled or praised, and our inner experiences will accompany us. Slowly, we will realize that only by learning to give ourselves likes, knowing our goals, making plans, and filling in our actions can we fulfill them. So everything, whether it's praise or admiration, criticism or contempt, or apathy, other people's emotions and opinions, can no longer affect our emotions when our self-worth is well established. So there is an ancient saying, 'Don't be surprised by favor or disgrace, watch the flowers bloom and fall; leave or stay as you please, let the clouds roll and relax.'. The cultivation of our inner self is accompanied by our self-awareness and the extension of our practice - it turns out that wise people are those who have learned to praise their true skills. As long as it is real, even if it is not satisfactory at first, the stage of life that is gradually repaired from that real foundation will play the beautiful notes of the world, satisfying oneself and others.

5 books for the soul

There is a mine for silver and a place where gold is refined.Iron is taken from the earth,and copper is smelted from ore.

——Old Uncle 28:1, 2

After obtaining the certificate of psychological counselor, if you think you can throw away your doctoral and master's hats as freely as you imagine, and then wield your sword like a hero to make a lot of money, then you are completely wrong.

Have you ever asked your heart, 'Are you ready?' and then heard it calmly, confidently answer, 'Yes, I am ready.'.

Once you embark on this path, I believe every psychologist who has fully experienced it will deeply understand this sentence: "This is a path that few people have taken.

When you encounter negative emotions: While being able to withstand the infection and transmission of negative energy, you need to use the skills of a counselor to accompany and infect the visitors in front of you with your true inner soul energy - calm and peaceful. He will not force you to change or rush to criticize your similarities and differences, but accept you unconditionally like all beings. Maintain neutrality and empathy, rarely express direct evaluations unless it is an emergency or special situation.

2. Neurosis walking with you and me: If the visitor is troubled, nervous, anxious, depressed, fearful, obsessive, paranoid, dissociative, transitional, or neurasthenic, in a painful self torture and struggle, or still stuck in a quagmire, or on the brink of collapse, the visitor comes with negative emotions and symptoms. As a competent psychologist, what should you do?

Firstly, you need to extensively study the treatment techniques of various schools of psychology, as different schools of psychology have different interpretations and treatment methods for the mechanisms of neurosis. However, after more than 100 years abroad and just a few decades of practice and development domestically, psychological therapy technology has gradually integrated, compromised, and cooperated into a more extensive, comprehensive, and practical model. The choice of which treatment method is currently the most effective is a "technique" that we have learned to help others and ourselves, but it cannot be imposed on patients.

Just like how we often hear our parents depriving and invading us of our choices, explaining it with just one sentence, 'I'm for your own good,' I believe it can no longer be accepted by mature individuals, let alone children living in adult shells?

In the short 50 minute treatment time, we may be their father, mother, and idealized intimate guardians after their regression, but while empathizing, we should not forget the rules and the responsibilities and identities of psychologists. Always remember that I am a psychological counselor, a 50 minute psychological companion listener wrapped in technical skills after removing all authority and glamorous halos.

3. Personality disorder is not something I can choose, it should be: Personality, also known as personality, is a person's fixed behavior pattern and habitual way of dealing with people and things in daily activities, which is a comprehensive of all psychological characteristics. The formation of personality is closely related to innate physiological characteristics and postnatal living environment.

This group of visitors clearly deviates from normal and deeply rooted behavior patterns, exhibiting maladaptive qualities. Their personalities are abnormal in terms of content, quality, or overall personality. As a result, patients suffer and/or cause pain to others, or have adverse effects on individuals or society. Personality abnormalities hinder their emotional and volitional activities, undermine the purposefulness and unity of their behavior, give people a unique and distinctive feeling, and are particularly prominent in interpersonal interactions.

This characteristic usually begins in childhood, adolescence, or early adulthood, and if we have to define it, it belongs to lifelong symptoms.

But why do we still need psychological counseling?

For these types of visitors, as a psychological counselor, what you need to do is not to lead them into the misconception of removing symptoms, obstacles, and returning to the normal zone, nor to tell them, "You're not good, you're wrong

But rather standing from the perspective of the visitor, even connecting and empathizing with their own spiritual understanding, helping them find a path to create beauty from those symptoms and difficult lifestyles.

In this world, life exists in various forms.

Here, I would like to apply the basic treatment principle of Morita therapy: 'Let nature take its course and do what is right'. Don't force it, do what we can. If we cannot choose our own personality disorders, but at least what we can master and choose is to try to avoid the dark boulders lying on the path of developing the light of life, and find a secluded path, even if it is really narrow, as long as we use it well, we can still use this path to reach the other side of life's meaning and realize our self-worth.

At that time, we can even walk through our long lives with symptoms and look back on the past. We can say to our current selves that we have grown much more than our past selves.

So do you love your current self?

If the answer is yes and indifferent, then our growth is worth it and valuable. Regardless of whether we have symptoms, are different from ordinary people, are difficult, trapped, and insecure like ants, we can still feel the equality and preciousness of life. We can calmly say to ourselves that even if we are ants, even if we do not have the usual happiness of others, I have achieved it compared to our past and present selves. That is far superior to ordinary people's willpower and ability to pursue happiness.

The three types of people mentioned above are all symptomatic, some of whom even hover at the boundary of mental illness. As psychotherapists, what can we do to alleviate their symptoms and how can we help them learn skills for growth and happiness.

These skills are by no means' cold in a day '.

I often see many psychologists who love psychology and are full of longing and confusion about this path. However, how to walk on this path, how to read and learn, are all realities worth carefully planning and considering.

What can be explored here is that psychology is vast and profound, and different schools of thought may be a biased division of knowledge at the boundary. A true psychologist is ultimately integrative, but also precise in their expertise, like parents or doctors.

To achieve these two points, it is necessary to combine your own strengths and advantages.

Firstly, search for a psychological topic that you enjoy, then follow the clues to find out which school it belongs to, study it, understand it, and consider its practicality. This way, you will feel interested in long-term focused learning and gain a strong internal drive to persistently learn it well.

Secondly, it is recommended to seek guidance from truly excellent teachers. Note that what I want to emphasize is that truly good teachers should not just aim for a glamorous "fame". Sometimes, it is not difficult to find that a true master may be famous or low-key, and it does not necessarily require multiple certificates and glamorous fame to indicate that they are "experts" or "masters".

The bias of "certificates" is something that every psychologist needs to explore on their personal growth path. What does the certificate mean behind it? What exactly do you want to get?

For example, college students must have more knowledge than high school students, and they must have a high personal and social value for society and those around them. For those who are far away, look at the peasant emperor Zhu Yuanzhang, and for those who have not finished college, look at Bill Gates... Let's not talk about far away here. The main point is that what is truly good is the strength and the height of one's soul as a psychological counselor, that is, the establishment of the superego (conscience) and mature self affirmation value and self-concept.

Whether the teacher is good or not can actually be felt through conversation.

I have read a lengthy classic book called "Sense and Sensibility" before, and it is not an exaggeration to describe one of the characteristics of this profession with these five words: Does it meet your need for good empathy, while also adhering to the principles of an excellent psychologist, firmly using geography and wisdom to analyze your conflicts? Can he withstand your sudden anger and irrational slander? Do you still uphold the original intention of being a psychologist with integrity and a love for every life, crossing oneself and crossing others.

Lastly, besides being good, you also need to find something that suits your development and your own characteristics to develop. With the guidance of a good teacher, it is not difficult to learn this subject well. But it's really hard to find good teachers, those who are too famous and very expensive. For example, as we all know about psychoanalysis, Professor Zeng Qifeng, if you were to use him as a supervisor for a case, in addition to paying attention to internal analysis of whether your self is suitable for him, you also need to prepare a lot of money for at least three years. Can your income and expenses be balanced? These are all things that must be considered, long-term considerations.

The language of a qualified and excellent psychological counselor should be similar to Zen music, which means treating all sounds as beautiful sounds, turning abusive voices into compassion and acceptance, blessing and praying for slanderers, and truly accompanying them with technology and soul. After achieving these, don't forget that you also need personal experience and growth, because we are also human beings.

With this article, I would like to send it to every psychologist, wishing them to embark on a path that suits them, complete integration, apply what they have learned to their own growth, improve themselves, and help suitable visitors at the same time!

6 Behind High Quality Labels - Restoring the 'omnipotent' Me in Others' Eyes

For she is more profitable than silver and yields better returns than gold.

——The Old Proverbs 3:14

Introduction: Some of us have been given the labels of "elite," "high-quality," and "gold medal" boys and girls since our student days because of our outstanding performance. However, how can we remove the "sugar coating" of these beautiful value labels and restore the true appearance of boys and girls?

Case: Zhengjie, a senior high school student, has been ranked first in elementary, middle, and high school. This first place is not only reflected in his textbook grades, but also in the 2500 meter long-distance race that many students cannot pass. He has even won awards in mathematics and physics competitions at or above the provincial level. Whether it is in morality, intelligence, physical fitness, aesthetics, or labor, he always ranks first.

If I don't become the first place, I will feel like my life has no meaning, "he said when he came to the consultation room.

At present, the third year of high school is about to enter the final preparation period. Although the new education policies are based on the actual situation of candidates in various regions, and pay more attention to adaptability and fairness, it is not particularly difficult to get into a better university. However, for Zhengjie, who always wants to maintain the "first place", it has become an increasingly troublesome thing for him.

He began to feel nervous, constantly anxious, and even frequently tense his muscles, to the point where he often had the same nightmare:

In his dream, he saw a donkey in a daze, carrying heavy goods on its back, struggling step by step towards the mountains. The donkey's back had been scarred by years of trekking on the rocky steps of the mountains, and it couldn't breathe. Just as it was about to stop and catch its breath, pairs of dark eyes would appear in the surrounding jungle, staring at it tightly. This feeling made it want to escape, but the road beneath its feet continued to stretch as if there was no end.

Every time he wakes up, he feels back and waist pain, as if those things were carried by him, not the donkey in his dream.

This dream lasted intermittently for a month because he couldn't rest well at night and couldn't concentrate in class during the day. Although his grades were not greatly affected for the time being, he often worried that one day his grades would plummet and he would no longer be associated with the high-quality label of "first place". Finally, one day, he was late for school.

Faced with the smiling faces of his parents and teachers who trusted, tolerated, and eagerly hoped for him, he became increasingly distressed. He could hardly forgive himself, let alone accept his lateness - "You're actually late, you're no longer the first!" Such voices repeatedly appeared in his mind. As the college entrance examination approached, he couldn't even read, enduring almost indescribable pain and torment.

He felt that the experience of being late made him feel ashamed and almost collapse.

[Analysis]

According to Freud's psychoanalytic perspective, the material of dreams comes from real life and expresses the needs of the subconscious. However, these real materials have been processed through the conscious, preconscious, and subconscious stages, and have been replaced and distorted. From Zhengjie's dream, it is not difficult to see that he is under tremendous pressure inside. The weight carried by the donkey in the dream may reflect the elements that an excellent student like him has been carrying since childhood, such as individual excellence, parents' expectations, classmates' envy and attention, teachers' love, etc. These have also invisibly transformed into the "dark" eyes in

Zhengjie's dream, making him want to escape but have to move forward. And behind these elements, it reflects the culture that our current society believes in.

Firstly, core beliefs can influence behavior, and context is merely a trigger.

The culture we believe in often leads to behavioral responses within a certain system framework. In today's society, values such as "elite culture" and "gold medalists" are prevalent. Under normal circumstances, these value frameworks carry a distinct and positive energy, and are deeply ingrained in our lives, work, and even students. Senior high school students like Zhengjie believe in this culture and are deeply influenced by it.

Under normal circumstances, a good core belief is beneficial for a person and even a society to have a positive outlook on life and values, as it encourages people to strive for excellence. However, such a core concept will bring low variable pressure of continuous value-added to people, and it gradually completes the original accumulation unconsciously.

The case of Zhengjie highlights the principle of "boiling frogs in warm water". His positive progress also brings a certain degree of anxiety and pressure, which slowly accumulate in his body and are not easily perceived by the body.

After experiencing a situation similar to 'being late for high school', his accumulated stress was elevated to its peak, which was revealed through abnormal bodily regulation, leading to the collapse of his stress regulation mechanism.

The voice of 'You're actually late, you're no longer the first!' repeatedly appeared in his mind. In Zhengjie's opinion, it was the awkward situation of being late that made him negative and pessimistic, but in reality, what really put pressure on him was his excessive belief in 'refined English'.

Existentialism says, "Life does not need meaning, existence itself is the only meaning." When the core concept of "elite culture" collides with the survival concept of "basic existence," it loses the high-quality value and meaning it was created with. Because this is no longer a matter of 'Huashan discusses swords and strives for the top spot in the world', but rather a theme about how a person needs to first ensure their existence.

We all have different beliefs, and from a psychological perspective, there is no right or wrong in belief itself. In the case of Zhengjie, due to the attention of his parents, teachers, and classmates from childhood to adulthood, he firmly attached himself with the labels of "quality" and "first place", and constantly gave himself such hints. Therefore, in his core philosophy, he will always be equated with the label of "first place" as a top performer, and this core philosophy has led to his continuous achievement of excellent results, which has deepened his conviction and strengthened him.

The Analects of Confucius: Advanced "says," If we go too far, we will go too far; if we slow down, things will come to an end. "When we excessively believe in a certain belief, it may lead to serious problems such as anxiety, shame, coercion, and excessive pressure, and even cause a" crisis of existence. "Therefore, the degree or direction in which such core beliefs are revered needs to be appropriately adjusted and rationalized.

Secondly, everyone has the desire to love beauty, and it is easy to overlook the needs of students themselves when riding a tiger: advocating beauty is human nature. Among the crowd, the most outstanding type of people are actually more likely to attract public attention, ranging from business elites and talented newcomers to leading dancers in daily life. If we focus on the level of students, the student with the most beautiful handwriting, exquisite word selection, logical reasoning, clever ideas, and clever answers in the homework book corrected by the teacher is also more likely to win the favor of the teacher.

In Zhengjie's dream, the gaze of those pairs of eyes made the already struggling donkey take another step, unable to stop. Due to being outstanding individuals from a young age, excessive external expectations and attention can easily lead students to neglect their basic needs of physical fatigue and not adjust their ways of rest and learning appropriately. And physical health is the most fundamental need for all development and growth.

Thirdly, the internal driving force to strive for first place is a demand that needs to be paid attention to. There are still differences in the areas of concern for parents and teachers of high school seniors

If I don't become the first place, I will feel that my life has no meaning. "This sentence from Zhengjie actually reflects his hidden need for attention from others. From a deeper psychological perspective, the inner needs that require attention may also be related to the intimate family relationships that students are in. As parents of high school seniors, do they overly focus on their children's grades and often overlook their inner needs? Is the child's academic performance the sole criterion for measuring their comprehensive development in morality, intelligence, and physical fitness? School teachers, due to their limited social roles, may easily judge students' developmental status by focusing on their classroom performance and test scores; But parents cannot simply interact with their children in this way. Because guardians, like parents, are not only teachers of their children, but also parents who lead by example. Therefore, simply expressing concern for children through academic performance can easily overlook the need for emotional interaction between parents and children. And this latter is precisely the kind of attention that school teachers cannot handle competently.

[Countermeasure]

The ancients said, "Those who are capable can establish their own country, while those who are incapable can do their own good." The existence of these two is of equal importance.

Just like the pharaoh's pyramid, the last stone brick left at the top of the pyramid drew a perfect conclusion to the great miracle of this world. However, compared to the millions of stone bricks at the lower levels of the pyramid, their composition is essentially the same - they are all bricks and tools for building the pyramid. If there is no accumulation, arrangement, and combination of stone bricks descending step by step, then the existence of the stone bricks at the top of the pyramid will have no meaning.

This metaphor, whether applied to any group we come into contact with, demonstrates the same principle. Third year high school students are also like a small social group, each person is like a brick in a pyramid, and their essence is interconnected - first of all, we are students. Secondly, it is the highly competitive students in their senior year of high school, and finally, it is the individual traits of the students. That is to say, we must first clarify our sense of existence in order to develop our own characteristics on this basis.

1. Reject excessive beliefs, the existence of life is the foundation of everything:

Every spiritual belief has its limitations, just like a learning philosophy that is suitable for student A may not necessarily work for student B; The learning philosophy that worked for student A in the past may not necessarily work for student A now and in the future. Human beings are individuals who constantly learn, accept, and absorb, and the core concepts of cognition should also be appropriately adjusted according to the individual's applicability in order to adapt to the development of the body, mind, and spirit. Zhengjie is in this situation, 'must be the first'. He once made the core belief of always being the 'first' his learning belief, but due to excessive conviction, his body experienced a series of negative emotional reactions such as insomnia, compulsion, and shame under long-term stress mechanisms. The advice of a psychotherapist is to reject negative misleading and suggestive information. You're actually late, you're no longer the number one! "Students like Zhengjie, facing the approaching lateness of exams, may feel both anxious and ashamed, thus expanding this negative perception and unconsciously transforming it into the only standard for measuring student value.

This is the tampering mode of human automatic thinking, and also the self-defense experience that most people have had. Just, what is reality? What is our exaggerated imagination? These cannot be judged solely by listening to the voice of the heart, but need to rely on intuitive thinking, rational thinking, logical causality, experiences in learning and life, and right and wrong concepts to make clear, precise judgments for us and rationalize our cognition.

2. There are no two identical leaves in the world: every student must have their own characteristics, and these characteristics are what our hobbies and strengths point to. There is no one in this world who knows oneself better than oneself. Our hobbies can be diverse, but they are not comprehensive. Even if they exist, they are only short-term investments. As a vital sign, human energy is limited. If we calculate based on 100 points, assuming we use 40 points to meet our needs for food, clothing, housing, and transportation, how should the remaining 60 points of energy be allocated scientifically? The spirit and motivation of students like Zhengjie to strive for excellence are commendable, but we cannot ignore that we only have 60 minutes of energy at our disposal. From the theoretical analysis of psychoanalysis, if limited energy is excessively consumed, people are more likely to suffer from various neurological disorders, and the body will also experience various negative symptoms under the accumulated "negative asset" energy, which will affect our development. A more scientific and reasonable suggestion is to focus your energy on your strengths and plan scientifically and reasonably. In general, as long as you find the right method, it is not difficult to achieve a proportional relationship between effort and reward. So, instead of having the label of 'omnipotence', it's better to stand out and develop one's own advantages.

Some students may think that they have no advantages or strengths, but in fact, it's not that they don't have them, it's just that you haven't discovered them yet. Human potential is powerful and profound. There is an ancient saying that goes, "I am naturally talented and useful." By discovering one's unique strengths and improving one's learning, one can achieve twice the result with half the effort.

3. Learn to admit defeat, accept the feeling of loss, and embrace your imperfections. There was once a film called 'Life Remote Control', which mainly tells the story of an architect who owns a family of three and a stable

job. Just like many middle-class Americans, life is quite ordinary. But the male protagonist, who is facing a midlife crisis, is not willing to live like this. He wants to be promoted, get a job with an annual salary of one million yuan, become a CEO, have a wife who is less nagging, and have a daughter who grows up quickly and no longer burdens his increasingly tired body and mind. These wishes were all fulfilled in an instant when he accidentally obtained a small remote control. He finally got everything he wanted, as if all the gains were the perfection he had dreamed of, but as long as he pressed the start button, he couldn't start over after fast forwarding. Soon, the male protagonist grew tired of such acquisition and possession, as all of his gains had no process.

There is no feeling of hardship, no loss, no setback, no competition, and no joy after harvest. He seems to have obtained the cheat code for the game, and life continues, but all the driving forces and experiential feelings of exploration have been completely skipped.

Just like drinking a glass of water, when we are thirsty, we will find water to drink, boil it, wait, mix it to the appropriate temperature, then pick up the cup and slowly drink it, feeling the water molecules pass through our taste buds and slide down our esophagus... Perhaps throughout the whole process, we will also feel that the water is too cold or too hot and need to be re mixed until it is suitable, finally meeting our thirst needs.

This process is experience, if we skip the process of finding and drinking water, then all our gains can only be translated into simple characters, lifeless.

Only by experiencing setbacks can we recognize our shortcomings and think of ways to make up for and improve; Only by tasting the bitter taste can we cherish the beautiful sweet fruit more. If you have never lost in life, and if you have not been overly protected, then you are likely to live forever in an invincible fantasy world. However, that is not reality, let alone a complete life.

If we believe that we never make mistakes and cannot make mistakes, then we are "saints", not people in real life. Accept your ordinary side, accept the sense of loss, and embrace your imperfections. Only then can you be closer to perfection.

4. Starting with behavioral relaxation: Exam anxiety is an emotional response that not only affects students' academic performance, but also their learning efficiency. In severe cases, it can greatly impact students' mental health.

The human body is a natural absorber, which gradually absorbs the stress encountered in daily life, work, and study. However, when it reaches its peak, the body will experience maladaptive reactions. The same principle applies to relaxing the body first, taking appropriate rest, and practicing relaxation training for a certain amount of time and frequency every day. Starting with muscle relaxation and doing the opposite, through the relaxation of the body's muscles, accumulated pressure can also be relieved, achieving the goal of relieving anxiety in studying, preparing for exams, and preparing for exams. It should be understood that the beliefs we uphold can provide us with a template for living better, as they can guide our daily behavior to achieve self actualization goals. However, these beliefs are based on survival and have value and meaning. Therefore, first of all, we need to learn to be aware of the moderate satisfaction of our body's basic needs in order to pursue a higher level of spiritual motivation. Students who do not respect the natural process of life can easily gain more than they lose in the end.

Moderate attention and care from parents are the strong backing for children.

As the saying goes, 'Every family has difficult scriptures to recite, and everyone has difficult songs to sing.' . Even the most beautiful and happy families will have some indescribable conflicts and unhappiness. As guardians (parents), when we encounter some unpleasant emotional experiences, we should not shift these negative feelings onto our children to bear. As an adult and a parent of a high school senior, it is even more important to take responsibility for and handle one's negative emotions. Only by taking care of their own negative emotions such as anxiety, anger, and depression can parents better assume the role of guardians who care about their children's physical and mental well-being. As a student, the college entrance examination is a turning point in life. As a whole family, isn't it also a turning point in the future of the family?

As parents, it is important to clarify that focusing solely on a child's grades as a synonym for "caring" and "caring" for the child is not advisable. A psychologist once conducted an experiment in which two groups of students with the same IQ, one group of teachers and parents adopted an encouraging educational strategy, and the other group did not encourage. After a period of time, the group with higher test results received the most encouragement. Encouragement cannot be interpreted as material encouragement in a biased way. Spiritual encouragement needs to be greater than material encouragement, which is obviously more scientific.

After all, although home is the least rational place, it is also the warmest harbor and the "Eden" where parents and children grow up together.

Explanation of this issue's "Psychology Gate":

Mr. Yang Jiang once said in her centenary speech: Heaven will not allow all happiness to be concentrated on one person. With so much, there will inevitably be less. Maintaining a mindset of contentment and happiness is the best way to temper the mind and purify the soul.

A person gains varying degrees of cultivation and benefits through different levels of exercise. Like spices, the more crushed and finely ground they are, the stronger their fragrance becomes. We once longed so much for the waves of fate, only to realize in the end that the most beautiful scenery in life is actually inner calmness and composure... We once hoped so much for external recognition, only to realize in the end that the world belongs to us and has nothing to do with others.

(Mr. Yang Jiang's words in this paragraph are only for her self reflection as a wise elder. As for how to comprehend the people and things we see in our eyes, including wisdom, knowledge, and cognition, different people have their own opinions. Let's allow ourselves to contemplate.)

7 Reflection on the Death Case of Two Young Children in Chongqing

The lamp of the wicked is snuffed out;the flame of his fire stops burning.

——Old Uncle 18:5

On the afternoon of November 2, 2020, at around 3:30 pm, the suspect Zhang Bo took advantage of his mother Liu Weihua's absence and hugged Zhang Mujia and Zhang Muji, who were playing in the bedroom, with both legs. He threw the two of them downstairs from the bay window of the second bedroom, causing Zhang Mujia to die on the spot. Zhang Muji was sent to the hospital for rescue but died despite efforts. Two vivid little lives left this world in such a tragic way

After the neighbor reported the case, Zhang Bo still sat on the ground downstairs in the community, crying loudly. At this moment, his heart was performing a big play for everyone.

Zhang Bo married Chen Meilin on August 17, 2017. After marriage, they gave birth to a daughter named Zhang Mujia in March 2018 and a son named Zhang Muji in January 2019. Around April 2019, Zhang Bo began to conceal his married and childless identity and pursue his online lover Ye Chengchen. At the end of the same year, Ye Chengchen learned that Zhang Bo had children and continued to associate with him.

In February 2020, Zhang Bocai and his first wife Chen Meilin reached an agreement to divorce. The two parties agreed that their daughter Zhang Moujia would be raised by his wife, and their son Zhang Mouyi would be raised by Zhang Bo before the age of six and by his wife Chen Meilin after the age of six.

So, after the divorce, Zhang Bo lived with his son Zhang Mouyi and mother

Liu Weihua. This tragic case of two young children falling to their deaths occurred at this time.

Everything starts with Ye Chengchen, this online lover. Since she met Zhang Bo, Ye Chengchen has repeatedly stated that she and her parents cannot accept the fact that Zhang Bo has children. The two of them conspired to kill Zhang Bo's child when they met in Changshou District around February 2020. Subsequently, Ye Chengchen conspired with Zhang Bo through multiple face-to-face meetings, WeChat chats, and other means to kill two children, and agreed to use accidental falls to kill Zhang Moujia and Zhang Mouyi. In June of the same year, Ye Chengchen repeatedly urged Zhang Bo to commit the crime through WeChat. In October of the same year, Zhang Bo and Ye Chengchen agreed to bring Zhang Mujia to their home under the pretext of buying clothes for her, intending to kill her. The plan was blocked because Chen Meilin was always present, and the murder plan was accurately executed on November 2, 2020

This case has inevitably triggered our contemplation from a rational psychological analysis perspective. Everyone says that tigers do not eat their own offspring. So, what exactly is the reason for Zhang Bo's insane behavior as a father?

From the communication with Ye Chengchen, it is not difficult to find from the case materials provided by the prosecutor's office that she had repeatedly urged Zhang Bo to commit the crime through face-to-face interviews, WeChat, and other means. It is not difficult to analyze that Zhang Bo actually faced a lot of pressure during these conversations and exchanges. Everyone, as long as they survive in society, will face pressure to some extent. Imagine that when a person is under immense pressure, they will expose various problems. When we are completely controlled and powerless, the pressure will devour our rationality and wisdom, and brilliantly play the role of a "killer" in life.

Each of us should have the correct way to relieve stress, treating it as negative energy and expelling it from the body. But what about someone who doesn't experience this kind of stress? That was undoubtedly a fatal self destruction.

Here, a brief discussion on the impact of stress on people is only from a psychological and emotional perspective, and not to defend a father like Zhang Bo who is insane. We all know that despite being encouraged and urged by Ye Chengchen, he is a fully capable person, and his evil deeds are controlled and manipulated by criminal psychology. This is a conscious crime that deserves the most fair and severe trial and punishment under the law.

But such people usually resort to violent crimes to relieve their immense inner pressure, which is the most foolish way to relieve stress.

So, what does pressure really affect us?

From the perspective of emotions and psychological signs, when we encounter stress, we may become angry, sweaty palms, insomnia, easy to cry, anxious, neurotic, easily upset, impatient, have difficulty maintaining clear thinking, forgetful, memory loss, inability to make decisions, persistent worry, loss of sensitivity to humor, and so on.

So how do we deal with stress correctly?

1. Know yourself: As the ancient saying goes, "A person is wise and self aware. The first principle of stress management is to 'know yourself'. What kind of person am I? What is my personality like? Am I a stress sensitive personality?

Previous studies have shown a close correlation between personality and stress. Personality is an important component of coping with stress, and some people tend to belong to a stress prone personality; Secondly, individuals with stress sensitive personalities are usually the most susceptible to suggestion. This is one of the reasons why Zhang Bo's plan to kill his son went so smoothly with just half a year of encouragement and urging from Ye Chengchen.

And these types of people, or those with serious psychological problems, are prone to developing a criminal mentality. This type of person's mental health is greatly tormented, as they lack the light in their body, mind, and spirit that can reflect their own behavior. Therefore, they either continue to torment themselves internally or harbor evil thoughts and turn to attacking outward. Jung once said, "Healthy people do not torment others, often those who have been tormented become tormentors

If this type of person has even a little bit of self-awareness, such as Zhang Bo, who realizes that he has been immersed in the pressure of his online lover encouraging him to kill his child during this period, and starts a scientific psychological counseling journey, I think there is an 80% chance that such a tragedy will not happen.

Unfortunately, this type of person usually doesn't do anything until their criminal mentality dominates them. The criminal aggression of individuals with stress prone personalities is often associated with anxiety. Attacking and implementing plans are the main ways for this type of stress susceptible individuals to express their anxiety.

They often have a little person deep inside them, informing them of the urgency of time. In order to be more efficient, they set plans, goals, standards, and deadlines, and the pressure from within keeps pushing them to achieve their ultimate goal.

2. Understand how to withstand the tests and hardships of life. It has to be said that before meeting Ye Chengchen, Zhang Bo's life was filled with happiness among ordinary people, although he may not have felt this inner detachment and abundance. After all, they had two children with their ex-wife in just two years. Is there no love in such a family? The answer is yes, but our lives always have to settle over time in order to become more and more fragrant like spices. With this settling, we can taste a perfect "good" character. Unfortunately, even pressure sensitive individuals like Zhang Bo have not been able to experience these perceptions.

For example, if he divorces Chen Meilin, everything will have to start over. Will I be happy in the future? If we hadn't encountered someone like Ye Chengchen, who had no bottom line and also had a criminal mentality, but another gentle and elegant woman, he and Chen Meilin could have "parted ways and settled down separately".

For example, my wife and I had another argument, and I'm really tired of this endless argument. So what should I do?

......

These thoughts seem to always lead him towards negative emotions.

But in fact, we understand that although we face life's challenges and changes, setbacks or hardships time and time again, perhaps sometimes we may become at a loss, most of the time, we will not immediately give up our aspirations and desires for life. So, we will actively adjust our inner energy and make some optimistic and positive assumptions:

If my lifestyle could change a bit

If I could be intimate with my lover, I would help him with more household chores

If I have time, I can take a break and relax.

......

The above assumptions are ideas that we should cherish, because they are the medicine to withstand the tests and hardships of life.

3. Reduce anxiety through exercise. We should all understand the value of exercise. The positive emotional energy experienced after physical exercise is stronger than just watching sports, which increases the positive energy of psychological state and relaxes the body.

4. Change cognition and unleash cognitive potential: It is necessary to mention the emotional ABC theory created by American psychologist Ellis, who believes that triggering event A is only an indirect cause of triggering emotional and behavioral consequences C, while the direct cause of C is the individual's belief B based on their cognition and evaluation of triggering event A. This is also known as erroneous beliefs or irrational beliefs. Only by changing cognitive beliefs can the occurrence of C be effectively avoided.

Finally, breathing, relaxation, and meditation can unlock the potential of cognition, allowing the radiance of our body, mind, and spirit to illuminate ourselves.

The best touchstone for true love is nothing more than that, even in times of hardship, pain, sorrow, falling into a low point, or suffering physical and mental trauma, I can love you unconditionally, but... please remember, my dear, what I cultivate is unconditional love, but not bottomless love. So, this love, you must cherish and cherish it, because... it is so heavy, steady, powerful, inclusive, and nourishing, becoming the fountain of true love that gives birth to the power of the soul in our souls.

8 Sometimes we need to learn to mourn and mourn

I will speak out in the anguish of my spirit, I will complain in the bitterness of my soul.

——**Old Uncle 7:11**

According to preliminary statistics, since July 16th, as of 12:00 on the 25th, this round of heavy rainfall has caused 63 deaths and 5 missing persons in Henan Province due to disasters

"Xiao Nan's younger brother bought a meal, and two more stops later, her sister will have a warm dinner; her husband specially sent a pair of green rubber shoes to Xiao Yue, because of the rainstorm, her wife left work early; the road rain was too heavy, Adi told her husband 'Don't drive', and she caught the subway at the evening peak..."

They all boarded the 0501 subway at the same time, but the subway that was hit by floods had no terminus.

When Hu He first came to the consultation room, he refused to ask me any questions about the news of his wife's death.

What exactly happened that day? Can you talk about it

He looked extremely angry and said, 'I don't know, I don't know anything, don't ask me!'

We were silent for a while, and I let this silence continue. Then I asked softly, "Can you tell me what that thing means to you

After a while, he slowly said, 'Since that incident, I have to grab something in my hand every night to fall asleep. These days have been very difficult for me, as if I have lost my soul...' As the saying goes, a man's tears are not light, but at this point, he still sobbed and cried.

If I had driven to pick her up that day, she might not have gotten on that subway

Have I completely lost her, teacher

I handed him a cup of warm tea and nodded.

Post traumatic stress disorder (PTSD) refers to a mental disorder in which an individual experiences, witnesses, or encounters one or more actual deaths, threats of death, serious injuries, or threats to physical integrity involving themselves or others, resulting in delayed onset and sustained existence.

The causes of post-traumatic stress disorder (PTSD) can be classified into three categories: (a) natural disasters such as floods, fires, earthquakes, hurricanes, and tornadoes; (b) Unexpected events, such as car crashes, explosions, or shootings; (c) Human activities such as rape, robbery, assault, abduction, or abuse.

After a traumatic event, individuals may experience a decrease in response to immediate environmental stimuli, accompanied by mental numbness or emotional apathy.

"In fact, we are experiencing losses for many times, such as the flood this time, the COVID-19 epidemic, the Wenchuan earthquake in 2008, etc.," I said slowly, "everything will change with time, but such changes will take a little time."

I haven't told the child yet, his mother is no longer here... because I don't know what to say

Your symptoms such as numbness, avoidance, anxiety, and difficulty falling asleep are all normal symptoms of PTSD. I sympathize with you, and I understand your current sadness. Can you talk about how your wife went to work that day

Okay... it was such an ordinary day, but I never expected the morning goodbye to be gone forever

The core symptoms of PTSD are divided into three groups: traumatic re experience symptoms, avoidance and numbness symptoms, and increased alertness symptoms. But the clinical manifestations of children and adults are not completely the same, and some symptoms are unique to children.

We can use many methods to help visitors recover their memories and deal with grief, including dreams, associations, fantasies, images, and old medical memories.

So how should we deal with grief?

Accept the reality of loss and face the fact that this person has passed away; Replace the initial denial and evasion with loss.

Experience the pain of sadness. Admitting and overcoming this pain is necessary, otherwise he will prove his existence through self defeating behavior.

Adapt to an environment where the deceased is no longer present. Survivors must face the reality that many roles played by the deceased in their original lives no longer exist.

Get rid of the emotions of the deceased and immerse yourself in another relationship. The initial instinctive reaction to losing a loved one may make a person feel like they will never love others again, but survivors must have an open mind towards new relationships or opportunities.

When dealing with memories related to the deceased, one must accept the pain of losing loved ones.

To openly express regret, hostility, and guilt, and to be able to publicly mourn.

To be able to understand the strong sadness of losing a loved one. For example, as in the case, being aware of these symptoms such as anxiety, difficulty sitting or standing, and disbelief may temporarily affect one's ability to initiate or maintain normal behavioral patterns.

Being able to tolerate anger towards the deceased, oneself, or others; Reposition your responsibility and don't think that you should be able to prevent death to some extent.

Mr. Hu, you should know that life is impermanent. In the face of life, we are all fragile and helpless. Because we are humans, not gods, in the face of life and death, we must allow ourselves to be so helpless

Yes, what I most want now is how to tell my child about this matter

So how can we help children smoothly complete the process of mourning?

Firstly, parents should tell him what exactly happened? Provide true and accurate information about where the mother went in the case, allow him to cry or ask various questions, and involve the child in the mourning ceremony at home.

Secondly, survivors should accompany their children steadily. For survivors, sometimes they do not pay attention to their emotions, let alone adjust their state in a timely manner, and let their children take on the responsibility of taking care of their parents, which is the least appropriate. So, for survivors, the most important thing is to adjust their own state and emotions. Those who can receive psychological counseling should actively seek psychological counseling, making themselves a good container that can bear the emotions of children crying and crying, and accompany them steadily. This is very important.

Explanation of this issue's "Psychology Gate":

In life, as long as we are alive, there will be joys, sorrows, joys, sorrows, separations, and reunions. It can be said that from birth, the most essential thing we lack is to experience loss and grief. It can make us sad beyond words, and even lose some social function. Sometimes, we feel lonely and helpless in this world, with nowhere to lean. But as long as this sadness and sorrow are expressed and seen, the thick warmth will surely light up a healing light in our hearts, drive away our coldness and loneliness, and make us no longer afraid of sadness.

Because the universe and I love you.

(Due to confidentiality principles, all cases in the article are virtual simulations)

9 Why do some people find it difficult to establish intimate relationships with others?

Surely no one lays a hand on a broken man when he cries for help in his distress.

——Old Uncle 30:24

Some people are born with 'social anxiety disorder', making a lot of friends is not difficult; Some people find it difficult to make friends in reality.

This group of people may feel fearful about the upcoming relationship, or they may not be able to release themselves in front of others; Otherwise, there is a lack of awareness of boundaries between people, and one's own boundary awareness is extremely poor. They tend to excessively expose their privacy in crowds, causing discomfort among others; Or perhaps I don't know how to develop an intimate relationship with someone I like

The above situations can be attributed to two reasons:

Some people are afraid to get close to others and cannot release themselves in front of them, completely because subconsciously, they have extremely serious anxiety and unease about the harm they may suffer in this relationship. Due to severe anxiety or insecurity, they are unable to develop intimate relationships between people, which we commonly refer to as 'social anxiety'. Some people may even experience hand tremors, body tremors, rapid heartbeat, headaches, stomach pains, heartbeats, or inexplicable rashes, loss of appetite, and other physical discomfort due to the fear of interacting with others. However, strangely enough, when they go to the hospital for examination, all physical indicators are normal.

But as soon as one approaches a group of people or is about to develop a slightly closer relationship with them, similar symptoms as mentioned above will appear.

Frank Victor once wrote a book called "The Quest for Life", which summarized that there are two types of human pain.

One is that you have already been injured, but you are unaware of it. You haven't experienced some painful feelings that you are experiencing, which is often a state of self feeling good. Ask him, "How is your work relationship?" He says, "No problem." Then ask him, "How have you been lately? Have you encountered anything unpleasant?" He says, "I have a lot of nerves and nothing special." These types of people, after actually experiencing painful experiences, do not have any painful reactions in their consciousness. But signals similar to the above can appear on his body, such as headaches, fever, and accelerated heartbeat

These types of people are "silly" in life and self evaluate themselves as "neurotic", so why things are not a problem in front of them is not considered a problem. But in fact, what he didn't know was that everything he had experienced had already caused him psychological damage, and it was usually very significant that would be transmitted through physical signals. This situation, we call it 'mind body integration', is where your body helps you metabolize emotions, metabolize or express something, which is called somatization in psychology.

For example, Xiao A lost his parents and brothers in the flood, leaving him the only one in the family. During this period of losing loved ones, he should still go to work, go home, and eat. Others may sympathize with his experience, but he chuckled and said, 'It's okay.'. He thinks he is very strong, at least able to eat, drink, and sleep. But after a while, when he met a girl he liked and wanted to confess to her, he would always have headaches or stomach pains. So much so that it delayed the opportunity to confess. It's strange to say that as soon as he thought about not confessing his feelings today, his physical problems immediately disappeared. After going to the hospital for examination, there is still no problem and everything is normal.

Xiao A's situation is that our bodies rely on pain to prevent us from feeling emotional pain, because the intimate relationship that is about to develop with the girl and the positive interaction established will trigger Xiao A's subconscious pain of losing all his loved ones overnight. It's just this kind of pain that people like Xiao A usually don't feel, because it's called hidden trauma.

The second type mentioned by Frank is explicit trauma. You can feel that you have been hurt, offended, falsely accused, betrayed, and so on in this relationship. This type of explicit trauma is easier to handle compared to the previous type of implicit trauma.

And what about implicit trauma? The pain it causes often far exceeds the human body's capacity to bear. This pain becomes an intangible pain in your subconscious, a hidden 'devil' in your personality, causing some personality disorders and even mental disorders.

The above are all situations where we dare not try to establish a relationship. Ultimately, it is due to our fear of being hurt, such as having nowhere to heal after being injured, lacking sufficient social support systems to rely on, and so on.

So in a relationship, let's talk about another situation:

2. We dare to try, even though we are afraid of fear, we are still willing to take that step.

For example, if we want to start a new relationship, but the worst-case scenario is that we are deceived, slandered, attacked, and so on. We are hurt, but these people often have sufficient social support systems to heal and do not feel helpless or helpless.

Now, let's talk about how to heal injuries?

In life, we all have very important interpersonal relationships to maintain. A healthy and normal person, in a healthy and virtuous cycle of relationships, requires both effort and reward. You can't assume that I only need to give or I only need to reap in any relationship. That is an imbalanced relationship, an unhealthy relationship, and it will inevitably not last. When we have both giving and receiving in a relationship, we can feel this balance. When you encounter explicit pain, please entrust the pain to this relationship to bear, let this relationship help you, reflect on you, help you learn from the past, and let you be heard.

But if you have hidden trauma, you have physical sensations, inexplicable pain or discomfort in your body, some pain may even get out of control or abnormal physical state, or you have done many things but often feel powerless, and you feel like you can't live comfortably.

So, at this point, you need to find an experienced psychological counselor to accompany you for counseling. Only in this way can you open up and activate the hidden traumas that have been forgotten in your subconscious. Only then can you fearlessly walk into the sunshine, metabolize the things left by those traumas in your psyche, and receive true healing.

Explanation of this issue's "Psychology Gate":

Only by having a mirror that reflects the depths of your soul can you straighten your clothes, truly understand yourself, see yourself clearly, understand who you are and who you can become. For any relationship, you can understand your true needs and the needs of others in a relationship, become more fearless, and fully enjoy the warmth of a relationship, welcoming the spring of your soul.

10 Can painting therapies really heal wounded souls?

Sometimes, when doing psychological counseling, counselors may encounter small visitors or visitors with expression barriers who cannot accurately express what they want to express deep inside.

At this point, experienced psychological counselors usually use painting therapy for talks.

Using painting to replace some language expression, expressing negative emotions such as worry, fear, anxiety, or a lifeless heart through painting, is the norm.

Using painting or appreciating artworks as an outlet for emotions.

According to research, appreciating world-renowned paintings can effectively change our brain waves. We can find patterns in painting that perfectly match our body, mind, and spirit, and release ourselves.

Based on past consulting experience, let's appreciate and analyze the following world-renowned paintings together, hoping to bring you a different feeling.

The first famous painting:

The painting depicts a static sunflower in an ordinary vase. The sunflowers in the painting bloom abundantly in the bottle, swaying in various postures under the warm sunshine, giving the whole picture a warm and positive feeling.

Imagine that on a busy day, we have to go through so many things that it's difficult for a heart to have a moment of peace. When we drag our exhausted bodies back home, if we can find a peaceful place in our hearts, wouldn't it be very pleasant and comfortable?

In the silent blooming time of sunflowers, the slanting afternoon sun shines on the body, and in the light fragrance of flowers, it seems that the body and mind that have experienced turmoil can also be healed in that moment. The trauma in a certain part of my heart seems to be gradually healing under the sunshine.

So the entire painting mostly uses the color of sunshine, giving people warmth and peace.

The second famous painting:

This is a young girl swinging on a swing, lively and cute. She lifted one foot and kicked her shoes away, and her playfulness unconsciously permeated the entire picture. She smiled among the flower branches, her dancing skirt filled with her joy. To her right were two little angels dancing their wings around her.

This is like implying that all the good luck and beauty in this world are bestowed upon her.

In order to highlight the liveliness of the girl, her long dress was chosen in a bright pink orange color.

Can you notice the emotional changes brought by the main color tone of the previous painting and this painting?

Different colors can have different effects on people's emotions. Does the bright pink orange color in the painting also make your emotions jump with excitement? This is the energy flow that this painting brings us.

The experiment of the medical school of Amsterdam University in the Netherlands shows that the identical psychotherapeutic drugs can excite people by wrapping them in red sugar, but can have a sedative effect by wrapping them in blue or green sugar.

This indicates that the red tone can indeed bring people an "uplifting" and "upward" effect.

This is based on scientific evidence. When the human eye receives light, it stimulates the retina to secrete adrenaline, which in turn accelerates blood circulation, raises our body temperature and blood pressure, and stimulates nerve tissue.

That's why most antidepressants prefer to be wrapped in red sugar coating.

When feeling down or exhausted, in addition to ensuring sufficient sleep, appreciating famous paintings in red tones is also very effective.

The third famous painting:

In the painting, there is an interaction between one or two animals and a little girl. Behind them is a wide grassy slope, with one or two secluded small houses, and a young woman leisurely walking by the houses

Does this composition really help people relax?

When you rescue yourself from the sound of "fighting" in the daytime and plan to empty yourself, isn't appreciating such a leisurely painting particularly relaxing?

Animals and humans are a part of nature, and many studies have shown that people who frequently interact with animals are less likely to suffer from depression, anxiety, or autism. In the process of interacting with animals, it is an incredibly comfortable and silent expression, but also filled with the flow of love.

The negative emotions and many troubles seemed to disappear without a trace in that moment.

Finally, based on real-life cases, from appreciating famous paintings to truly practicing painting therapy, I have applied painting therapy to several children aged 5-6. Because children in this age group have insufficient language skills to express their experiences and struggles, the use of painting therapy has indeed achieved good therapeutic effects at this moment.

Children can use painting to depict what kind of terrible events they have experienced, so much so that even after a long time, such events still leave a deep impression in their little minds. Of course, these events also cause significant psychological harm to them.

But in the process of painting, their negative emotions such as anxiety, fear, helplessness, etc. were well supported and nurtured, and we thus established a better and stronger working alliance.

So, when feeling depressed or frustrated and unable to speak to others, you may try to appreciate a world-renowned painting or paint a brightly colored artwork. Fill it with various colors you want to use, and you will find that your self is better released, and thus you will gain peace of mind and body.

11 What kind of intimate relationship is considered a high-quality relationship?

There are many types of interactions between people, both intimate and distant. Different relationships lead to different social distances. Regardless, deep down in our hearts, we still crave to establish good or even high-quality intimate relationships.

So, what constitutes a high-quality intimate relationship?

1. Consciousness and consciousness have a communicative relationship.

Whether it's a group relationship of two, three, or multiple people, we can express our own opinions in their interactions. These opinions have both the same and different perspectives as our conscious level. But these exchanges allow for seeking common ground while reserving differences. They can be unique or united. Therefore, such communication can be considered as positive flow and will not form obstacles in the communication. And in this way, the cognition of these people in the group, their views on the whole world, their life experiences and principles, and even their opinions on how much money it costs to buy a product can all complement each other. They can form resonance within a region. That is to say, the cognition shared by these people can be diverse, but they will always resonate within a unified cognitive range.

2. Emotions between each other can be heard and seen.

For example, when Little A just lost his beloved little dog, he was very sad. However, when he told Little B about it, Little B was willing to listen and could see Little A's sadness. Through his caring eyes, language, and expressions, Little A could see himself grieving for the passing of the little dog. Between Xiao A and Xiao B, emotions can be well reflected and accommodated here.

Not only can they share happy things with each other, but they can also share sad things.

Just like the example above, when Little A's pain and sadness are heard, seen, and accepted, Little B will also have similar painful experiences in his heart and be willing to share them. Xiao A and Xiao B are willing to face each other's pain, sadness, helplessness, and even feelings of despair together.

On the other hand, if Xiao A shares his sadness and pain, he actually hopes to receive a warm response from Xiao B when he brings up this matter to Xiao B. However, if Xiao B cannot bear the pain of Xiao A's wounds at all, he avoids, escapes, or even speaks harshly, "Go talk to someone else, don't tell me this kind of thing

He thought that as long as these wounds were not mentioned, Xiao A's inner pain could be healed without medication?

At the end of the day, the main reason for this situation is that Little B is afraid to face the same wounds in his heart. Once the information he receives from outside causes pain, sadness, despair, and other emotions, Little B will avoid wrapping himself up. He doesn't know how to deal with these wounds in his heart, so when Little A tells him, he will adopt an attitude of avoidance or even harsh words to avoid the old wounds in his heart.

In other words, Little B is not very good at dealing with his negative emotions, and he cannot face a helpless and fragile self.

Xiao A couldn't express himself well in such a situation.

A good confidant needs to be a container that can withstand all your negative emotions. You need to be seen, warmed, reflected, embraced, and accepted.

High quality interaction between friend groups requires meeting the above three requirements.

So, what kind of high-quality communication is needed between spouses and parents in the family? In addition to achieving the first three, it is also necessary to achieve the fourth:

That is the contact between limbs.

For example, a warm embrace, holding hands, patting the head or shoulder, etc., such physical contact can give warmth and encouragement, and such intimate contact is also a natural need for high-quality relationships in a family.

12 May I have a life like a dandelion

Why do I always keep thinking repeatedly?

Every day before going to bed, I almost always make this reasoning: What if we look at our eyes? We must close our eyelids in order to fall asleep. But what if we don't have eyelids?

If that's the case, even reluctantly, the eyes have to see things. But why can't the pupils look at the eyelids? Otherwise, even if I close my eyelids, I can still see the inner layer of my eyelids. Even if I don't want to, I have to look. What should I do

Every time I think about these things, I feel like I have no way out. So I fell into a long period of insomnia. Some of us may frequently immerse ourselves in similar reasoning, painful experiences that have already occurred, or fantasies that have not yet occurred, thinking repeatedly, minute after minute, hour after hour... over and over again.

However, these thoughts are meaningless for our current lives, yet we cannot control ourselves from thinking about these issues, wasting a lot of our lives in vain. Although I know it's true, I still can't help but think and keep thinking, even to the point where I can't help myself. What's going on here? This is a type of obsessive-compulsive disorder, characterized by endless thoughts and concerns.

So, how is the concept of coercion formed?

So far, the narrative suggests that "obsessive thoughts are thoughts that one feels uncomfortable with, presented in a compulsive manner deep within oneself

Many people with a compulsive mindset stubbornly believe that these sudden thoughts that enter their minds are foreign objects of thought, and they try every means possible to expel them from their bodies, like excrement. But the more one thinks like this, the more serious the problem becomes. This is the self-defense concept of people with obsessive-compulsive disorder, especially when we are completely controlled by the symptoms. This may make us trapped in it and completely unable to see the underlying problems. Once we seek medical treatment, we always ask the doctor to treat these symptoms.

But in fact, to truly alleviate the symptoms of obsessive-compulsive disorder, the focus of treatment should be on breaking the mechanism of "being bound". Patients who are bound by symptoms are actually a manifestation of strong desire to live.

The key is how to convey this subtle 'inner feeling' to patients.

2. Compulsive ideas are not foreign objects of thought, but rather mistaking the unpleasant emotions that everyone experiences in daily life as pathological or abnormal. This is the pain caused by struggling desperately to eliminate fear, worry, and other psychological factors.

For example, Xiao A often feels excruciating pain when his eyes catch a glimpse of his nose tip. He doesn't want to think this way, but the more he doesn't want to, the easier it is to see his nose tip. He also becomes more anxious and cannot calm down to study or work. In the end, he even stops his normal life and work, and focuses all day on how to prevent himself from seeing his nose tip.

Alternatively, if Little B is often nervous in class and doesn't recognize words and phrases, he often warns himself not to be nervous. However, the more he pays attention to non nervous questions, the more nervous he becomes. Eventually, when the teacher asks questions in class, he can't even say simple words and phrases. This situation became increasingly serious, to the point where he later took a leave of absence from school and was unable to study normally at home.

……

The ancients said: Lanterns do not know when their feet are black.

In Morita therapy, it is believed that the true cause of neurosis is the individual's hypochondriacal quality.

Even though outsiders can see it clearly, people with obsessive-compulsive disorder are constantly entangled in their own symptoms, trapped in a cocoon and suffering greatly. If patients are made aware of the true cause of their illness, a considerable number of them will suddenly realize it.

This is like some people treating their shadow as a "devil", afraid and fearful. Once they know that the shadow belongs to everyone and there is no harm, the fear naturally disappears.

Furthermore, from a psychoanalytic perspective, we can see the symptom of exhaustive thinking in obsessive-compulsive disorder: some people, because they repeatedly think about problems that have no practical significance, keep thinking until they become confused.

Subconsciously, it's about piling up one's thoughts, thinking that if you can't think anymore, then you can't think anymore.

In fact, it is evading the essence of problem formation.

Why would he treat himself like this?

Because if he could still think, he could clearly feel many desires and impulses, relationships, narcissism, and other factors that he was not allowed by reality, so he avoided them.

Another possibility is that he cannot face the situation where he loses control, so he immerses himself in the A-Q spirit or the fantasy of Zhuge Liang afterwards, in order to escape the pain and sadness of being attacked in reality. The essence of psychoanalysis is that symptoms are subconscious conflicts, and if they are made conscious, the pain naturally decreases or even disappears.

So, what should we do if we suffer from obsessive-compulsive disorder?

Patients with obsessive-compulsive disorder often suffer from certain concepts or physiological reactions.

Behavioral therapy believes that human psychology and behavior are formed through conditioned learning in the postnatal environment, and similarly, pathological thinking and bad behavior are also formed through conditioned reflexes.

That's why some OCD patients may have a clear understanding of their underlying causes and reasoning, but they still experience relapse and stagnation.

It is emphasized here that positive reinforcement methods must be used to enhance healthy behavior, aversion therapy to downplay and suppress pathological behavior, and sometimes exposure therapy and desensitization therapy are carried out with the courage to die.

Behavioral therapy reveals the root cause of obsessive-compulsive disorder stubbornness.

The Morita therapy emphasizes "letting nature take its course and doing what it should", but at the same time, it also emphasizes "focusing on practice", "enduring pain and living with symptoms", and "every day is a good day". It believes that purpose oriented and behavior oriented approaches are the key to breaking the interaction between spirits, and emphasizes "not asking about symptoms".

In the traditional treatment method of Morita therapy, except for the first week of bed rest, most of the time is spent on various tasks and life experiences.

So, strictly speaking, focusing on behavioral practice, developing plans, and getting us moving is a great way to alleviate obsessive-compulsive disorder.

In fact, sometimes we just think about it, why don't we live like a dandelion, rising and falling with the wind, and adapting to the situation?

This article only briefly describes the methods for treating obsessive-compulsive disorder. If one really suffers from obsessive-compulsive disorder, 'Rome wasn't built in a day', and this simple text cannot explain it clearly. It is recommended to follow medical advice carefully. May all patients with obsessive-compulsive disorder meet a healthy self soon, gather courage, and live a precious, healthy, and free spirited life.

13 Consultation Notes: How Counselors Overcome Choice Conflicts in Consultation

Case: Xiao A is a newly hired psychological counselor. Although he is a novice, fortunately he is enthusiastic and good at exploring, which allows him to empathize and accept even when facing some difficult counseling processes.

Before encountering Little B's visit, he did not feel that it was difficult to engage in this profession.

On that day, Little B visited with questions and showed some symptoms of anxiety. He urgently wants Little A to answer his questions immediately and provide guidance for his helpless life.

Looking at Little B's expectant gaze, Little A wanted to immediately empathize with his distress and respond positively. But he immediately thought of a textbook that explicitly stated that guidance cannot be given immediately. Counselors should follow the principle of moderation during the counseling process and guide visitors to self-awareness and self-awareness in order to achieve improvement in real life.

So, Little A was caught in a long thought process of whether to give an immediate response or to follow the principle of moderation, while Little B's repeated questioning and his anxious emotions forced Little A into a dilemma.

He didn't know how to choose. This consultation also resulted in the failure of the collaboration, and Xiao A felt a sense of powerlessness that he had never experienced before. He even began to doubt whether he was truly suitable for this profession.

When a consultant is unable to freely choose between providing timely responses to visitors or adhering to moderation principles, conflict arises.

From the above case, it can be clearly felt that Xiao A was caught in a dilemma of choice during this consultation, and one of his conflicts arose. This is a problem that many novice consultants are prone to encounter.

Firstly, we should not let the mentor tell you how to choose, whether to respond to visitors in a timely manner or to follow the principle of moderation. Instead, we should analyze from a deeper level why you have such a situation? Why am I unable to provide a response or adhere to the principle of moderation in the current situation.

Here, based on my mentor's notes, I have summarized the following two explanations:

Firstly, perhaps this is not a conflict between these two scenarios, such as giving a response or moderation. But there is a conflict within you that has not been integrated:

So, am I responding promptly and empathizing with the visitor based on their actual situation? According to the repeated instructions in textbooks or from a mentor, one should adhere to the principle of moderation.

This kind of conflict may involve not only this matter, but also other places where conflicts arise.

For example, when Little A responds and explains to Visitor Little B in a timely manner, they face a new conflict of whether to explain empathy or the impact of early relationships on the present. Because empathy occurs in the present moment, is that explaining the relationship between you and him, or explaining the relationship between him and his caregiver?

This is obviously a completely new conflict that two consultants, Xiao A, may face, and in the subsequent consultation process, there may be a third, fourth, fifth... or even more conflicts. Whenever it comes to choosing between A or B, these unfree hesitations will appear in your mind, making you unsure which one to choose.

The first explanation is that the occurrence of this situation has nothing to do with these two conflicts, but rather a conflict within you is projected onto these two things.

Secondly, perhaps on the surface, it may appear that events are chosen in conflict, but in reality, it is a conflict between people.

For example, a mentor taught you that the more flexible you are in handling the specific situation of each case, the better. When visitors need you to respond in a timely manner, you can forget about the moderation principles that textbooks require you to follow.

But at the same time, as time goes by and you continue to study psychological counseling, several other mentors have also told you that there are some basic settings of psychological therapy that still need to be followed in psychological counseling work.

So, whether it's what is said in textbooks or the knowledge taught by mentors, such conflicts are internalized by you as your own conflicts. As a result, the consultant faces numerous difficulties in specific operations and is unsure of what to do?

These situations, especially for novice counselors who have difficulty making choices, can become even more troublesome.

So, how should we handle this situation of conflicting choices correctly?

Firstly, regardless of which one you choose, try to reduce your anxiety as much as possible.

If you are a consultant with ten years of consulting experience, you will understand whether you should remain silent or provide timely and reasonable explanations and responses at a specific time. Having the operations of predecessors at the forefront, such a tailored approach based on specific practical situations can greatly alleviate the anxiety of novice counselors and better facilitate their work in the negotiation alliance.

Secondly, not responding to specific questions, but responding in a different way to express a certain degree of empathy.

For example, when Xiao A encounters Xiao B's repeated questioning and has already clearly felt Xiao B's anxiety and impatience, it is particularly necessary to respond to him. We can say this: "I know you really want to know my response, but I want to communicate with you because I am not very familiar with your expression. I don't know what I should give you feedback on. So the best way is for you to tell me more about you. I believe that after I have a better understanding of you, I will naturally know what to give you feedback on

Thirdly, take careful notes of the consultation and analyze every detail that requires your attention, including emotional reactions, visitor demands, and the causes of the current problem.

Maintaining a good habit of taking consultation notes can help you analyze the information you receive from visitors more clearly, so that when necessary, you can provide meaningful responses and make visitors feel respected, alleviating their anxiety.

In addition, maintaining the habit of taking consultation notes can show visitors your serious attitude towards the negotiation alliance, which is more conducive to establishing a good working alliance relationship and making novice consultants more confident during the consultation process.

Explanation of this issue's "Psychology Gate":

Only with a pragmatic, open, and sincere attitude, patient listening, and advanced deep empathy that penetrates through the life scripts of various visitors, can you open the mirror of reflection in your soul with a clear, rational, and wise heart, and see what kind of voice each different soul and need is making.

14 How to get out of an anxious state of mind?

When An visited, he appeared anxious and restless, unable to calm down completely. In addition, her eyes turned blue, she was listless, and her hands trembled uncontrollably. She said to me, "Help me, do something quickly? Let it stop

Although I have gained a lot of consulting experience, I still feel a sense of powerlessness when facing her symptoms. Then I said, 'Okay, you lie down on our sofa first and talk about what's going on?'

Perhaps it was my orderly tone and peaceful mindset that made An realize something. Suddenly, she burst into tears and took a long time to say, "I... I just want to live and work peacefully like you

Can't An live and work peacefully?

I slowly fell into contemplation as she recounted.

It has been some time since An visited, and she often couldn't sleep at night. Her heart was pounding uncontrollably, as if she didn't want to jump out.

I asked her what she was thinking when she didn't sleep at night.

She said she often can't sleep because of some trivial matters, such as whether the windows are tightly closed or not? Has the gas been checked? There is a dripping sound in the kitchen, it should be because the faucet is not turned off properly.

Her partner beside her let out a subtle and even snoring sound, but she envied him for sleeping so soundly. However, she kept her eyes open and kept tossing and turning, thinking about the sesame sized things mentioned earlier, and couldn't sleep.

I told her that this is already a symptom of persistent anxiety and insomnia.

She felt at a loss. I continued to ask her, what do you most want to do now to make yourself feel better? She answered without hesitation, sleeping.

So I allowed her to take a short nap on the sofa in the consultation room, as long as it made her feel better.

But she still kept her tired eyes open, hoarse voice chattering incessantly, and she still couldn't sleep.

How can I end this? How can I stop worrying about what I have to do? Even worse, these meaningless things are either out of my control or haven't happened yet

Since knowing it is meaningless, why do you still want to control it? "I asked her.

Because I want to control my thoughts, "was her answer," I want to become more relaxed and confident, just like a teacher

I attempted hypnosis relaxation therapy for her. I made her imagine herself coming to a beautiful seaside, with the sea breeze gently brushing her hair, seagulls soaring in the sky, and the sound of the sea gently undulating and the tide rising and falling, echoing in her ears time and time again

Then, I told her that you want to free yourself from the constant anxiety, to stop the cycle of spells that you constantly imagine in bed when you dream back at midnight, to open your eyes in the morning and easily harvest the beauty of the day, no longer troubled by the fear and anxiety caused by depressing possibilities and upcoming obstacles

You need to take the first step bravely. It's a hopeful step

Firstly, let's understand how anxious thinking works.

Normally, we all know that when we face a situation, our brain first becomes anxious before thinking.

We often first examine the environment to determine if there is any danger, even when encountering friendly people or being in a safe state.

Our brain tends to perceive threats first, and its response to negative information is actually stronger compared to positive information.

In fact, we tend to focus more on negative emotions because we tend to excessively search for so-called 'FUD factors': fear, uncertainty, and doubt.

And this is the 'negative tendency' of our brain. If subjected to prolonged negative stress, the brain cannot reach a resting state, making it difficult to relax and enter deep sleep, making it even less likely for you to restore a calm emotional state. Your body is tense and trapped in rumination, which can make you feel very upset.

In this state, the brain re forms new neural pathways and plans a new roadmap towards future perspectives, emotions, thoughts, perceptions, and behaviors that are influenced by the current mental state, but the roadmap is drawn in the current poor mental state.

Your brain begins to weave various life shocks into a restrictive pattern of beliefs and rules about life.

This pattern can trigger anxious, fearful, and emotional thinking, disrupt your thinking, hinder your perseverance to the end, and undermine your confidence and satisfaction.

Your self-defense habits will only make your interpersonal relationships worse, your health damaged, your work not going smoothly, and your emotions numb.

Secondly, anxiety often leaves you trapped in worries and uncertainties about reality or fantasy, making arbitrary negative judgments and unable to pause halfway to reflect on reality.

This kind of restlessness makes you constantly want to solve problems and seek a way out, but never think about finding ease and liberation.

If you are in an anxious state, you may find yourself constantly trying to find all the things that could get worse, so that you can be prepared to face them. But the fact is, such a way of thinking will only make people struggle in distress and unable to escape.

So, what can we do when we are anxious to regain calmness? To alleviate anxiety, we need to use intervention methods to calm the brain.

Through practice, you can unblock your brain again. This process is called self-directed neural plasticity.

Your emotions, behavior patterns, attitudes, and perspectives are all related to your mental state.

How and where to place your attention determines your mental state for most of the time.

Only by shifting your focus can you change your current mental state.

By self-regulation and control over beliefs, feelings, and behaviors, you can make changes and maintain a happier mental state for a long time.

Being plagued by anxiety is because your brain keeps playing the movie 'My Worst Future', which can lead you into a crisis storm.

Only when you learn to consciously control yourself and engage in self-regulation, can you have a clearer understanding of the world and approach your experiences more rationally.

Just like An during the Buddha's visit, if she sets aside all the restless thoughts that keep her up at night and approaches these issues with an open-minded attitude, then these problems are not worth mentioning in her eyes and cannot bother her anymore.

3. Your physical condition reflects your mental state.

You are well aware that anxiety can cause gastrointestinal discomfort or headaches. Your mental state reflects your physical condition at every moment, sending unconscious thoughts and emotions that guide your behavior.

When you unconsciously bring calm thoughts into your brain, no matter what, you can create amazing changes in your nervous system. You can indeed change your mental state and restructure your thinking to alter your physical condition by unclogging your brain.

Charlie Chaplin wrote in his poem "When I Started Loving Myself":

I only live in the present moment

Entering into everything that is happening

I live fully every day

Day after day, like this

And I understand

This is perfect

Explanation of this issue's "Psychology Gate":

Every relationship, no matter how beautiful, has a day to say goodbye, perhaps earlier or later. However, this does not mean that we know that this relationship is destined to end, so we should not choose to start. On the contrary, every relationship brings different tasks and missions, and they can always teach us something in different forms, such as... seeing the wounds left in our souls, or helping us grow

So, with a grateful heart, we should fully open up and accept every wonderful encounter, fully experience it, and discover our ability to love others. At the same time, we should also see and perceive that we are deeply loved by others.

www.ingramcontent.com/pod-product-compliance
Lightning Source LLC
Chambersburg PA
CBHW081152070526
44583CB00021B/2801